Programming
Pearls
Second Edition

Programming
Pearls

Second Edition

JON BENTLEY

Bell Labs, Lucent Technologies
Murray Hill, New Jersey

ACM Press
New York, New York

✦Addison-Wesley

Boston • San Francisco • New York • Toronto • Montreal
London • Munich • Paris • Madrid
Capetown • Sydney • Tokyo • Singapore • Mexico City

This book is published as part of ACM Press Books—a collaboration between the Association for Computing (ACM) and Addison-Wesley. ACM is the oldest and largest educational and scientific society in the information technology field. Through its high-quality publications and services, ACM is a major force in advancing the skills and knowledge of IT professionals throughout the world. For further information about ACM, contact:

ACM Member Services
1515 Broadway, 17th Floor
New York, NY 10036-5701
Phone: 1-212-626-0500
Fax: 1-212-944-1318
E-mail: ACMHELP@ACM.org

ACM European Service Center
108 Cowley Road
Oxford OX4IJF
United Kingdom
Phone: 144-1865-382338
Fax: 144-1865-381338
E-mail: acm.europe@acm.org
URL: http://www.acm.org

The publisher offers discounts on this book when ordered in quantity for special sales. For more information, please contact:

U.S. Corporate and Government Sales
(800) 382-3419
corpsales@pearsontechgroup.com

For sales outside of the U.S., please contact:

International Sales
(317) 581-3793
international@pearsontechgroup.com.

Visit Addison-Wesley on the Web: www.awprofessional.com

This book was typeset in Times Roman and Lucida Sans Typewriter by the author.

Text printed on recycled and acid-free paper.

ISBN 0-201-65788-0

Text printed in the United States at RR Donnelley Crawfordsville in Crawfordsville, Indiana.

17th Printing   October 2008

PREFACE

Computer programming has many faces. Fred Brooks paints the big picture in *The Mythical Man Month*; his essays underscore the crucial role of management in large software projects. At a finer grain, Steve McConnell teaches good programming style in *Code Complete*. The topics in those books are the key to good software and the hallmark of the professional programmer. Unfortunately, though, the workman-like application of those sound engineering principles isn't always thrilling — until the software is completed on time and works without surprise.

About the Book

The columns in this book are about a more glamorous aspect of the profession: programming pearls whose origins lie beyond solid engineering, in the realm of insight and creativity. Just as natural pearls grow from grains of sand that have irritated oysters, these programming pearls have grown from real problems that have irritated real programmers. The programs are fun, and they teach important programming techniques and fundamental design principles.

Most of these essays originally appeared in my "Programming Pearls" column in *Communications of the Association for Computing Machinery*. They were collected, revised and published as the first edition of this book in 1986. Twelve of the thirteen pieces in the first edition have been edited substantially for this edition, and three new columns have been added.

The only background the book assumes is programming experience in a high-level language. Advanced techniques (such as templates in C++) show up now and then, but the reader unfamiliar with such topics will be able to skip to the next section with impunity.

Although each column may be read by itself, there is a logical grouping to the complete set. Columns 1 through 5 form Part I of the book. They review programming fundamentals: problem definition, algorithms, data structures and program verification and testing. Part II is built around the theme of efficiency, which is sometimes important in itself and is always a fine springboard into interesting programming problems. Part III applies those techniques to several substantial problems in sorting, searching and strings.

One hint about reading the essays: don't go too fast. Read them carefully, one per sitting. Try the problems as they are posed — some of them look easy until you've butted your head against them for an hour or two. Afterwards, work hard on the problems at the end of each column: most of what you learn from this book will come out the end of your pencil as you scribble down your solutions. If possible, discuss your ideas with friends and colleagues before peeking at the hints and solutions in the back of the book. The further reading at the end of each chapter isn't intended as a scholarly reference list; I've recommended some good books that are an important part of my personal library.

This book is written for programmers. I hope that the problems, hints, solutions, and further reading make it useful for individuals. The book has been used in classes including Algorithms, Program Verification and Software Engineering. The catalog of algorithms in Appendix 1 is a reference for practicing programmers, and also shows how the book can be integrated into classes on algorithms and data structures.

The Code

The pseudocode programs in the first edition of the book were all implemented, but I was the only person to see the real code. For this edition, I have rewritten all the old programs and written about the same amount of new code. The programs are available at

```
www.programmingpearls.com
```

The code includes much of the scaffolding for testing, debugging and timing the functions. The site also contains other relevant material. Because so much software is now available online, a new theme in this edition is how to evaluate and use software components.

The programs use a terse coding style: short variable names, few blank lines, and little or no error checking. This is inappropriate in large software projects, but it is useful to convey the key ideas of algorithms. Solution 5.1 gives more background on this style.

The text includes a few real C and C++ programs, but most functions are expressed in a pseudocode that takes less space and avoids inelegant syntax. The notation *for* $i = [0, n)$ iterates i from 0 through $n-1$. In these *for* loops, left and right parentheses denote open ranges (which do not include the end values), and left and right square brackets denote closed ranges (which do include the end values). The phrase *function*(i, j) still calls a function with parameters i and j, and *array*$[i, j]$ still accesses an array element.

This edition reports the run times of many programs on ''my computer'', a 400MHz Pentium II with 128 megabytes of RAM running Windows NT 4.0. I timed the programs on several other machines, and the book reports the few substantial differences that I observed. All experiments used the highest available level of compiler optimization. I encourage you to time the programs on your machine; I bet that you'll find similar ratios of run times.

To Readers of the First Edition

I hope that your first response as you thumb through this edition of the book is, "This sure looks familiar." A few minutes later, I hope that you'll observe, "I've never seen that before."

This version has the same focus as the first edition, but is set in a larger context. Computing has grown substantially in important areas such as databases, networking and user interfaces. Most programmers should be familiar users of such technologies. At the center of each of those areas, though, is a hard core of programming problems. Those programs remain the theme of this book. This edition of the book is a slightly larger fish in a much larger pond.

One section from old Column 4 on implementing binary search grew into new Column 5 on testing, debugging and timing. Old Column 11 grew and split into new Columns 12 (on the original problem) and 13 (on set representations). Old Column 13 described a spelling checker that ran in a 64-kilobyte address space; it has been deleted, but its heart lives on in Section 13.8. New Column 15 is about string problems. Many sections have been inserted into the old columns, and other sections were deleted along the way. With new problems, new solutions, and four new appendices, this edition of the book is 25 percent longer.

Many of the old case studies in this edition are unchanged, for their historical interest. A few old stories have been recast in modern terms.

Acknowledgments for the First Edition

I am grateful for much support from many people. The idea for a *Communications of the ACM* column was originally conceived by Peter Denning and Stuart Lynn. Peter worked diligently within ACM to make the column possible and recruited me for the job. ACM Headquarters staff, particularly Roz Steier and Nancy Adriance, have been very supportive as these columns were published in their original form. I am especially indebted to the ACM for encouraging publication of the columns in their present form, and to the many *CACM* readers who made this expanded version necessary and possible by their comments on the original columns.

Al Aho, Peter Denning, Mike Garey, David Johnson, Brian Kernighan, John Linderman, Doug McIlroy and Don Stanat have all read each column with great care, often under extreme time pressure. I am also grateful for the particularly helpful comments of Henry Baird, Bill Cleveland, David Gries, Eric Grosse, Lynn Jelinski, Steve Johnson, Bob Melville, Bob Martin, Arno Penzias, Marilyn Roper, Chris Van Wyk, Vic Vyssotsky and Pamela Zave. Al Aho, Andrew Hume, Brian Kernighan, Ravi Sethi, Laura Skinger and Bjarne Stroustrup provided invaluable help in bookmaking, and West Point cadets in EF 485 field tested the penultimate draft of the manuscript. Thanks, all.

Acknowledgments for the Second Edition

Dan Bentley, Russ Cox, Brian Kernighan, Mark Kernighan, John Linderman, Steve McConnell, Doug McIlroy, Rob Pike, Howard Trickey and Chris Van Wyk have all read this edition with great care. I am also grateful for the particularly helpful comments of Paul Abrahams, Glenda Childress, Eric Grosse, Ann Martin, Peter McIlroy, Peter Memishian, Sundar Narasimhan, Lisa Ricker, Dennis Ritchie, Ravi Sethi, Carol Smith, Tom Szymanski and Kentaro Toyama. I thank Peter Gordon and his colleagues at Addison-Wesley for their help in preparing this edition.

Murray Hill, New Jersey   J. B.
December, 1985
August, 1999

CONTENTS

PART I: **PRELIMINARIES**

These five columns review the basics of programming. Column 1 is the history of a single problem. A combination of careful problem definition and straightforward programming techniques led to an elegant solution. The column illustrates the central theme of this book: thinking hard about a real case study can be fun and can also lead to practical benefits.

Column 2 examines three problems, with an emphasis on how algorithmic insights can yield simple and effective code. Column 3 surveys the crucial role that the structure of data can play in software design.

Column 4 introduces program verification as a tool for writing correct code. Verification techniques are used extensively as we derive subtle (and fast) functions in Columns 9, 11 and 14. Column 5 shows how we implement those abstract programs in real code: we use scaffolding to probe a function, to bombard it with test cases, and to measure its performance.

External Mergesort:

eg. Data size = 900 MB
    RAM size = 100 MB

1. Read 100MB, do quicksort
2. write sorted chunk into temp file
3. Repeat 1 & 2 for all chunks (now needs merge)
4. Read 10 MB of each chunk & set 10MB for output
5. Perform 9-way merge
   a) keep writing sorted data to output

COLUMN 1: **CRACKING THE OYSTER**

The programmer's question was simple: "How do I sort a disk file?" Before I tell you how I made my first mistake, let me give you a chance to do better than I did. What would you have said?

1.1 A Friendly Conversation

My mistake was to answer his question. I gave him a thumbnail sketch of how to implement a Merge Sort on disk. My suggestion that he dig into an algorithms text met with less than enthusiasm — he was more concerned about solving the problem than furthering his education. I then told him about a disk sorting program in a popular programming book. The program consisted of about two hundred lines of code in a dozen functions; I estimated that implementing and testing the code would have taken the programmer at most a week.

I thought that I had solved his problem, but his hesitation led me back to the right track. The conversation then went something like this, with my questions in *italics*.

Why do you want to write your own sort at all? Why not use a sort provided by your system?

I need the sort in the middle of a large system, and for obscure technical reasons, I can't use the system file-sorting program.

What exactly are you sorting? How many records are in the file? What is the format of each record?

The file contains at most ten million records; each record is a seven-digit integer.

Wait a minute. If the file is that small, why bother going to disk at all? Why not just sort it in main memory?

Although the machine has many megabytes of main memory, this function is part of a big system. I expect that I'll have only about a megabyte free at that point.

Is there anything else you can tell me about the records?

Each one is a seven-digit positive integer with no other associated data, and no integer can appear more than once.

The context makes the problem clearer. In the United States, telephone numbers consist of a three-digit "area code" followed by seven additional digits. Telephone calls to numbers with the "toll-free" area code of 800 (the only such code at the time) were not charged. A real database of toll-free telephone numbers includes a great deal of information: the toll-free telephone number, the real number to which calls are routed (sometimes several numbers, with rules on which calls go where when), the name and address of the subscriber, and so on.

The programmer was building a small corner of a system for processing such a database, and the integers to be sorted were toll-free telephone numbers. The input file was a list of numbers (with all other information removed), and it was an error to include the same number twice. The desired output was a file of the numbers, sorted in increasing numeric order. The context also defines the performance requirements. During a long session with the system, the user requested a sorted file roughly once an hour and could do nothing until the sort was completed. The sort therefore couldn't take more than a few minutes, while ten seconds was a more desirable run time.

1.2 Precise Problem Statement

To the programmer these requirements added up to, "How do I sort a disk file?" Before we attack the problem, let's arrange what we know in a less biased and more useful form.

Input: A file containing at most n positive integers, each less than n, where $n = 10^7$. It is a fatal error if any integer occurs twice in the input. No other data is associated with the integer.

Output: A sorted list in increasing order of the input integers.

Constraints: At most (roughly) a megabyte of storage is available in main memory; ample disk storage is available. The run time can be at most several minutes; a run time of ten seconds need not be decreased.

Think for a minute about this problem specification. How would you advise the programmer now?

1.3 Program Design

The obvious program uses a general disk-based Merge Sort as a starting point but trims it to exploit the fact that we are sorting integers. That reduces the two hundred lines of code by a few dozen lines, and also makes it run faster. It might still take a few days to get the code up and running.

A second solution makes even more use of the particular nature of this sorting problem. If we store each number in seven bytes, then we can store about 143,000 numbers in the available megabyte. If we represent each number as a 32-bit integer, though, then we can store 250,000 numbers in the megabyte. We will therefore use a program that makes 40 passes over the input file. On the first pass it reads into memory any integer between 0 and 249,999, sorts the (at most) 250,000 integers and writes them to the output file. The second pass sorts the integers from 250,000 to 499,999, and so on to the 40th pass, which sorts 9,750,000 to 9,999,999. A Quicksort would be quite efficient for the main-memory sorts, and it requires only twenty lines of code (as we'll see in Column 11). The entire program could therefore be implemented in a page or two of code. It also has the desirable property that we no longer have to worry about using intermediate disk files; unfortunately, for that benefit we pay the price of reading the entire input file 40 times.

A Merge Sort program reads the file once from the input, sorts it with the aid of work files that are read and written many times, and then writes it once.

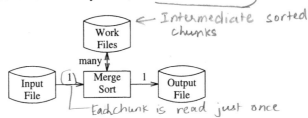
← *Intermediate sorted chunks*
Each chunk is read just once

The 40-pass algorithm reads the input file many times and writes the output just once, using no intermediate files.

We would prefer the following scheme, which combines the advantages of the previous two. It reads the input just once, and uses no intermediate files.

We can do this only if we represent all the integers in the input file in the available megabyte of main memory. Thus the problem boils down to whether we can represent at most ten million distinct integers in *about* eight million available bits. Think about an appropriate representation.

1.4 Implementation Sketch

Viewed in this light, the *bitmap* or *bit vector* representation of a set screams out to be used. We can represent a toy set of nonnegative integers less than 20 by a string of 20 bits. For instance, we can store the set {1, 2, 3, 5, 8, 13} in this string:

        0 1 1 1 0 1 0 0 1 0 0 0 0 1 0 0 0 0 0 0

The bits representing numbers in the set are 1, and all other bits are 0.

In the real problem, the seven decimal digits of each integer denote a number less than ten million. We'll represent the file by a string of ten million bits in which the ith bit is on if and only if the integer i is in the file. (The programmer found two million spare bits; Problem 5 investigates what happens when a megabyte is a firm limit.) This representation uses three attributes of this problem not usually found in sorting problems: the input is from a relatively small range, it contains no duplicates, and no data is associated with each record beyond the single integer.

Given the bitmap data structure to represent the set of integers in the file, the program can be written in three natural phases. The first phase initializes the set to empty by turning off all bits. The second phase builds the set by reading each integer in the file and turning on the appropriate bit. The third phase produces the sorted output file by inspecting each bit and writing out the appropriate integer if the bit is one. If n is the number of bits in the vector (in this case 10,000,000), the program can be expressed in pseudocode as:

```
/* phase 1: initialize set to empty */
    for i = [0, n)
        bit[i] = 0
/* phase 2: insert present elements into the set */
    for each i in the input file
        bit[i] = 1
/* phase 3: write sorted output */
    for i = [0, n)
        if bit[i] == 1
            write i on the output file
```

(Recall from the preface that the notation *for* $i = [0, n)$ iterates i from 0 to $n - 1$.)

This sketch was sufficient for the programmer to solve his problem. Some of the implementation details he faced are described in Problems 2, 5 and 7.

1.5 Principles

The programmer told me about his problem in a phone call; it took us about fifteen minutes to get to the real problem and find the bitmap solution. It took him a couple of hours to implement the program in a few dozen lines of code, which was far superior to the hundreds of lines of code and the week of programming time that we had feared at the start of the phone call. And the program was lightning fast: while a Merge Sort on disk might have taken many minutes, this program took little more than the time to read the input and to write the output — about ten seconds. Solution 3 contains timing details on several programs for the task.

Those facts contain the first lesson from this case study: careful analysis of a small problem can sometimes yield tremendous practical benefits. In this case a few minutes of careful study led to an order of magnitude reduction in code length, programmer time and run time. General Chuck Yeager (the first person to fly faster than sound) praised an airplane's engine system with the words "simple, few parts, easy to maintain, very strong"; this program shares those attributes. The program's specialized structure, however, would be hard to modify if certain dimensions of the specifications were changed. In addition to the advertising for clever programming, this case illustrates the following general principles.

The Right Problem. Defining the problem was about ninety percent of this battle

— I'm glad that the programmer didn't settle for the first program I described. Problems 10, 11 and 12 have elegant solutions once you pose the right problem; think hard about them before looking at the hints and solutions.

The Bitmap Data Structure. This data structure represents a dense set over a finite domain when each element occurs at most once and no other data is associated with the element. Even if these conditions aren't satisfied (when there are multiple elements or extra data, for instance), a key from a finite domain can be used as an index into a table with more complicated entries; see Problems 6 and 8.

Multiple-Pass Algorithms. These algorithms make several passes over their input data, accomplishing a little more each time. We saw a 40-pass algorithm in Section 1.3; Problem 5 encourages you to develop a two-pass algorithm.

A Time-Space Tradeoff and One That Isn't. Programming folklore and theory abound with time-space tradeoffs: by using more time, a program can run in less space. The two-pass algorithm in Solution 5, for instance, doubles a program's run time to halve its space. It has been my experience more frequently, though, that reducing a program's space requirements also reduces its run time.† The space-efficient structure of bitmaps dramatically reduced the run time of sorting. There were two reasons that the reduction in space led to a reduction in time: less data to process means less time to process it, and keeping data in main memory rather than on disk avoids the overhead of disk accesses. Of course, the mutual improvement was possible only because the original design was far from optimal.

A Simple Design. Antoine de Saint-Exupéry, the French writer and aircraft designer, said that, "A designer knows he has arrived at perfection not when there is no longer anything to add, but when there is no longer anything to take away." More programmers should judge their work by this criterion. Simple programs are usually more reliable, secure, robust and efficient than their complex cousins, and easier to build and to maintain.

Stages of Program Design. This case illustrates the design process that is described in detail in Section 12.4.

1.6 Problems

Hints for and solutions to selected problems can be found in sections at the back of the book.

1. If memory were not scarce, how would you implement a sort in a language with libraries for representing and sorting sets?

---

† Tradeoffs are common to all engineering disciplines; automobile designers, for instance, might trade reduced mileage for faster acceleration by adding heavy components. Mutual improvements are preferred, though. A review of a small car I once drove observed that "the weight saving on the car's basic structure translates into further weight reductions in the various chassis components — and even the elimination of the need for some, such as power steering".

2. How would you implement bit vectors using bitwise logical operations (such as and, or and shift)?

3. Run-time efficiency was an important part of the design goal, and the resulting program was efficient enough. Implement the bitmap sort on your system and measure its run time; how does it compare to the system sort and to the sorts in Problem 1? Assume that n is 10,000,000, and that the input file contains 1,000,000 integers.

4. If you take Problem 3 seriously, you will face the problem of generating k integers less than n without duplicates. The simplest approach uses the first k positive integers. This extreme data set won't alter the run time of the bitmap method by much, but it might skew the run time of a system sort. How could you generate a file of k unique random integers between 0 and $n - 1$ in random order? Strive for a short program that is also efficient.

5. The programmer said that he had about a megabyte of free storage, but the code we sketched uses 1.25 megabytes. He was able to scrounge the extra space without much trouble. If the megabyte had been a hard and fast boundary, what would you have recommended? What is the run time of your algorithm?

6. What would you recommend to the programmer if, instead of saying that each integer could appear at most once, he told you that each integer could appear at most ten times? How would your solution change as a function of the amount of available storage?

7. [R. Weil] The program as sketched has several flaws. The first is that it assumes that no integer appears twice in the input. What happens if one does show up more than once? How could the program be modified to call an error function in that case? What happens when an input integer is less than zero or greater than or equal to n? What if an input is not numeric? What should a program do under those circumstances? What other sanity checks could the program incorporate? Describe small data sets that test the program, including its proper handling of these and other ill-behaved cases.

8. When the programmer faced the problem, all toll-free phone numbers in the United States had the 800 area code. Toll-free codes now include 800, 877 and 888, and the list is growing. How would you sort all of the toll-free numbers using only a megabyte? How can you store a set of toll-free numbers to allow very rapid lookup to determine whether a given toll-free number is available or already taken?

9. One problem with trading more space to use less time is that initializing the space can itself take a great deal of time. Show how to circumvent this problem by designing a technique to initialize an entry of a vector to zero the first time it is accessed. Your scheme should use constant time for initialization and for each vector access, and use extra space proportional to the size of the vector. Because this method reduces initialization time by using even more space, it should be considered only when space is cheap, time is dear and the vector is sparse.

10. Before the days of low-cost overnight deliveries, a store allowed customers to order items over the telephone, which they picked up a few days later. The store's database used the customer's telephone number as the primary key for retrieval (customers know their phone numbers and the keys are close to unique). How would you organize the store's database to allow orders to be inserted and retrieved efficiently?

11. In the early 1980's Lockheed engineers transmitted daily a dozen drawings from a Computer Aided Design (CAD) system in their Sunnyvale, California, plant to a test station in Santa Cruz. Although the facilities were just 25 miles apart, an automobile courier service took over an hour (due to traffic jams and mountain roads) and cost a hundred dollars per day. Propose alternative data transmission schemes and estimate their cost.

12. Pioneers of human space flight soon realized the need for writing implements that work well in the extreme environment of space. A popular urban legend asserts that the United States National Aeronautics and Space Administration (NASA) solved the problem with a million dollars of research to develop a special pen. According to the legend, how did the Soviets solve the same problem?

1.7 Further Reading

This little exercise has only skimmed the fascinating topic of specifying a program. For a deep insight into this crucial activity, see Michael Jackson's *Software Requirements & Specifications*, published by Addison-Wesley in 1995. The tough topics in the book are presented as a delightful collection of independent but reinforcing little essays.

In the case study described in this column, the programmer's main problem was not so much technical as psychological: he couldn't make progress because he was trying to solve the wrong problem. We finally solved his problem by breaking through his conceptual block and solving an easier problem. *Conceptual Blockbusting* by James L. Adams (the third edition was published by Perseus in 1986) studies this kind of leap and is generally a pleasant prod towards more creative thinking. Although it was not written with programmers in mind, many of its lessons are particularly appropriate for programming problems. Adams defines conceptual blocks as ''mental walls that block the problem-solver from correctly perceiving a problem or conceiving its solution''; Problems 10, 11 and 12 encourage you to bust some.

AHA! ALGORITHMS

The study of algorithms offers much to the practicing programmer. A course on the subject equips students with functions for important tasks and techniques for attacking new problems. We'll see in later columns how advanced algorithmic tools sometimes have a substantial influence on software systems, both in reduced development time and in faster execution speed.

As crucial as those sophisticated ideas are, algorithms have a more important effect at a more common level of programming. In his book *Aha! Insight* (from which I stole my title), Martin Gardner describes the contribution I have in mind: "A problem that seems difficult may have a simple, unexpected solution." Unlike the advanced methods, the *aha!* insights of algorithms don't come only after extensive study; they're available to any programmer willing to think seriously before, during and after coding.

2.1 Three Problems

Enough generalities. This column is built around three little problems; try them before you read on.

A. Given a sequential file that contains at most four billion 32-bit integers in random order, find a 32-bit integer that isn't in the file (and there must be at least one missing — why?). How would you solve this problem with ample quantities of main memory? How would you solve it if you could use several external "scratch" files but only a few hundred bytes of main memory?

B. Rotate a one-dimensional vector of n elements left by i positions. For instance, with $n=8$ and $i=3$, the vector *abcdefgh* is rotated to *defghabc*. Simple code uses an n-element intermediate vector to do the job in n steps. Can you rotate the vector in time proportional to n using only a few dozen extra bytes of storage?

C. Given a dictionary of English words, find all sets of anagrams. For instance, "pots", "stop" and "tops" are all anagrams of one another because each can be formed by permuting the letters of the others.

2.2 Ubiquitous Binary Search

I'm thinking of an integer between 1 and 100; you guess it. Fifty? Too low. Seventy-five? Too high. And so the game goes, until you guess my number. If my integer is originally between 1 and n, then you can guess it in $\log_2 n$ guesses. If n is a thousand, ten guesses will do, and if n is a million, you'll need at most twenty.

This example illustrates a technique that solves a multitude of programming problems: *binary search*. We initially know that an object is within a given range, and a probe operation tells us whether the object is below, at, or above a given position. Binary search locates the object by repeatedly probing the middle of the current range. If the probe doesn't find the object, then we halve the current range and continue. We stop when we find what we're looking for or when the range becomes empty.

The most common application of binary search in programming is to search for an element in a sorted array. When looking for the entry 50, the algorithm makes the following probes.

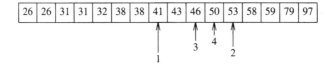

A binary search program is notoriously hard to get right; we'll study the code in detail in Column 4.

Sequential search uses about $n/2$ comparisons on the average to search a table of n elements, while binary search never uses more than about $\log_2 n$ comparisons. That can make a big difference in system performance; this anecdote from a *Communications of the ACM* case study describing ''The TWA Reservation System'' is typical.

> We had one program that was doing a linear search through a very large piece of memory almost 100 times a second. As the network grew, the average CPU time per message was up 0.3 milliseconds, which is a huge jump for us. We traced the problem to the linear search, changed the application program to use a binary search, and the problem went away.

I've seen that same story in many systems. Programmers start with the simple data structure of sequential search, which is often fast enough. If it becomes too slow, sorting the table and using a binary search can usually remove the bottleneck.

But the story of binary search doesn't end with rapidly searching sorted arrays. Roy Weil applied the technique in cleaning an input file of about a thousand lines that contained a single bad line. Unfortunately, the bad line wasn't known by sight; it could be identified only by running a (starting) portion of the file through a program and seeing a wildly erroneous answer, which took several minutes. His predecessors at debugging had tried to spot it by running a few lines at a time through the program, and they had been making progress towards a solution at a snail's pace. How did Weil find the culprit in just ten runs of the program?

With this warmup, we can tackle Problem A. The input is on a sequential file (think of a tape or disk — although a disk may be randomly accessed, it is usually much faster to read a file from beginning to end). The file contains at most four billion 32-bit integers in random order, and we are to find one 32-bit integer not present. (There must be at least one missing, because there are 2^{32} or 4,294,967,296 such integers.) With ample main memory, we could use the bitmap technique from Column 1 and dedicate 536,870,912 8-bit bytes to a bitmap representing the integers seen so far. The problem, however, also asks how we can find the missing integer if we have only a few hundred bytes of main memory and several spare sequential files. To set this up as a binary search we have to define a range, a representation for the elements within the range, and a probing method to determine which half of a range holds the missing integer. How can we do this?

We'll use as the range a sequence of integers known to contain at least one missing element, and we'll represent the range by a file containing all the integers in it. The insight is that we can probe a range by counting the elements above and below its midpoint: either the upper or the lower range has at most half the elements in the total range. Because the total range has a missing element, the smaller half must also have a missing element. These are most of the ingredients of a binary search algorithm for the problem; try putting them together yourself before you peek at the solutions to see how Ed Reingold did it.

These uses of binary search just scratch the surface of its applications in programming. A root finder uses binary search to solve a single-variable equation by successively halving an interval; numerical analysts call this the bisection method. When the selection algorithm in Solution 11.9 partitions around a random element and then calls itself recursively on all elements on one side of that element, it is using a "randomized" binary search. Other uses of binary search include tree data structures and program debugging (when a program dies a silent death, where do you probe the source text to home in on the guilty statement?). In each of these examples, thinking of the program as a few embellishments on top of the basic binary search algorithm can give the programmer that all-powerful *aha!*

2.3 The Power of Primitives

Binary search is a solution that looks for problems; we'll now study a problem that has several solutions. Problem B is to rotate the n-element vector x left by i positions in time proportional to n and with just a few dozen bytes of extra space. This problem arises in applications in various guises. Some programming languages provide rotation as a primitive operation on vectors. More importantly, rotation corresponds to swapping adjacent blocks of memory of unequal size: whenever you drag-and-drop a block of text elsewhere in a file, you ask the program to swap two blocks of memory. The time and space constraints are important in many applications.

One might try to solve the problem by copying the first i elements of x to a temporary array, moving the remaining $n - i$ elements left i places, and then copying the first i from the temporary array back to the last positions in x. However, the i extra locations used by this scheme make it too space-expensive. For a different approach, we could define a function to rotate x left one position (in time proportional to n) and call it i times, but that would be too time-expensive.

To solve the problem within the resource bounds will apparently require a more complicated program. One successful approach is a delicate juggling act: move $x[0]$ to the temporary t, then move $x[i]$ to $x[0]$, $x[2i]$ to $x[i]$, and so on (taking all indices into x modulo n), until we come back to taking an element from $x[0]$, at which point we instead take the element from t and stop the process. When i is 3 and n is 12, that phase moves the elements in this order.

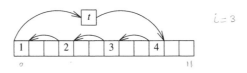

If that process didn't move all the elements, then we start over at $x[1]$, and continue until we move all the elements. Problem 3 challenges you to reduce this idea to code; be careful.

A different algorithm results from a different view of the problem: rotating the vector x is really just swapping the two segments of the vector ab to be the vector ba, where a represents the first i elements of x. Suppose a is shorter than b. Divide b into b_l and b_r so that b_r is the same length as a. Swap a and b_r to transform ab_lb_r into b_rb_la. The sequence a is in its final place, so we can focus on swapping the two parts of b. Since this new problem has the same form as the original, we can solve it recursively. This algorithm can lead to an elegant program (Solution 3 describes an iterative solution due to Gries and Mills), but it requires delicate code and some thought to see that it is efficient enough.

The problem looks hard until you finally have the *aha!* insight: let's view the problem as transforming the array ab into the array ba, but let's also assume that we have a function that reverses the elements in a specified portion of the array. Starting with ab, we reverse a to get a^rb, reverse b to get a^rb^r, and then reverse the whole thing to get $(a^rb^r)^r$, which is exactly ba. This results in the following code for rotation; the comments show the results when $abcdefgh$ is rotated left three elements.

```
reverse(0, i-1)      /* cbadefgh */
reverse(i, n-1)      /* cbahgfed */
reverse(0, n-1)      /* defghabc */
```

Doug McIlroy gave this hand-waving example of rotating a ten-element array up five positions; start with your palms towards you, left over right.

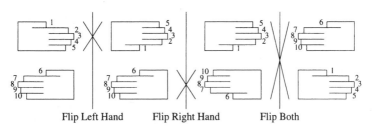

Flip Left Hand   Flip Right Hand   Flip Both

The reversal code is time- and space-efficient, and is so short and simple that it's pretty hard to get wrong. Brian Kernighan and P. J. Plauger used precisely this code in their 1981 *Software Tools in Pascal* to move lines within a text editor. Kernighan reports that it ran correctly the first time it was executed, while their previous code for a similar task based on linked lists contained several bugs. This code is used in several text processing systems, including the text editor with which I originally typed this column. Ken Thompson wrote the editor and the reversal code in 1971, and claims that it was part of the folklore even then.

2.4 Getting It Together: Sorting

Let's turn now to Problem C. Given a dictionary of English words (one word per input line in lower case letters), we must find all anagram classes. There are several good reasons for studying this problem. The first is technical: the solution is a nice combination of getting the right viewpoint and then using the right tools. The second reason is more compelling: wouldn't you hate to be the only person at a party who didn't know that "deposit", "dopiest", "posited" and "topside" are anagrams? And if those aren't enough, Problem 6 describes a similar problem in a real system.

Many approaches to this problem are surprisingly ineffective and complicated. Any method that considers all permutations of letters for a word is doomed to failure. The word "cholecystoduodenostomy" (an anagram in my dictionary of "duodenocholecystostomy") has 22! permutations, and a few multiplications showed that $22! \approx 1.124 \times 10^{21}$. Even assuming the blazing speed of one picosecond per permutation, this will take 1.1×10^9 seconds. The rule of thumb that "π seconds is a nanocentury" (see Section 7.1) tells us that 1.1×10^9 seconds is a few decades. And any method that compares all pairs of words is doomed to at least an overnight run on my machine — there are about 230,000 words in the dictionary I used, and even a simple anagram comparison takes at least a microsecond, so the total time is roughly

230,000 words × 230,000 comparisons/word × 1 microsecond/comparison

$= 52,900 \times 10^6$ microseconds $= 52,900$ seconds ≈ 14.7 hours

Can you find a way to avoid both the above pitfalls?

The *aha!* insight is to sign each word in the dictionary so that words in the same anagram class have the same *signature*, and then bring together words with equal signatures. This reduces the original anagram problem to two subproblems: selecting a signature and collecting words with the same signature. Think about these problems before reading further.

For the first problem we'll use a signature based on sorting†: order the letters within the word alphabetically. The signature of "deposit" is "deiopst", which is also the signature of "dopiest" and any other word in that class. To solve the second problem, we'll sort the words in the order of their signatures. The best description I have heard of this algorithm is Tom Cargill's hand waving: sort this way (with a horizontal wave of the hand) then that way (a vertical wave). Section 2.8 describes an implementation of this algorithm.

2.5 Principles

Sorting. The most obvious use of sorting is to produce sorted output, either as part of the system specification or as preparation for another program (perhaps one that uses binary search). But in the anagram problem, the ordering was not of interest; we sorted to bring together equal elements (in this case signatures). Those signatures are yet another application of sorting: ordering the letters within a word provides a *canonical form* for the words within an anagram class. By placing extra keys on each record and sorting by those keys, a sort function can be used as a workhorse for rearranging data on disk files. We'll return to the subject of sorting several times in Part III.

Binary Search. The algorithm for looking up an element in a sorted table is remarkably efficient and can be used in main memory or on disk; its only drawback is that the entire table must be known and sorted in advance. The strategy underlying this simple algorithm is used in many other applications.

Signatures. When an equivalence relation defines classes, it is helpful to define a signature such that every item in a class has the same signature and no other item does. Sorting the letters within a word yields one signature for an anagram class; other signatures are given by sorting and then representing duplicates by a count (so the signature of "mississippi" might be "i4m1p2s4", or "i4mp2s4" if 1's are deleted) or by keeping a 26-integer array telling how many times each letter occurs. Other applications of signatures include the Federal Bureau of Investigation's method for indexing fingerprints and the Soundex heuristic for identifying names that sound alike but are spelled differently.

NAME	SOUNDEX SIGNATURE
Smith	s530
Smythe	s530
Schultz	s243
Shultz	s432

Knuth describes the Soundex method in Chapter 6 of his *Sorting and Searching*.

---

† This anagram algorithm has been independently discovered by many people, dating at least as far back as the mid-1960's.

Problem Definition. Column 1 showed that determining what the user really wants to do is an essential part of programming. The theme of this column is the next step in problem definition: what primitives will we use to solve the problem? In each case the *aha!* insight defined a new basic operation to make the problem trivial.

A Problem Solver's Perspective. Good programmers are a little bit lazy: they sit back and wait for an insight rather than rushing forward with their first idea. That must, of course, be balanced with the initiative to code at the proper time. The real skill, though, is knowing the proper time. That judgment comes only with the experience of solving problems and reflecting on their solutions.

2.6 Problems

1. Consider the problem of finding all the anagrams of a given input word. How would you solve this problem given only the word and the dictionary? What if you could spend some time and space to process the dictionary before answering any queries?

2. Given a sequential file containing 4,300,000,000 32-bit integers, how can you find one that appears at least twice?

3. We skimmed two vector rotation algorithms that require subtle code; implement each as a program. How does the greatest common divisor of i and n appear in each program?

4. Several readers pointed out that while all three rotation algorithms require time proportional to n, the juggling algorithm is apparently twice as fast as the reversal algorithm: it stores and retrieves each element of the array just once, while the reversal algorithm does so twice. Experiment with the functions to compare their speeds on real machines; be especially sensitive to issues surrounding the locality of memory references.

5. Vector rotation functions change the vector *ab* to *ba*; how would you transform the vector *abc* to *cba*? (This models the problem of swapping nonadjacent blocks of memory.)

6. In the late 1970's, Bell Labs deployed a "user-operated directory assistance" program that allowed employees to look up a number in a company telephone directory using a standard push-button telephone.

1	2 ABC	3 DEF
4 GHI	5 JKL	6 MNO
7 PRS	8 TUV	9 WXY
*	0 OPER	#

To find the number of the designer of the system, Mike Lesk, one pressed "LESK*M*" (that is, "5375*6*") and the system spoke his number. Such services are now ubiquitous. One problem that arises in such systems is that different names may have the same push-button encoding; when this happens in Lesk's system, it asks the user for more information. Given a large file of names, such as a standard metropolitan telephone directory, how would you locate these "false matches"? (When Lesk did this experiment on such telephone directories, he found that the incidence of false matches was just 0.2 percent.) How would you implement the function that is given a push-button encoding of a name and returns the set of possible matching names?

7. In the early 1960's, Vic Vyssotsky worked with a programmer who had to transpose a 4000-by-4000 matrix stored on magnetic tape (each record had the same format in several dozen bytes). The original program his colleague suggested would have taken fifty hours to run; how did Vyssotsky reduce the run time to half an hour?

8. [J. Ullman] Given a set of n real numbers, a real number t, and an integer k, how quickly can you determine whether there exists a k-element subset of the set that sums to at most t?

9. Sequential search and binary search represent a tradeoff between search time and preprocessing time. How many binary searches need be performed in an n-element table to buy back the preprocessing time required to sort the table?

10. On the day a new researcher reported to work for Thomas Edison, Edison asked him to compute the volume of an empty light bulb shell. After several hours with calipers and calculus, the fresh hire returned with the answer of 150 cubic centimeters. In a few seconds, Edison computed and responded "closer to 155" — how did he do it?

2.7 Further Reading

Section 8.8 describes several good books on algorithms.

2.8 Implementing an Anagram Program *[Sidebar]*†

I organized my anagram program as a three-stage "pipeline" in which the output file of one program is fed as the input file to the next. The first program *sign*s the words, the second *sort*s the signed file, and the third *squash*es the words in an anagram class onto one line. Here's the process on a six-word dictionary.

---

† Sidebars in magazine columns are offset from the text, often in a bar at the side of the page. While they aren't an essential part of the column, they provide perspective on the material. In this book they appear as the last section in a column, marked as a "sidebar".

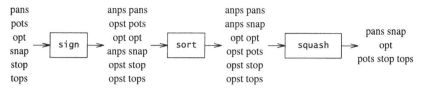

pans	anps pans	anps pans	
pots	opst pots	anps snap	pans snap
opt	opt opt	opt opt	opt
snap	anps snap	opst pots	pots stop tops
stop	opst stop	opst stop	
tops	opst tops	opst tops	

The output contains three anagram classes.

The following C *sign* program assumes that no word contains more than one hundred letters and that the input file contains only lower-case letters and newline characters. (I therefore preprocessed the dictionary with a one-line command to change upper-case characters to lower case.)

```
int charcomp(char *x, char *y) { return *x - *y; }

#define WORDMAX 100
int main(void)
{   char word[WORDMAX], sig[WORDMAX];
    while (scanf("%s", word) != EOF) {
        strcpy(sig, word);
        qsort(sig, strlen(sig), sizeof(char), charcomp);
        printf("%s %s\n", sig, word);
    }
    return 0;
}
```

The *while* loop reads one string at a time into *word* until it comes to the end of the file. The *strcpy* function copies the input word to the word *sig*, whose characters are then sorted by calling the C Standard Library *qsort* (the parameters are the array to be sorted, its length, the number of bytes per sort item, and the name of the function to compare two items, in this case, characters within the word). Finally, the *printf* statement prints the signature followed by the word itself and a newline.

The system *sort* program brings together all words with the same signature; the *squash* program prints them on a single line.

```
int main(void)
{   char word[WORDMAX], sig[WORDMAX], oldsig[WORDMAX];
    int linenum = 0;
    strcpy(oldsig, "");
    while (scanf("%s %s", sig, word) != EOF) {
        if (strcmp(oldsig, sig) != 0 && linenum > 0)
            printf("\n");
        strcpy(oldsig, sig);
        linenum++;
        printf("%s ", word);
    }
    printf("\n");
    return 0;
}
```

The bulk of the work is performed by the second *printf* statement; for each input line, it writes out the second field followed by a space. The *if* statement catches the changes between signatures: if *sig* changes from *oldsig* (its previous value), then a newline is printed (as long as this record isn't the first in the file). The last *printf* writes a final newline character.

After testing those simple parts on small input files, I constructed the anagram list by typing

```
sign <dictionary | sort | squash >gramlist
```

That command feeds the file *dictionary* to the program *sign*, pipes *sign*'s output into *sort*, pipes *sort*'s output into *squash*, and writes *squash*'s output in the file *gramlist*. The program ran in 18 seconds: 4 in *sign*, 11 in *sort* and 3 in *squash*.

I ran the program on a dictionary that contains 230,000 words; it does not, however, include many -s and -ed endings. The following were among the more interesting anagram classes.

```
subessential suitableness
canter creant cretan nectar recant tanrec trance
caret carte cater crate creat creta react recta trace
destain instead sainted satined
adroitly dilatory idolatry
least setal slate stale steal stela tales
reins resin rinse risen serin siren
constitutionalism misconstitutional
```

COLUMN 3: **DATA STRUCTURES PROGRAMS**

Most programmers have seen them, and most good programmers realize they've written at least one. They are huge, messy, ugly programs that should have been short, clean, beautiful programs. I've seen several programs that boil down to code like this

```
if (k ==   1) c001++
if (k ==   2) c002++
   ...
if (k == 500) c500++
```

Although the programs actually accomplished slightly more complicated tasks, it isn't misleading to view them as counting how many times each integer between 1 and 500 was found in a file. Each program contained over 1000 lines of code. Most programmers today instantly realize that they could accomplish the task with a program just a tiny fraction of the size by using a different data structure — a 500-element array to replace the 500 individual variables.

Hence the title of this column: a proper view of data does indeed structure programs. This column describes a variety of programs that were made smaller (and better) by restructuring their internal data.

3.1 A Survey Program

The next program we'll study summarized about twenty thousand questionnaires filled out by students at a particular college. Part of the output looked like this:

	Total	US Citi	Perm Visa	Temp Visa	Male	Female
African American	1289	1239	17	2	684	593
Mexican American	675	577	80	11	448	219
Native American	198	182	5	3	132	64
Spanish Surname	411	223	152	20	224	179
Asian American	519	312	152	41	247	270
Caucasian	16272	15663	355	33	9367	6836
Other	225	123	78	19	129	92
Totals	19589	18319	839	129	11231	8253

For each ethnic group, the number of males plus the number of females is a little less than the total because some people didn't answer some questions. The real output was more complicated. I've shown all seven rows plus the total row, but only the six columns that represent the totals and two other categories, citizenship status and sex. In the real problem there were twenty-five columns that represented eight categories and three similar pages of output: one apiece for two separate campuses, and one for the sum of the two. There were also a few other closely related tables to be printed, such as the number of students that declined to answer each question. Each questionnaire was represented by a record in which entry 0 contained the ethnic group encoded as an integer between 0 and 7 (for the seven categories and "refused"), entry 1 contained the campus (an integer between 0 and 2), entry 2 contained citizenship status, and so on through entry 8.

The programmer coded the program from the systems analyst's high-level design; after working on it for two months and producing a thousand lines of code, he estimated that he was half done. I understood his predicament after I saw the design: the program was built around 350 distinct variables — 25 columns times 7 rows times 2 pages. After variable declarations, the program consisted of a rat's nest of logic that decided which variables to increment as each input record was read. Think for a minute about how you would write the program.

The crucial decision is that the numbers should be stored as an array. The next decision is harder: should the array be laid out according to its output structure (along the three dimensions of campus, ethnic group and the twenty-five columns) or its input structure (along the four dimensions of campus, ethnic group, category and value within category)? Ignoring the campus dimension, the approaches can be viewed as

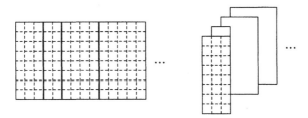

Both approaches work; the three-dimensional (left) view in my program resulted in a little more work when the data was read and a little less work when it was written. The program took 150 lines of code: 80 to build tables, 30 to produce the output I described, and 40 to produce other tables.

The count program and the survey program were two needlessly big programs; both contained numerous variables that were replaced by a single array. Reducing the length of the code by an order of magnitude led to correct programs that were developed quickly and could be easily tested and maintained. And although it didn't matter much in either application, both small programs were more efficient in run time and space than the big programs.

Why do programmers write big programs when small ones will do? One reason is that they lack the important laziness mentioned in Section 2.5; they rush ahead to code their first idea. But in both cases I've described, there was a deeper problem: the programmers thought about their problems in languages in which arrays are typically used as fixed tables that are initialized at the beginning of a program and never altered. In his book described in Section 1.7, James Adams would say that the programmers had "conceptual blocks" against using a dynamic array of counters.

There are many other reasons that programmers make these mistakes. When I prepared to write this column I found a similar example in my own code for the survey program. The main input loop had forty lines of code in eight five-statement blocks, the first two of which could be expressed as

```
ethnicgroup = entry[0]
campus = entry[1]
if entry[2] == refused
    declined[ethnicgroup, 2]++
else
    j = 1 + entry[2]
    count[campus, ethnicgroup, j]++
if entry[3] == refused
    declined[ethnicgroup, 3]++
else
    j = 4 + entry[3]
    count[campus, ethnicgroup, j]++
```

I could have replaced forty of those lines with six, after initializing the array *offset* to contain 0, 0, 1, 4, 6, ...

```
for i = [2, 8]
    if entry[i] == refused
        declined[ethnicgroup, i]++
    else
        j = offset[i] + entry[i]
        count[campus, ethnicgroup, j]++
```

I had been so satisfied to get one order-of-magnitude reduction in code length that I missed another one staring me in the face.

3.2 Form-Letter Programming

You've just typed your name and password to log in to the web site of your favorite store. The next page you see looks something like

```
Welcome back, Jane!
We hope that you and all the members
of the Public family are constantly
reminding your neighbors there
on Maple Street to shop with us.
As usual, we will ship your order to
    Ms. Jane Q. Public
    600 Maple Street
    Your Town, Iowa 12345
  ...
```

As a programmer, you realize that behind the scenes a computer looked up your user name in a database and retrieved fields like

```
Public|Jane|Q|Ms.|600|Maple Street|Your Town|Iowa|12345
```

But how exactly did the program construct that customized web page from your database record? The hasty programmer may be tempted to write a program that begins something like

```
read lastname, firstname, init, title, streetnum,
    streetname, town, state, zip
print "Welcome back,", firstname, "!"
print "We hope that you and all the members"
print "of the", lastname, "family are constantly"
print "reminding your neighbors there"
print "on", streetname, "to shop with us."
print "As usual, we will ship your order to"
print "    ", title, firstname, init ".", lastname
print "    ", streetnum, streetname
print "    ", town ",", state, zip
  ...
```

Such a program is tempting but tedious.

A more elegant approach involves writing a *form letter generator* that relies on a *form letter schema* like

```
Welcome back, $1!
We hope that you and all the members
of the $0 family are constantly
reminding your neighbors there
on $5 to shop with us.
As usual, we will ship your order to
    $3 $1 $2. $0
    $4 $5
    $6, $7 $8
  ...
```

The notation $\$i$ refers to the ith field in the record, so $\$0$ is the last name, and so on. The schema is interpreted by the following pseudocode, which assumes that a literal $\$$ character is written in the input schema as $\$\$$.

```
read fields from database
loop from start to end of schema
    c = next character in schema
    if c != '$'
        printchar c
    else
        c = next character in schema
        case c of
            '$':        printchar '$'
            '0' - '9':  printstring field[c]
            default:    error("bad schema")
```

The schema is represented in the program as one long array of characters in which text lines are ended by newline characters. (Perl and other scripting languages make this even easier; we can use variables like *$lastname*.)

Writing the generator and the schema will probably be easier than writing the obvious program. Separating the data from the control will pay off handsomely: if the letter is redesigned then the schema can be manipulated with a text editor, and the second specialized page will be simple indeed to prepare.

The concept of a report schema could have greatly simplified a 5300-line Cobol program I once maintained. The program's input was a description of a family's financial status; its output was a booklet summarizing the status and recommending future policy. Some numbers: 120 input fields; 400 output lines on 18 pages; 300 lines of code to clean the input data, 800 lines for computation, and 4200 lines to write the output. I estimate that the 4200 lines of output code could have been replaced by an interpreter of at most a few dozen lines of code and a schema of 400 lines; the computational code would have remain unchanged. Originally writing the program in that form would have resulted in Cobol code that was at most one-third the size and much easier to maintain.

3.3 An Array of Examples

Menus. I wanted the user of my Visual Basic program to be able to choose one of several possibilities by clicking a menu item. I browsed through an excellent collection of sample programs, and found one that allowed the user to select one of eight options. When I inspected the code behind the menu, item 0 looked like this:

```
sub menuitem0_click()
    menuitem0.checked = 1
    menuitem1.checked = 0
    menuitem2.checked = 0
    menuitem3.checked = 0
    menuitem4.checked = 0
    menuitem5.checked = 0
    menuitem6.checked = 0
    menuitem7.checked = 0
```

Item 1 was almost the same, with the following changes:

```
sub menuitem1_click()
    menuitem0.checked = 0
    menuitem1.checked = 1
    ...
```

And so on for items 2 through 7. Altogether, the selection menu items used about 100 lines of code.

I've written code like that myself. I started off with two items on the menu, and the code was reasonable. As I added the third, fourth and later items, I was so excited about the functionality behind the code that I didn't stop to clean up the mess.

With a little perspective, we can move most of that code into the single function *uncheckall* that sets each *checked* field to 0. The first function then becomes:

```
sub menuitem0_click()
    uncheckall
    menuitem0.checked = 1
```

But we are still left with seven other similar functions.

Fortunately, Visual Basic supports arrays of menu items, so we can replace the eight similar functions with one:

```
sub menuitem_click(int choice)
    for i = [0, numchoices)
        menuitem[i].checked = 0
    menuitem[choice].checked = 1
```

Gathering repeated code into a common function reduced 100 lines of code to 25, and judicious use of arrays dropped that to 4 lines. The next selection is much simpler to add, and potentially buggy code is now crystal clear. This approach solved my problem in just a few lines of code.

Error Messages. Dirty systems have hundreds of error messages scattered throughout the code, mixed in with other output statements; clean systems have them accessed through a single function. Consider the difficulty of performing the following requests under the "dirty" and "clean" organizations: produce a list of all possible error messages, change each "serious" error message to sound an alarm, and translate the error messages into French or German.

Date Functions. Given a year and day of the year, return the month and day of the month; for instance, the 61st day of 2004 is the 1st day of the 3rd month. In their *Elements of Programming Style*, Kernighan and Plauger present a fifty-five line program for this task taken straight from someone else's programming text. They then give a five-line program for the task, using an array of twenty-six integers. Problem 4 introduces the representation issues that abound in date functions.

Word Analysis. Many computing problems arise in the analysis of English words. We'll see in Section 13.8 how spelling checkers use "suffix stripping" to condense their dictionaries: they store the single word "laugh" without storing all its various endings ("-ing", "-s", "-ed", etc.). Linguists have developed a substantial body of rules for such tasks. Doug McIlroy knew that code was the wrong vessel for such rules when he built the first real-time text-to-speech synthesizer in 1973; he instead wrote it using 1000 lines of code and a 400-line table. When someone modified the program without adding to the tables, that resulted in 2500 extra lines of code to do twenty percent more work. McIlroy asserts that he could probably do the expanded task now using fewer than 1000 lines by adding even more tables. To try your own hand on a similar set of rules, see Problem 5.

3.4 Structuring Data

What is well-structured data? The standards have risen steadily over time. In the early years, structured data meant well-chosen variable names. Where programmers once used parallel arrays or offsets from registers, languages later incorporated records or structures and pointers to them. We learned to replace code for manipulating data with functions with names like *insert* or *search*; that helped us to change representations without damaging the rest of the program. David Parnas extended that approach to observe that the data a system is to process gives deep insight into a good module structure.

"Object-Oriented Programming" took the next step. Programmers learned to identify the fundamental objects in their design, publish to the world an abstraction and the essential operations on it, and hide the implementation details from view. Languages like Smalltalk and C++ allowed us to encapsulate those objects in classes; we'll study this approach in detail as we investigate set abstractions and implementations in Column 13.

3.5 Powerful Tools for Specialized Data

In the bad old days, programmers built each application from scratch. Modern tools allow programmers (and others) to build applications with minimal effort. The little list of tools in this section is indicative, not exhaustive. Each tool exploits one view of data to solve a particular but common problem. Languages such as Visual Basic, Tcl and various shells provide the "glue" for joining these objects.

Hypertext. In the early 1990's, when web sites were numbered in the thousands, I was entranced by the reference books that were just coming out on CD-ROMs. The collection of data was stunning: encyclopedias, dictionaries, almanacs, telephone directories, classical literature, textbooks, system reference manuals, and more, all in the palm of my hand. The user interfaces for the various data sets were, unfortunately, equally stunning: every program had its own quirks. Today, I have access to all that data (and more) on CDs and the web, and the interface is usually the web browser of my choice. That makes life better for user and implementer alike.

Name-Value Pairs. A bibliographic database might have entries like this:

```
%title    The C++ Programming Language, Third Edition
%author   Bjarne Stroustrup
%publisher Addison-Wesley
%city     Reading, Massachusetts
%year     1997
```

Visual Basic takes this approach to describe controls in an interface. A text box in the upper-left corner of a form can be described with the following properties (names) and settings (values):

Height	495
Left	0
Multiline	False
Name	txtSample
Top	0
Visible	True
Width	215

(The complete text box contains three dozen pairs.) To widen the text box, for example, I might drag the right edge with the mouse, or enter a larger integer to replace 215, or use the run-time assignment

```
txtSample.Width = 400
```

The programmer may choose the most convenient way to manipulate this simple but powerful structure.

Spreadsheets. Keeping track of our organization's budget looked difficult to me. Out of habit, I would have built a large program for the job, with a clunky user interface. The next programmer took a broader view, and implemented the program as a spreadsheet, supplemented by a few functions in Visual Basic. The interface was totally natural for the accounting people who were the main users. (If I had to write the college survey program today, the fact that it is an array of numbers would encourage me to try to put it into a spreadsheet.)

Databases. Many years ago, after scribbling details about his first dozen jumps in a paper log book, a programmer decided that he wanted to automate his skydiving records. A few years earlier, that would have involved laying out a complex record format, and then building by hand (or by a "Report Program Generator") programs to enter, update and retrieve the data. At the time, he and I were both awe-struck by his use of a new-fangled commercial database package for the job: he was able to define new screens for database operations in minutes rather than days.

Domain-Specific Languages. Graphical user interfaces (GUIs) have fortunately replaced many old, clunky textual languages. But special-purpose languages are still useful in certain applications. I despise having to use a mouse to poke at a faux calculator on the screen when I really want to type straightforward mathematics like

```
n = 1000000
47 * n * log(n)/log(2)
```

Rather than specifying a query with baroque combinations of text boxes and operator buttons, I prefer to write in a language like

```
(design or architecture) and not building
```

Windows that were formerly specified by hundreds of lines of executable code are now described in dozens of lines of Hypertext Markup Language (HTML). Languages may be out of vogue for general user input, but they are still potent devices in some applications.

3.6 Principles

While the stories in this column span several decades and a dozen languages, the moral of each is the same: *don't write a big program when a little one will do.* Most of the structures exemplify what Polya calls the Inventor's Paradox in his *How to Solve It*: "the more general problem may be easier to solve". In programming this means that it may be harder to solve a 23-case problem directly than to write a general program to handle the n-case version, and then apply it to the case that $n = 23$.

This column has concentrated on just one contribution that data structures can make to software: reducing big programs to small programs. Data structure design can have many other positive impacts, including time and space reduction and increased portability and maintainability. Fred Brooks's comment in Chapter 9 of his *Mythical Man Month* is stated for space reduction, but it is good advice for programmers who desire the other attributes as well:

> The programmer at wit's end for lack of space can often do best by disentangling himself from his code, rearing back, and contemplating his data. Representation *is* the essence of programming.

Here are a few principles for you to ponder as you rear back.

Rework repeated code into arrays. A long stretch of similar code is often best expressed by the simplest of data structures, the array.

Encapsulate complex structures. When you need a sophisticated data structure, define it in abstract terms, and express those operations as a class.

Use advanced tools when possible. Hypertext, name-value pairs, spreadsheets, databases, languages and the like are powerful tools within their specialized problem domains.

Let the data structure the program. The theme of this column is that data can structure a program by replacing complicated code with an appropriate data structure. Although the particulars change, the theme remains: before writing code, good programmers thoroughly understand the input, the output and the intermediate data structures around which their programs are built.

3.7 Problems

1. As the second edition of this book goes to press, individual income in the United
    States is taxed at five different rates, the maximum of which is around forty per-
    cent. The situation was formerly more complicated, and more expensive. A pro-
    gramming text gave the following twenty-five *if* statements as a reasonable
    approach for calculating the 1978 United States Federal Income Tax. The rate
    sequence .14, .15, .16, .17, .18, ... exhibits jumps larger than .01 later in the
    sequence. Any comments?

    ```
    if income <= 2200
        tax = 0
    else if income <= 2700
        tax =           .14 * (income - 2200)
    else if income <= 3200
        tax =      70 + .15 * (income - 2700)
    else if income <= 3700
        tax =     145 + .16 * (income - 3200)
    else if income <= 4200
        tax =     225 + .17 * (income - 3700)
        ...
    else
        tax = 53090 + .70 * (income - 102200)
    ```

2. A kth-order linear recurrence with constant coefficients defines a series as

    $$a_n = c_1 a_{n-1} + c_2 a_{n-2} + \cdots + c_k a_{n-k} + c_{k+1},$$

    where $c_1, ..., c_{k+1}$ are real numbers. Write a program that with input k, a_1, ...,
    a_k, c_1, ..., c_{k+1}, and m produces the output a_1 through a_m. How difficult is that
    program compared to a program that evaluates one particular fifth-order recur-
    rence, but does so without using arrays?

3. Write a "banner" function that is given a capital letter as input and produces as
    output an array of characters that graphically depicts that letter.

4. Write functions for the following date problems: given two dates, compute the
    number of days between them; given a date, return its day of the week; given a
    month and year, produce a calendar for the month as an array of characters.

5. This problem deals with a small part of the problem of hyphenating English
    words. The following list of rules describes some legal hyphenations of words
    that end in the letter "c":

    > et-ic al-is-tic s-tic p-tic -lyt-ic ot-ic an-tic n-tic c-tic at-ic h-nic n-ic m-ic l-lic b-lic -clic
    > l-ic h-ic f-ic d-ic -bic a-ic -mac i-ac

    The rules must be applied in the above order; thus the hyphenations "eth-nic"
    (which is caught by the rule "h-nic") and "clinic" (which fails that test and falls
    through to "n-ic"). How would you represent such rules in a function that is
    given a word and must return suffix hyphenations?

6. Build a "form-letter generator" that can prepare a customized document for each record in a database (this is often referred to as a "mail-merge" feature). Design small schemas and input files to test the correctness of your program.

7. Typical dictionaries allow one to look up the definition of a word, and Problem 2.1 describes a dictionary that allows one to look up the anagrams of a word. Design dictionaries for looking up the proper spelling of a word and for looking up the rhymes of a word. Discuss dictionaries for looking up an integer sequence (such as 1, 1, 2, 3, 5, 8, 13, 21, ...), a chemical structure, or the metrical structure of a song.

8. [S. C. Johnson] Seven-segment devices provide an inexpensive display of the ten decimal digits:

The seven segments are usually numbered as

$$3\ \overline{\underset{1}{2}}\ 4$$
$$5\ \underset{0}{}\ 6$$

Write a program that displays a 16-bit positive integer in five seven-segment digits. The output is an array of five bytes; bit i of byte j is one if and only if the ith segment of digit j should be on.

3.8 Further Reading

Data may structure programs, but only wise programmers structure large software systems. Steve McConnell's *Code Complete* was published by Microsoft Press in 1993. The subtitle accurately describes this 860-page volume: *A Practical Handbook of Software Construction*. It provides a fast track to wisdom for programmers.

Chapters 8 through 12 on "Data" are most relevant to this column. McConnell moves from basics such as declaring data and choosing data names to advanced topics including table-driven programs and abstract data types. His Chapters 4 through 7 on "Design" elaborate on the theme of this column.

The knowledge required to build a software project spans a wide range, from tasteful construction of small functions to managing big software projects. Especially when combined with his *Rapid Development* (Microsoft Press, 1996) and *Software Project Survival Guide* (Microsoft Press, 1998), McConnell's work covers the two extremes, and most of the territory in between. His books are fun to read, but you never forget that he is speaking from hard-won personal experience.

WRITING CORRECT PROGRAMS

In the late 1960's people were talking about the promise of programs that verify the correctness of other programs. Unfortunately, in the intervening decades, with precious few exceptions, there is still little more than talk about automated verification systems. In spite of unrealized expectations, though, research on program verification has given us something far more valuable than a black box that gobbles programs and flashes "good" or "bad" — we now have a fundamental understanding of computer programming.

The purpose of this column is to show how that fundamental understanding can help real programmers write correct programs. One reader characterized the approach that most programmers grow up with as "write your code, throw it over the wall, and have Quality Assurance or Testing deal with the bugs." This column describes an alternative. Before we get to the subject itself, we must keep it in perspective. Coding skill is just one small part of writing correct programs. The majority of the task is the subject of the three previous columns: problem definition, algorithm design, and data structure selection. If you perform those tasks well, writing correct code is usually easy.

4.1 The Challenge of Binary Search

Even with the best of designs, every now and then a programmer has to write subtle code. This column is about one problem that requires particularly careful code: binary search. After reviewing the problem and sketching an algorithm, we'll use verification principles as we write the program.

We first met this problem in Section 2.2; we are to determine whether the sorted array $x[0..n-1]$ contains the target element t.† Precisely, we know that $n \geq 0$ and that

---

† See Problem and Solution 5.1 if you need help in criticizing these short variable names, the form of the binary search function definition, error handling and other issues of style that are critical to the success of large software projects.

$x[0] \le x[1] \le x[2] \le \ldots \le x[n-1]$; when $n=0$ the array is empty. The types of t and the elements of x are the same; the pseudocode should work equally well for integers, floats or strings. The answer is stored in the integer p (for position): when p is -1 the target t is not in $x[0..n-1]$, otherwise $0 \le p \le n-1$ and $t = x[p]$.

Binary search solves the problem by keeping track of the range within the array that holds t (if t is anywhere in the array). Initially, the range is the entire array. The range is shrunk by comparing its middle element to t and discarding half the range. The process continues until t is discovered in the array or until the range in which it must lie is known to be empty. In a table of n elements, binary search uses roughly $\log_2 n$ comparisons.

Most programmers think that with the above description in hand, writing the code is easy. They're wrong. The only way you'll believe this is by putting down this column right now and writing the code yourself. Try it.

I've assigned this problem in courses for professional programmers. The students had a couple of hours to convert the description above into a program in the language of their choice; a high-level pseudocode was fine. At the end of the specified time, almost all the programmers reported that they had correct code for the task. We would then take thirty minutes to examine their code, which the programmers did with test cases. In several classes and with over a hundred programmers, the results varied little: ninety percent of the programmers found bugs in their programs (and I wasn't always convinced of the correctness of the code in which no bugs were found).

I was amazed: given ample time, only about ten percent of professional programmers were able to get this small program right. But they aren't the only ones to find this task difficult: in the history in Section 6.2.1 of his *Sorting and Searching*, Knuth points out that while the first binary search was published in 1946, the first published binary search without bugs did not appear until 1962.

4.2 Writing the Program

The key idea of binary search is that we always know that if t is anywhere in $x[0..n-1]$, then it must be in a certain range of x. We'll use the shorthand *mustbe(range)* to mean that if t is anywhere in the array, then it must be in *range*. We can use this notation to convert the above description of binary search into a program sketch.

```
initialize range to 0..n-1
loop
    { invariant: mustbe(range) }
    if range is empty,
        break and report that t is not in the array
    compute m, the middle of the range
    use m as a probe to shrink the range
        if t is found during the shrinking process,
        break and report its position
```

The crucial part of this program is the *loop invariant*, which is enclosed in curly braces. This *assertion* about the program state is called an *invariant* because it is true at the beginning and end of each iteration of the loop; it formalizes the intuitive notion we had above.

We'll now refine the program, making sure that all actions respect the invariant. The first issue we must face is the representation of *range*: we'll use two indices *l* and *u* (for "lower" and "upper") to represent the range *l..u*. (A binary search function in Section 9.3 represents a range by its beginning position and its length.) The logical function *mustbe*(*l*, *u*) says that if *t* is anywhere in the array, it must be in the (closed) range *x*[*l..u*].

Our next job is the initialization; what values should *l* and *u* have so that *mustbe*(*l*, *u*) is true? The obvious choice is 0 and $n - 1$: *mustbe*(0, $n - 1$) says that if *t* is anywhere in *x*, then it is in $x[0..n - 1]$, which is precisely what we know at the beginning of the program. Initialization therefore consists of the assignments $l = 0$ and $u = n - 1$.

The next tasks are to check for an empty range and to compute the new midpoint, *m*. The range *l..u* is empty if $l > u$, in which case we store the special value -1 in *p* and terminate the loop, which gives

```
if l > u
    p = -1; break
```

The *break* statement terminates the enclosing *loop*. This statement computes *m*, the midpoint of the range:

```
m = (l + u) / 2
```

The "/" operator implements integer division: 6/2 is 3, as is 7/2. Our expanded program is now

```
l = 0; u = n-1
loop
    { invariant: mustbe(l, u) }
    if l > u
        p = -1; break
    m = (l + u) / 2
    use m as a probe to shrink the range l..u
        if t is found during the shrinking process,
        break and note its position
```

Refining the last three lines in the loop body will involve comparing *t* and *x*[*m*] and taking appropriate action to maintain the invariant. Thus the code will have the general form

```
case
    x[m] <  t:   action a
    x[m] == t:   action b
    x[m] >  t:   action c
```

For action b, we know that t is in position m, so we set p to m and *break* the loop. Because the other two cases are symmetric, we'll focus on the first and trust that the last will follow by symmetry (this is part of the reason we'll verify the code precisely in the next section).

If $x[m]<t$, then we know that $x[0]\leq x[1]\leq...\leq x[m]<t$, so t can't be anywhere in $x[0..m]$. Combining this with the knowledge that t is not outside $x[l..u]$, we know that if it is anywhere, then it must be in $x[m+1..u]$, which we write as $mustbe(m+1, u)$. We then reestablish the invariant $mustbe(l, u)$ by setting l to $m+1$. Putting these cases into the previous code sketch gives the final function.

```
l = 0; u = n-1
loop
    { mustbe(l, u) }
    if l > u
        p = -1; break
    m = (l + u) / 2
    case
        x[m] <  t:   l = m+1
        x[m] == t:   p = m; break
        x[m] >  t:   u = m-1
```

It's a short program: a dozen lines of code and one invariant assertion. The basic techniques of program verification — stating the invariant precisely and keeping an eye towards maintaining the invariant as we wrote each line of code — helped us greatly as we converted the algorithm sketch into pseudocode. This process gives us some confidence in the program, but we are by no means certain of its correctness. Spend a few minutes determining whether the code behaves as specified before reading further.

4.3 Understanding the Program

When I face a subtle programming problem, I try to derive code at about the level of detail we just saw. I then use verification methods to increase my confidence that it is correct. We'll use verification at this level in Columns 9, 11 and 14.

In this section we'll study a verification argument for the binary search code at a picky level of detail — in practice I'd do a much less formal analysis. The version of the program on the next page is (far too) heavily annotated with assertions that formalize the intuitive notions that we used as we originally wrote the code.

While the development of the code was top-down (starting with the general idea and refining it to individual lines of code), this analysis of correctness will be bottom-up: we'll start with the individual lines of code and see how they work together to solve the problem.

> **Warning**
> Boring material ahead.
> Skip to Section 4.4
> when drowsiness strikes.

We'll start with lines 1 through 3. The assertion in line 1 that $mustbe(0, n-1)$ is true by the definition of *mustbe*: if t is anywhere in the array, then it must be in $x[0..n-1]$. The assignments in line 2 of $l = 0$ and $u = n-1$ therefore give the assertion in line 3: $mustbe(l, u)$.

We come now to the hard part: the loop in lines 4 through 27. Our argument for its correctness has three parts, each of which is closely related to the loop invariant:

Initialization. The invariant is true when the loop is executed for the first time.

Preservation. If the invariant holds at the beginning of an iteration and the loop body is executed, then the invariant will remain true after the loop body finishes execution.

Termination. The loop will terminate and the desired result will hold (in this case, the desired result is that p has the correct value). Showing this will use the facts established by the invariant.

For initialization we note that the assertion in line 3 is the same as that in line 5. To establish the other two properties, we'll reason from line 5 through to line 27. When we discuss lines 9 and 21 (the *break* statements) we will establish termination properties, and if we make it all the way to line 27, we will have established preservation, because it is the same as line 5.

```
 1.    { mustbe(0, n-1) }
 2.    l = 0; u = n-1
 3.    { mustbe(l, u) }
 4.    loop
 5.        { mustbe(l, u) }
 6.        if l > u
 7.            { l > u && mustbe(l, u) }
 8.            { t is not in the array }
 9.            p = -1; break
10.        { mustbe(l, u) && l <= u }
11.        m = (l + u) / 2
12.        { mustbe(l, u) && l <= m <= u }
13.        case
14.            x[m] <  t:
15.                    { mustbe(l, u) && cantbe(0, m) }
16.                    { mustbe(m+1, u) }
17.                    l = m+1
18.                    { mustbe(l, u) }
19.            x[m] == t:
20.                    { x[m] == t }
21.                    p = m; break
22.            x[m] >  t:
23.                    { mustbe(l, u) && cantbe(m, n) }
24.                    { mustbe(l, m-1) }
25.                    u = m-1
26.                    { mustbe(l, u) }
27.        { mustbe(l, u) }
```

A successful test in line 6 yields the assertion of line 7: if t is anywhere in the array then it must be between positions l and u, and $l > u$. Those facts imply line 8: t is not in the array. We thus correctly terminate the loop in line 9 after setting p to -1.

If the test in line 6 fails, we come to line 10. The invariant still holds (we've done nothing to change it), and because the test failed we know that $l \leq u$. Line 11 sets m to the average of l and u, truncated down to the nearest integer. Because the average is always between the two values and truncating can't move it below l, we have the assertion of line 12.

The analysis of the *case* statement in lines 13 through 27 considers each of its three possible choices. The easiest choice to analyze is the second alternative, in line 19. Because of the assertion in line 20, we are correct in setting p to m and terminating the loop. This is the second of two places where the loop is terminated, and both end it correctly, so we have established the termination correctness of the loop.

We come next to the two symmetric branches of the case statement; because we concentrated on the first branch as we developed the code, we'll turn our attention now to lines 22 through 26. Consider the assertion in line 23. The first clause is the invariant, which the loop has not altered. The second clause is true because $t < x[m] \leq x[m+1] \leq \ldots \leq x[n-1]$, so we know that t can't be anywhere in the array above position $m-1$; this is expressed with the shorthand *cantbe*$(m, n-1)$.

Logic tells us that if t must be between l and u and can't be at or above m, then it must be between l and $m-1$ (if it is anywhere in x); hence line 24. Execution of line 25 with line 24 true leaves line 26 true — that is the definition of assignment. This choice of the *case* statement therefore re-establishes the invariant in line 27.

The argument for lines 14 through 18 has exactly the same form, so we've analyzed all three choices of the *case* statement. One correctly terminates the loop, and the other two maintain the invariant.

This analysis of the code shows that if the loop terminates, then it does so with the correct value in p. It may still, however, have an infinite loop; indeed, that was the most common error in the programs written by the professional programmers.

Our halting proof uses a different aspect of the range $l..u$. That range is initially a certain finite size (n), and lines 6 through 9 ensure that the loop terminates when the range contains less than one element. To prove termination we therefore have to show that the range shrinks during each iteration of the loop. Line 12 tells us that m is always within the current range. Both looping branches of the *case* statement (lines 14 and 22) exclude the value at position m from the current range and thereby decrease its size by at least one. The program must therefore halt.

With this background, I feel pretty confident that we are able to move ahead with this function. The next column covers precisely this topic: implementing the function in C, then testing it to ensure that it is correct and efficient.

4.4 Principles

This exercise displays many strengths of program verification: the problem is important and requires careful code, the development of the program is guided by verification ideas, and the analysis of correctness employs general tools. The primary weakness of this exercise is its level of detail; in practice I would work at a less formal level. Fortunately, the details illustrate a number of general principles, including the following.

Assertions. The relations among input, program variables, and output describe the "state" of a program; assertions allow a programmer to enunciate those relations precisely. Their roles throughout a program's life are discussed in the next section.

Sequential Control Structures. The simplest structure to control a program is of the form "do this statement then that statement". We understand such structures by placing assertions between them and analyzing each step of the program's progress individually.

Selection Control Structures. These structures include *if* and *case* statements of various forms; during execution, one of many choices is selected. We show the correctness of such a structure by considering each of the several choices individually. The fact that a certain choice is selected allows us to make an assertion in the proof; if we execute the statement following *if $i > j$*, for instance, then we can assert that $i > j$ and use that fact to derive the next relevant assertion.

Iteration Control Structures. To prove the correctness of a loop we must establish three properties:

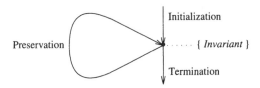

We first argue that the loop invariant is established by initialization, and then show that each iteration preserves its truth. These two steps show by mathematical induction that the invariant is true before and after each iteration of the loop. The third step is to argue that whenever execution of the loop terminates, the desired result is true. Together these establish that if the loop ever halts, then it does so correctly; we must prove that it does terminate by other means (the halting proof of binary search used a typical argument).

Functions. To verify a function, we first state its purpose by two assertions. Its *precondition* is the state that must be true before it is called, and its *postcondition* is what the function will guarantee on termination. Thus we might specify a C binary search function as follows:

```
int bsearch(int t, int x[], int n)
/* precondition: x[0] <= x[1] <= ... <= x[n-1]
   postcondition:
        result == -1     => t not present in x
        0 <= result < n  => x[result] == t
*/
```

These conditions are more a contract than a statement of fact: they say that if the function is called with the preconditions satisfied, then execution of the function will establish its postcondition. After I prove once that the body of the function has this property, I can use the stated relations between the pre- and postconditions without ever again considering the implementation. This approach to software development is often called "programming by contract".

4.5 The Roles of Program Verification

When one programmer tries to convince another that a piece of code is correct, the primary tool is usually the test case: execute the program by hand on one input. That's a powerful tool: it's good for detecting bugs, easy to use, and well understood. It is clear, however, that programmers have a deeper understanding of programs — if they didn't, they could never write them in the first place. One of the major benefits of program verification is that it gives programmers a language in which they can express that understanding.

Later in this book, especially in Columns 9, 11 and 14, we'll use verification techniques as we develop subtle programs. We'll use the language of verification to explain every line of code as it is written; it is particularly helpful to sketch an invariant for each loop. The important explanations end up in the program text as assertions; deciding which assertions to include in real software is an art that comes only with practice.

The language of verification is used often after the code is first written, starting during code walk-throughs. During testing, violations of the *assert* statements point the way to bugs, and examining the form of a violation shows how to remove one bug without introducing another. When you debug, fix both the code and the false assertion: understand the code at all times, and resist those foul urges to "just change it until it works". The next column illustrates several roles that assertions can play during testing and debugging. Assertions are crucial during maintenance of a program; when you pick up code that you've never seen before, and no one else has looked at for years, assertions about the program state can give invaluable insight.

These techniques are only a small part of writing correct programs; keeping the code simple is usually the key to correctness. On the other hand, several professional programmers familiar with these techniques have related to me an experience that is too common in my own programming: when they construct a program, the "hard" parts work the first time, while the bugs are in the "easy" parts. When they came to a hard part, they hunkered down and successfully used powerful formal techniques. In the easy parts, though, they returned to their old ways of programming, with the old results. I wouldn't have believed this phenomenon until it happened to me; such embarrassments are good motivation to use the techniques frequently.

4.6 Problems

1. As laborious as our proof of binary search was, it is still unfinished by some standards. How would you prove that the program is free of run-time errors (such as division by zero, word overflow, variables out of declared range, or array indices out of bounds)? If you have a background in discrete mathematics, can you formalize the proof in a logical system?

2. If the original binary search was too easy for you, try the variant that returns in p the position of the first occurrence of t in the array x (if there are multiple occurrences of t, the original algorithm returns an arbitrary one). Your code should make a logarithmic number of comparisons of array elements; it is possible to do the job in $\log_2 n$ such comparisons. *(section 9.3)*

3. Write and verify a recursive binary search program. Which parts of the code and proof stay the same as in the iterative version, and which parts change?

4. Add fictitious "timing variables" to your binary search program to count the number of comparisons it makes, and use program verification techniques to prove that its run time is indeed logarithmic.

5. Prove that this program terminates when its input x is a positive integer.

```
while x != 1 do
    if even(x)
        x = x/2
    else
        x = 3*x+1
```

6. [C. Scholten] David Gries calls this the "Coffee Can Problem" in his *Science of Programming*. You are initially given a coffee can that contains some black beans and some white beans and a large pile of "extra" black beans. You then repeat the following process until there is a single bean left in the can.

   Randomly select two beans from the can. If they are the same color, throw them both out and insert an extra black bean. If they are different colors, return the white bean to the can and throw out the black.

   Prove that the process terminates. What can you say about the color of the final remaining bean as a function of the numbers of black and white beans originally in the can?

7. A colleague faced the following problem in a program to draw lines on a bit-mapped display. An array of n pairs of reals (a_i, b_i) defined the n lines $y_i = a_i x + b_i$. The lines were ordered in the x-interval $[0,1]$ in the sense that $y_i < y_{i+1}$ for all values of i between 0 and $n-2$ and all values of x in $[0,1]$:

   Less formally, the lines don't touch in the vertical slab. Given a point (x,y), where $0 \le x \le 1$, he wanted to determine the two lines that bracket the point. How could he solve the problem quickly?

8. Binary search is fundamentally faster than sequential search: to search an n-element table, it makes roughly $\log_2 n$ comparisons while sequential search makes roughly $n/2$. While it is often fast enough, in a few cases binary search must be made faster yet. Although you can't reduce the logarithmic number of comparisons made by the algorithm, can you rewrite the binary search code to be faster? For definiteness, assume that you are to search a sorted table of $n = 1000$ integers.

9. As exercises in program verification, precisely specify the input/output behavior of each of the following program fragments and show that the code meets its specification. The first program implements the vector addition $a = b + c$.

```
i = 0
while i < n
    a[i] = b[i] + c[i]
    i = i+1
```

(This code and the next two fragments expand the *"for $i = [0, n)$"* loop to a *while* loop with an increment at the end.) The next fragment computes the maximum value in the array x.

```
max = x[0]
i = 1
while i < n do
    if x[i] > max
        max = x[i]
    i = i+1
```

This sequential search program returns the position of the first occurrence of t in the array $x[0..n-1]$.

```
i = 0
while i < n && x[i] != t
    i = i+1
if i >= n
    p = -1
else
    p = i
```

This program computes the nth power of x in time proportional to the logarithm of n. This recursive program is straightforward to code and to verify; the iterative version is subtle, and is left as an additional problem.

```
function exp(x, n)
        pre   n >= 0
        post result = x^n
    if n = 0
        return 1
    else if even(n)
        return square(exp(x, n/2))
    else
        return x*exp(x, n-1)
```

10. Introduce errors into the binary search function and see whether (and how) they are caught by attempting to verify the buggy code.

11. Write and prove the correctness of a recursive binary search function in C or C++ with this declaration:

```
int binarysearch(DataType x[], int n)
```

Use this function alone; do not call any other recursive functions.

4.7 Further Reading

The Science of Programming by David Gries is an excellent introduction to the field of program verification. It was published in paperback by Springer-Verlag in 1987. It starts with a tutorial on logic, goes on to a formal view of program verification and development, and finally discusses programming in common languages. In this column I've tried to sketch the potential benefits of program verification; the only way that most programmers will be able to use verification effectively is to study a book like Gries's.

COLUMN 5: **A SMALL MATTER OF PROGRAMMING**

So far, you've done everything right. You dug deep to define the right problem. You balanced the true requirements with a careful selection of algorithms and data structures. You used the techniques of program verification to write elegant pseudocode that you're pretty sure is correct. How do you incorporate the resulting gem into your big system? All that's left is, well, a small matter of programming.

Programmers are optimists, and they are tempted to take the easy path: code up the function, slip it into the system, and fervently hope that it runs. Sometimes that works. But the other 999 times out of 1000, it leads to disaster: one has to grope around in the huge system to manipulate the little function.

Wise programmers instead build *scaffolding* to give them easy access to the function. This column is devoted to implementing the binary search described in pseudocode in the last column as a trustworthy C function. (The code would be very similar in C++ or Java, and the approach works for most other languages.) Once we have the code, we'll probe it with scaffolding, then move on to test it more thoroughly and conduct experiments on its running time. For a tiny function, our path is long. The result, though, is a program we can trust.

5.1 From Pseudocode to C

We'll assume that the array x and the target item t are both of type *DataType*, which is defined by a C *typedef* statement like

```
typedef int DataType;
```

The defined type might be long integer, floating point, or whatever. The array is implemented by two global variables:

```
int n;
DataType x[MAXN];
```

(Although this is poor style for most C programs, it reflects the way that we access data within a C++ class; global variables can also result in smaller scaffolding.) Our goal is this C function:

45

```
int binarysearch(DataType t)
/* precondition: x[0] <= x[1] <= ... <= x[n-1]
   postcondition:
        result == -1     =>  t not present in x
        0 <= result < n  =>  x[result] == t
*/
```

Most of the pseudocode statements in Section 4.2 translate line-by-line into C (and most other languages, for that matter). Where the pseudocode stores a value in the answer variable *p*, the C program will *return* the value. Replacing the pseudocode *loop* with the C infinite loop *for* (;;) yields this code:

```
for (;;) {
    if (l > u)
        return -1;
    ... rest of loop ...
}
```

We can transform that to a *while* loop by reversing the test:

```
while (l <= u) {
    ... rest of loop ...
}
return -1;
```

The final program is then:

```
int binarysearch(DataType t)
    /* return (any) position if t in sorted x[0..n-1] or
       -1 if t is not present */
{   int l, u, m;
    l = 0;
    u = n-1;
    while (l <= u) {
        m = (l + u) / 2;
        if (x[m] < t)
            l = m+1;
        else if (x[m] == t)
            return m;
        else /* x[m] > t */
            u = m-1;
    }
    return -1;
}
```

5.2 A Test Harness

The first step in exercising the function is, of course, to walk through a few test cases by hand. Tiny cases (zero-, one- and two-element arrays) often suffice to smoke out bugs. On larger arrays such tests become tedious, so the next step is to build a driver to call the function. Five lines of C scaffolding can do the job:

```
while (scanf("%d %d", &n, &t) != EOF) {
    for (i = 0; i < n; i++)
        x[i] = 10*i;
    printf(" %d\n", binarysearch(t));
}
```

We can start with a C program of about two dozen lines: the *binarysearch* function
and the above code in the *main* function. We should expect to grow the program as
we add additional scaffolding.

When I type the input line ''2 0'', the program generates the two-element array
with $x[0]=0$ and $x[1]=10$, then reports (on the next, indented, line) that the result of
searching for 0 was that it was in location 0:

```
2  0
 0
2  10
 1
2  -5
 -1
2  5
 -1
2  15
 -1
```

The typed input is always in *italics*. The next pair of lines shows that 10 is correctly
found in location 1. The final six lines describe three correct unsuccessful searches.
The program thus correctly handles all possible searches in an array of two distinct
elements. As the program passed similar tests on inputs of other sizes, I grew more
and more confident of its correctness and more and more bored with this laborious
hand testing. The next section describes scaffolding to automate this job.

Not all testing proceeds this smoothly. Here is a binary search proposed by several professional programmers:

```
int badsearch(DataType t)
{   int l, u, m;
    l = 0;
    u = n-1;
    while (l <= u) {
        m = (l + u) / 2;
/* printf("   %d %d %d\n", l, m, u); */
        if (x[m] < t)
            l = m;
        else if (x[m] > t)
            u = m;
        else
            return m;
    }
    return -1;
}
```

(We'll return shortly to the commented-out *printf* statement.) Can you spot any problems in the code?

The program passed the first two little tests. It found 20 in position 2 of a 5-element array, and found 30 in position 3:

```
5  20
   2
5  30
   3
5  40
  . . .
```

When I searched for 40, though, the program went into an infinite loop. Why?

To solve the puzzle, I inserted the *printf* statement that appears as a comment above. (It is outdented to the left margin to show that it is scaffolding.) It displays the sequence of values of *l*, *m* and *u* for each search:

```
5  20
   0 2 4
   2
5  30
   0 2 4
   2 3 4
   3
5  40
   0 2 4
   2 3 4
   3 3 4
   3 3 4
   3 3 4
  . . .
```

The first search finds 20 on the first probe, and the second search finds 30 on the second probe. The third search is fine for the first two probes, but on the third probe goes into an infinite loop. We could have discovered that bug as we tried (in vain) to prove the termination of the loop.

When I have to debug a little algorithm deep inside a big program, I sometimes use debugging tools like single-stepping through the huge program. When I work on an algorithm using scaffolding like this, though, *print* statements are usually faster to implement and more effective than sophisticated debuggers.

5.3 The Art of Assertion

Assertions played several key roles as we developed the binary search in Column 4: they guided the development of the code, and they allowed us to reason about its correctness. We'll now insert them into the code to ensure that the run-time behavior matches our understanding.

We'll use an *assert* to state that we believe a logical expression to be true. The statement *assert*($n \geq 0$) will do nothing if n is zero or greater, but will raise an error of some sort if n is negative (perhaps invoking a debugger). Before reporting that binary search has found its target, we might make this assertion:

```
        ...
    else if (x[m] == t) {
        assert(x[m] == t);
        return m;
    } else
        ...
```

This weak assertion merely repeats the condition in the *if* statement. We might want to strengthen it to assert that the return value is in the input range:

```
    assert(0 <= m && m < n && x[m] == t);
```

When the loop terminates without finding the target value, we know that l and u have crossed, and we therefore know that the element is not in the array. We might be tempted to assert that we have found a pair of adjacent elements that bracket it:

```
    assert(x[u] < t && x[u+1] > t);
    return -1;
```

The logic is that if we see 1 and 3 adjacent in the sorted table, then we know with certainty that 2 is not present. This assertion will sometimes fail, though, even for a correct program; why?

When n is zero, the variable u is initialized to -1, so the indexing will access an element outside the array. To make the assertion useful, we must therefore weaken it by testing for the edges:

```
    assert((u < 0 || x[u] < t) && (u+1 >= n || x[u+1] > t));
```

This statement will indeed find some bugs in faulty searches.

We proved that the search always halts by showing that the range decreases in each iteration. We can check that property during execution with a little extra computation and an assertion. We initialize *size* to $n + 1$, then insert the following code after the *for* statement:

```
    oldsize = size;
    size = u - 1 + 1;
    assert(size < oldsize);
```

I would be embarrassed to admit in public how many times I've tried in vain to debug a ''broken'' binary search, only to find.that the array to be searched was not sorted. Once we define this function

```
int sorted()
{    int i;
     for (i = 0; i < n-1; i++)
         if (x[i] > x[i+1])
             return 0;
     return 1;
}
```

we can *assert(sorted())*. We should be careful, though, to make this pricey test only once before all searches. Including the test in the main loop could result in a binary search that runs in time proportional to $n \log n$.

Assertions are helpful as we test the function in its scaffolding, and as we move from component test through system test. Some projects define *assert* with a preprocessor so the assertions can be compiled away and thereby incur no run-time overhead. On the other hand, Tony Hoare once observed that a programmer who uses assertions while testing and turns them off during production is like a sailor who wears a life vest while drilling on shore and takes it off at sea.

Chapter 2 of Steve Maguire's *Writing Solid Code* (Microsoft Press, 1993) is devoted to the use of assertions in industrial-strength software. He describes in detail several war stories of the use of assertions in Microsoft's products and libraries.

5.4 Automated Testing

You've played with the program enough to be pretty sure it is correct, and you're bored feeding it cases by hand. The next step is to build scaffolding to attack it by machine. The main loop of the test function runs *n* from the smallest possible value (zero) to the largest reasonable value:

```
for n = [0, maxn]
    print "n=", n
    /* test value n */
```

The *print* statement reports the progress of the test. Some programmers hate it. it produces clutter but no substantial information. Others find solace in watching the progress of the test, and it can be useful to know what tests were passed when you see the first bug.

The first part of the testing loop examines the case in which all elements are distinct (it also puts a spare at the top of the array to ensure that the search does *not* locate it).

```
/* test distinct elements (plus one at the end) */
for i = [0, n]
    x[i] = 10*i
for i = [0, n)
    assert(s(10*i)      ==  i)
    assert(s(10*i - 5) == -1)
assert(s(10*n - 5) == -1)
assert(s(10*n)      == -1)
```

To make it easy to test various functions, we *define* the function to be tested:

```
#define s binarysearch
```

The assertions test every possible position for successful and unsuccessful searches, and the case that an element is in the array but outside the search bounds.

The next part of the testing loop probes an array of equal elements:

```
/* test equal elements */
for i = [0, n)
    x[i] = 10
if n == 0
    assert(s(10) == -1)
else
    assert(0 <= s(10) && s(10) < n)
assert(s(5) == -1)
assert(s(15) == -1)
```

This searches for the element that is there, and for a lesser and greater element.

These tests poke around most of the program. Testing n from zero to 100 covers the empty array, common sizes for bugs (zero, one and two), several powers of two, and many numbers one away from a power of two. The tests would have been dreadfully boring (and therefore error prone) by hand, but they used an insignificant amount of computer time. With *maxn* set to 1000, the tests require only a few seconds of run time on my computer.

5.5 Timing

The extensive testing supports our belief that the search is correct. How can we similarly bolster our belief that it does the job using about $\log_2 n$ comparisons? Here is the main loop of the timing scaffolding:

```
while read(algnum, n, numtests)
    for i = [0, n)
        x[i] = i
    starttime = clock()
    for testnum = [0, numtests)
        for i = [0, n)
            switch (algnum)
                case 1: assert(binarysearch1(i) == i)
                case 2: assert(binarysearch2(i) == i)
    clicks = clock() - starttime
    print algnum, n, numtests, clicks,
        clicks/(1e9 * CLOCKS_PER_SEC * n * numtests)
```

This code computes the average run time of a successful binary search in an array of n distinct elements. It first initializes the array, then performs a search for each element of the array a total of *numtests* times. The *switch* statement selects the algorithm to be tested (scaffolding should always be prepared to test several variants). The *print* statement reports the three input values and two output values: the raw number of clicks (it is always crucial to inspect those numbers), and a value easier to interpret (in this case, the average cost of a search in nanoseconds, given by the conversion factor *1e9* in the *print* statement).

Here is an interactive session with the program on a 400MHz Pentium II, with typed input, as usual, in *italics*:

```
1 1000 10000
1        1000    10000    3445    344.5
1 10000 1000
1        10000    1000    4436    443.6
1 100000 100
1        100000   100     5658    565.8
1 1000000 10
1        1000000 10       6619    661.9
```

The first line tests algorithm 1 (the *binarysearch* we've studied so far) on an array of size 1000, and performs the tests 10000 times. It takes 3445 clock ticks (reported on this system in milliseconds), which translates to an average cost of 344.5 nanoseconds per search. Each of the three subsequent trials increases n by a factor of 10, and decreases the number of tests by the same factor. The run time for a search seems to be roughly $50 + 30\log_2 n$ nanoseconds.

I next wrote a three-line program to generate input for the timing scaffolding. The output is plotted in the graph, which shows that the average search cost indeed grows as $\log n$. Problem 7 observes a potential timing bug in this scaffolding; be sure to study that before you put too much faith in such numbers.

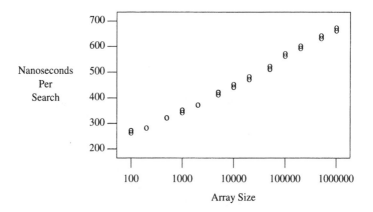

5.6 The Complete Program

I believe that the C implementation of binary search is correct. Why? I carefully derived the pseudocode in a convenient language, then used analytic techniques to verify its correctness. I translated it into C line-by-line, and fed the program inputs and watched the output. I sprinkled assertions through the code to ensure that my theoretical analysis matched the behavior in practice. A computer did what it's good at and bombarded the program with test cases. Finally, simple experiments showed that its run time was as low as theory predicted.

With this background, I'd feel comfortable using the code to search a sorted array in a big program. I'd be pretty surprised if a logic bug showed up in this C code. I wouldn't be shocked to find many other kinds of bugs, though. Did the caller remember to sort the table? Is − 1 the desired return value when the search item isn't in the table? If the target item occurs many times in the table, this code returns an arbitrary index; did the user really want the first or the last? And so on and so on.

Can you trust this code? You could take my word for it. (If you are inclined in this direction, I currently own a very nice bridge that you might be interested in purchasing.) Alternatively, you can get a copy of the program from this book's web site. It includes all of the functions we've seen so far, and several variants of binary search that we'll study in Column 9. Its main function looks like:

```
int main(void)
{   /* probe1(); */
    /* test(25); */
    timedriver();
    return 0;
}
```

By commenting out all but one call, you can play with particular inputs, deluge it with test cases, or run timing experiments.

5.7 Principles

This column has thrown a lot of effort at a little problem. The problem may be small, but it's not easy. Recall from Section 4.1 that while the first binary search was published in 1946, the first binary search that works correctly for all values of *n* did not appear until 1962. If early programmers had taken the approach in this column, it might not have taken them 16 years to derive a correct binary search.

Scaffolding. The best kind of scaffolding is usually that which is easiest to build. For some tasks, the easiest scaffolding consists of a graphical user interface implemented in a language like Visual Basic or Java or Tcl. In each of those languages, I've whipped up little programs in half an hour with point-and-click control and fancy visual output. For many algorithmic tasks, though, I find it easier to ignore those powerful tools in favor of the simpler (and more portable) command-line techniques that we've seen in this column.

Coding. I find it easiest to sketch a hard function in a convenient high-level pseudocode, then translate it into the implementation language.

Testing. One can test a component much more easily and thoroughly in scaffolding than in a large system.

Debugging. Debugging is hard when a program is isolated in its scaffolding, and much harder yet when it is embedded in its real environment. Section 5.10 tells tales of debugging large systems.

Timing. If run time doesn't matter, linear search is much simpler than binary search; many programmers can get it right on the first try. Because run time is important enough for us to introduce the additional complexity of binary search, we should conduct experiments to ensure that its performance is what we expect.

5.8 Problems

1. Comment on the programming style used in this column, and in this book, in general. Address issues such as the variable names, the form and specification of the binary search function, the code layout and so forth.

2. Translate the pseudocode description of binary search into languages other than C, and build scaffolding to test and debug your implementation. How do the language and system help and hinder?

3. Introduce errors into the binary search function. How are your errors caught by the tests? How does the scaffolding help you chase down the bugs? (This exercise is best carried out as a two-player game, in which the attacker introduces bugs that the defender must then track.)

4. Repeat Problem 3, but this time, leave the binary search code correct and introduce errors into the functions that call it (such as forgetting to sort the array).

5. [R. S. Cox] A common bug applies binary search to an unsorted array. Completely checking whether the array is sorted before each search has the exorbitant

cost of $n - 1$ extra comparisons. How can you add partial checking to the function at significantly less cost?

6. Implement a graphical user interface for studying binary search. Is the bang (in increased debugging effectiveness) worth the buck (in development time)?

7. The timing scaffolding in Section 5.5 has a potential timing bug: by searching for each element in order, we get particularly beneficial caching behavior. If we know that the searches in the potential application will exhibit similar locality, this is an accurate framework (but binary search is probably not the right tool for that job). If we expect the searches to probe the array randomly, though, then we should probably initialize and shuffle a permutation vector

```
for i = [0, n)
    p[i] = i
scramble(p, n)
```

and then perform the searches in a random order

```
assert(binarysearch1(p[i]) == p[i])
```

Measure the two versions to see if there is any difference in observed run times.

8. Scaffolding is underused and rarely described in public. Inspect any scaffolding you can find; desperation may drive you to this book's web site. Build scaffolding to test a complex function that you have written.

9. Download the *search.c* scaffolding program from this book's web site, and experiment to find the run time of binary search on your machine. What tools will you use to generate the input and to store and to analyze the output?

5.9 Further Reading

Kernighan and Pike's *Practice of Programming* was published by Addison-Wesley in 1999. They devote fifty pages to debugging (Chapter 5) and testing (Chapter 6). They cover important topics such as non-reproducible bugs and regression testing that are beyond the scope of this little column.

The nine chapters of their book will be interesting and fun for every practicing programmer. In addition to the two chapters mentioned above, other chapter titles include programming style, algorithms and data structures, design and implementation, interfaces, performance, portability and notation. Their book gives valuable insight into the craft and style of two journeymen programmers.

Section 3.8 of this book describes Steve McConnell's *Code Complete*. Chapter 25 of that book describes "Unit Testing" and Chapter 26 describes "Debugging".

5.10 Debugging [Sidebar]

Every programmer knows that debugging is hard. Great debuggers, though, can make the job look simple. Distraught programmers describe a bug that they've been chasing for hours, the master asks a few questions, and minutes later the programmers are staring at the faulty code. The expert debugger never forgets that there has to be a logical explanation, no matter how mysterious the system's behavior may seem when first observed.

That attitude is illustrated in an anecdote from IBM's Yorktown Heights Research Center. A programmer had recently installed a new workstation. All was fine when he was sitting down, but he couldn't log in to the system when he was standing up. That behavior was one hundred percent repeatable: he could always log in when sitting and never when standing.

Most of us just sit back and marvel at such a story. How could that workstation know whether the poor guy was sitting or standing? Good debuggers, though, know that there has to be a reason. Electrical theories are the easiest to hypothesize. Was there a loose wire under the carpet, or problems with static electricity? But electrical problems are rarely one-hundred-percent consistent. An alert colleague finally asked the right question: how did the programmer log in when he was sitting and when he was standing? Hold your hands out and try it yourself.

The problem was in the keyboard: the tops of two keys were switched. When the programmer was seated he was a touch typist and the problem went unnoticed, but when he stood he was led astray by hunting and pecking. With this hint and a convenient screwdriver, the expert debugger swapped the two wandering keytops and all was well.

A banking system built in Chicago had worked correctly for many months, but unexpectedly quit the first time it was used on international data. Programmers spent days scouring the code, but they couldn't find any stray command that would quit the program. When they observed the behavior more closely, they found that the program quit as they entered data for the country of Ecuador. Closer inspection showed that when the user typed the name of the capital city (Quito), the program interpreted that as a request to quit the run!

Bob Martin once watched a system "work once twice". It handled the first transaction correctly, then exhibited a minor flaw in all later transactions. When the system was rebooted, it once again correctly processed the first transaction, and failed on all subsequent transactions. When Martin characterized the behavior as having "worked once twice", the developers immediately knew to look for a variable that was initialized correctly when the program was loaded, but was not reset properly after the first transaction.

In all cases the right questions guided wise programmers to nasty bugs in short order: "What do you do differently sitting and standing? May I watch you logging in each way?" "Precisely what did you type before the program quit?" "Did the program ever work correctly before it started failing? How many times?"

Rick Lemons said that the best lesson he ever had in debugging was watching a magic show. The magician did a half-dozen impossible tricks, and Lemons found himself tempted to believe them. He then reminded himself that the impossible isn't possible, and probed each stunt to resolve its apparent inconsistency. He started with what he knew to be bedrock truth — the laws of physics — and worked from there to find a simple explanation for each trick. This attitude makes Lemons one of the best debuggers I've ever seen.

The best book I've seen on debugging is *The Medical Detectives* by Berton Roueché, published by Penguin in 1991. The heroes in the book debug complex systems, ranging from mildly sick people to very sick towns. The problem-solving methods they use are directly applicable to debugging computer systems. These true stories are as spellbinding as any fiction.

PART II: **PERFORMANCE**

A simple, powerful program that delights its users and does not vex its builders — that is the programmer's ultimate goal and the emphasis of the five previous columns.

We'll turn our attention now to one specific aspect of delightful programs: efficiency. Inefficient programs sadden their users with long waits and missed opportunities. These columns therefore describe several paths to performance.

Column 6 surveys the approaches and how they interact. The three subsequent columns discuss three methods for improving run time, in the order in which they are usually applied:

Column 7 shows how "back-of-the-envelope" calculations used early in the design process can ensure that the basic system structure is efficient enough.

Column 8 is about algorithm design techniques that sometimes dramatically reduce the run time of a module.

Column 9 discusses code tuning, which is usually done late in the implementation of a system.

To wrap up Part II, Column 10 turns to another important aspect of performance: space efficiency.

There are three good reasons for studying efficiency. The first is its intrinsic importance in many applications. I'm willing to bet that every reader of this book has at some time stared in frustration at a monitor, wishing fervently that the program were faster. A software manager I know estimates that half her development budget goes to performance improvement. Many programs have stringent time requirements, including real-time programs, huge database systems and interactive software.

The second reason for studying performance is educational. Apart from practical benefits, efficiency is a fine training ground. These columns cover ideas ranging from the theory of algorithms to common-sense techniques like "back-of-the-envelope" calculations. The major theme is fluidity of thinking; Column 6, especially, encourages us to look at a problem from many different viewpoints.

Similar lessons come from many other topics. These columns might have been built around user interfaces, system robustness or security. Efficiency has the advantage that it can be measured: we can all agree that one program is 2.5 times faster than another, while discussions on user interfaces, for instance, often get bogged down in personal tastes.

The most important reason for studying performance is described best in the immortal words of the 1986 film *Top Gun*: ''I feel the need ... the need for speed!''

COLUMN 6: **PERSPECTIVE ON PERFORMANCE**

The next three columns describe three different approaches to run-time efficiency. In this column we'll see how those parts fit together into a whole: each technique is applied at one of several *design levels* at which computer systems are built. We'll first study one particular program, and then turn to a more systematic view of the levels at which systems are designed.

6.1 A Case Study

Andrew Appel describes "An efficient program for many-body simulations" in the January 1985 *SIAM Journal on Scientific and Statistical Computing 6*, 1, pp. 85-103. By working on the program at several levels, he reduced its run time from a year to a day.

The program solved the classical "n-body problem" of computing interactions in a gravitational field. It simulated the motions of n objects in three-dimensional space, given their masses, initial positions and velocities; think of the objects as planets, stars or galaxies. In two dimensions, the input might look like

Appel's paper describes two astrophysical problems in which $n = 10,000$; by studying simulation runs, physicists could test how well a theory matches astronomical observations. (For more details on the problem and later solutions based on Appel's approach, see Pfalzner and Gibbon's *Many-Body Tree Methods in Physics*, published by Cambridge University Press in 1996.)

The obvious simulation program divides time into small "steps" and computes the progress of each object at each step. Because it computes the attraction of each object to every other, the cost per time step is proportional to n^2. Appel estimated that 1,000 time steps of such an algorithm with $n = 10,000$ would require roughly one year on his computer.

Appel's final program solved the problem in less than a day (for a speedup factor of 400). Many physicists have since used his techniques. The following brief survey of his program will ignore many important details that can be found in his paper; the important message is that a huge speedup was achieved by working at several different levels.

Algorithms and Data Structures. Appel's first priority was to find an efficient algorithm. He was able to reduce the $O(n^2)$ cost per time step to $O(n \log n)$† by representing the physical objects as leaves in a binary tree; higher nodes represent clusters of objects. The force operating on a particular object can be approximated by the force exerted by the large clusters; Appel showed that this approximation does not bias the simulation. The tree has roughly $\log n$ levels, and the resulting $O(n \log n)$ algorithm is similar in spirit to the divide-and-conquer algorithm in Section 8.3. This change reduced the run time of the program by a factor of 12.

Algorithm Tuning. The simple algorithm always uses small time steps to handle the rare case that two particles come close to one another. The tree data structure allows such pairs to be recognized and handled by a special function. That doubles the time step size and thereby halves the run time of the program.

Data Structure Reorganization. The tree that represents the initial set of objects is quite poor at representing later sets. Reconfiguring the data structure at each time step costs a little time, but reduces the number of local calculations and thereby halves the total run time.

Code Tuning. Due to additional numerical accuracy provided by the tree, 64-bit double-precision floating point numbers could be replaced by 32-bit single-precision numbers; that change halved the run time. Profiling the program showed that 98 percent of the run time was spent in one function; rewriting that code in assembly language increased its speed by a factor of 2.5.

Hardware. After all the above changes, the program still required two days of time on a departmental machine that cost a quarter of a million dollars, and several runs of the program were desired. Appel therefore moved the program to a slightly more expensive machine equipped with a floating point accelerator, which halved its run time again.

---

† The "big-oh" notation $O(n^2)$ can be thought of as "proportional to n^2"; both $15n^2 + 100n$ and $n^2/2 - 10$ are $O(n^2)$. More formally, $f(n) = O(g(n))$ means that $f(n) < cg(n)$ for some constant c and sufficiently large values of n. A formal definition of the notation can be found in textbooks on algorithm design or discrete mathematics, and Section 8.5 illustrates the relevance of the notation to program design.

The changes described above multiply together for a total speedup factor of 400; Appel's final program ran a 10,000-body simulation in about one day. The speedups were not free, though. The simple algorithm may be expressed in a few dozen lines of code, while the fast program required 1200 lines. The design and implementation of the fast program required several months of Appel's time. The speedups are summarized in the following table.

DESIGN LEVEL	SPEEDUP FACTOR	MODIFICATION
Algorithms and Data Structures	12	A binary tree reduces $O(n^2)$ time to $O(n \log n)$
Algorithm Tuning	2	Use larger time steps
Data Structure Reorganization	2	Produce clusters well-suited to the tree algorithm
System-Independent Code Tuning	2	Replace double-precision floating point with single precision
System-Dependent Code Tuning	2.5	Recode the critical function in assembly language
Hardware	2	Use a floating point accelerator
Total	400	

This table illustrates several kinds of dependence among speedups. The primary speedup is the tree data structure, which opened the door for the next three changes. The last two speedups, changing to assembly code and using the floating point accelerator, were in this case independent of the tree. The tree structure would have had less of an impact on the supercomputers of the time (with pipelined architectures well suited to the simple algorithm); algorithmic speedups are not necessarily independent of hardware.

6.2 Design Levels

A computer system is designed at many levels, ranging from its high-level software structure down to the transistors in its hardware. The following survey is an intuitive guide to design levels; please don't expect a formal taxonomy.†

Problem Definition. The battle for a fast system can be won or lost in specifying the problem it is to solve. On the day I wrote this paragraph, a vendor told me that he couldn't deliver supplies because a purchase order had been lost somewhere between

---

† I learned the theme of this column from Raj Reddy and Allen Newell's paper "Multiplicative speedup of systems" (in *Perspectives on Computer Science*, edited by A. K. Jones and published in 1977 by Academic Press). Their paper describes speedups at various design levels, and is especially rich in speedups due to hardware and system software.

my organization and my company's purchasing department. Purchasing was swamped with similar orders; fifty people in my organization alone had placed individual orders. A friendly chat between my management and purchasing resulted in consolidating those fifty orders into one large order. In addition to easing administrative work for both organizations, this change also sped up one small piece of a computer system by a factor of fifty. A good systems analyst keeps an eye out for such savings, both before and after systems are deployed.

Sometimes good specifications give users a little less than what they thought was needed. In Column 1 we saw how incorporating a few important facts about the input to a sorting program decreased both its run time and its code length by an order of magnitude. Problem specification can have a subtle interaction with efficiency; for example, good error recovery may make a compiler slightly slower, but it usually decreases its overall time by reducing the number of compilations.

System Structure. The decomposition of a large system into modules is probably the single most important factor in determining its performance. After sketching the overall system, the designer should do a simple "back-of-the-envelope" estimate to make sure that its performance is in the right ballpark; such calculations are the subject of Column 7. Because efficiency is much easier to build into a new system than to retrofit into an existing system, performance analysis is crucial during system design.

Algorithms and Data Structures. The keys to a fast module are usually the structures that represent its data and the algorithms that operate on the data. The largest single improvement in Appel's program came from replacing an $O(n^2)$ algorithm with an $O(n \log n)$ algorithm; Columns 2 and 8 describe similar speedups.

Code Tuning. Appel achieved a speedup factor of five by making small changes to code; Column 9 is devoted to that topic.

System Software. Sometimes it is easier to change the software on which a system is built than the system itself. Is a new database system faster for the queries that arise in this system? Would a different operating system be better suited to the real-time constraints of this task? Are all possible compiler optimizations enabled?

Hardware. Faster hardware can increase performance. General-purpose computers are usually fast enough; speedups are available through faster clock speeds on the same processor or multiprocessors. Sound cards, video accelerators and other cards offload work from the central processor onto small, fast, special-purpose processors; game designers are notorious for using those devices for clever speedups. Special-purpose digital signal processors (DSPs), for example, enable inexpensive toys and household appliances to talk. Appel's solution of adding a floating point accelerator to the existing machine was somewhere between the two extremes.

6.3 Principles

Because an ounce of prevention is worth a pound of cure, we should keep in mind an observation Gordon Bell made when he was designing computers for the Digital Equipment Corporation.

The cheapest, fastest and most reliable components of a computer system are those that aren't there.

Those missing components are also the most accurate (they never make mistakes), the most secure (they can't be broken into), and the easiest to design, document, test and maintain. The importance of a simple design can't be overemphasized.

But when performance problems can't be sidestepped, thinking about design levels can help focus a programmer's effort.

If you need a little speedup, work at the best level. Most programmers have their own knee-jerk response to efficiency: "change algorithms" or "tune the queueing discipline" spring quickly to some lips. Before you decide to work at any given level, consider all possible levels and choose the one that delivers the most speedup for the least effort.

If you need a big speedup, work at many levels. Enormous speedups like Appel's are achieved only by attacking a problem on several different fronts, and they usually take a great deal of effort. When changes on one level are independent of changes on other levels (as they often, but not always, are), the various speedups multiply.

Columns 7, 8 and 9 discuss speedups at three different design levels; keep perspective as you consider the individual speedups.

6.4 Problems

1. Assume that computers are now 1000 times faster than when Appel did his experiments. Using the same total computing time (about a day), how will the problem size n increase for the $O(n^2)$ and $O(n \log n)$ algorithms?

2. Discuss speedups at various design levels for some of the following problems: factoring 500-digit integers, Fourier analysis, simulating VLSI circuits, and searching a large text file for a given string. Discuss the dependencies of the proposed speedups.

3. Appel found that changing from double-precision arithmetic to single-precision arithmetic doubled the speed of his program. Choose an appropriate test and measure that speedup on your system.

4. This column concentrates on run-time efficiency. Other common measures of performance include fault-tolerance, reliability, security, cost, cost/performance ratio, accuracy, and robustness to user error. Discuss how each of these problems can be attacked at several design levels.

5. Discuss the costs of employing state-of-the-art technologies at the various design levels. Include all relevant measures of cost, including development time (calendar and personnel), maintainability and dollar cost.

6. An old and popular saying claims that "efficiency is secondary to correctness — a program's speed is immaterial if its answers are wrong". True or false?

7. Discuss how problems in everyday life, such as injuries suffered in automobile accidents, can be addressed at different levels.

6.5 Further Reading

Butler Lampson's "Hints for Computer System Design" appeared in *IEEE Software 1*, 1, January 1984. Many of the hints deal with performance; his paper is particularly strong at integrated hardware-software system design. As this book goes to press, a copy of the paper is available at *www.research.microsoft.com/~lampson/*.

COLUMN 7: **THE BACK OF THE ENVELOPE**

It was in the middle of a fascinating conversation on software engineering that Bob Martin asked me, "How much water flows out of the Mississippi River in a day?" Because I had found his comments up to that point deeply insightful, I politely stifled my true response and said, "Pardon me?" When he asked again I realized that I had no choice but to humor the poor fellow, who had obviously cracked under the pressures of running a large software shop.

My response went something like this. I figured that near its mouth the river was about a mile wide and maybe twenty feet deep (or about one two-hundred-and-fiftieth of a mile). I guessed that the rate of flow was five miles an hour, or a hundred and twenty miles per day. Multiplying

$$1 \text{ mile} \times 1/250 \text{ mile} \times 120 \text{ miles/day} \approx 1/2 \text{ mile}^3/\text{day}$$

showed that the river discharged about half a cubic mile of water per day, to within an order of magnitude. But so what?

At that point Martin picked up from his desk a proposal for the communication system that his organization was building for the Summer Olympic games, and went through a similar sequence of calculations. He estimated one key parameter as we spoke by measuring the time required to send himself a one-character piece of mail. The rest of his numbers were straight from the proposal and therefore quite precise. His calculations were just as simple as those about the Mississippi River and much more revealing. They showed that, under generous assumptions, the proposed system could work only if there were at least a hundred and twenty seconds in each minute. He had sent the design back to the drawing board the previous day. (The conversation took place about a year before the event, and the final system was used during the Olympics without a hitch.)

That was Bob Martin's wonderful (if eccentric) way of introducing the engineering technique of "back-of-the-envelope" calculations. The idea is standard fare in engineering schools and is bread and butter for most practicing engineers. Unfortunately, it is too often neglected in computing.

7.1 Basic Skills

These reminders can be helpful in making back-of-the-envelope calculations.

Two Answers Are Better Than One. When I asked Peter Weinberger how much water flows out of the Mississippi per day, he responded, "As much as flows in." He then estimated that the Mississippi basin was about 1000 by 1000 miles, and that the annual runoff from rainfall there was about one foot (or one five-thousandth of a mile). That gives

$$1000 \text{ miles} \times 1000 \text{ miles} \times 1/5000 \text{ mile/year} \approx 200 \text{ miles}^3/\text{year}$$

$$200 \text{ miles}^3/\text{year} / 400 \text{ days/year} \approx 1/2 \text{ mile}^3/\text{day}$$

or a little more than half a cubic mile per day. It's important to double check all calculations, and especially so for quick ones.

As a cheating triple check, an almanac reported that the river's discharge is 640,000 cubic feet per second. Working from that gives

$$640,000 \text{ ft}^3/\text{sec} \times 3600 \text{ secs/hr} \approx 2.3 \times 10^9 \text{ ft}^3/\text{hr}$$

$$2.3 \times 10^9 \text{ ft}^3/\text{hr} \times 24 \text{ hrs/day} \approx 6 \times 10^{10} \text{ ft}^3/\text{day}$$

$$6 \times 10^{10} \text{ ft}^3/\text{day} / (5000 \text{ ft/mile})^3 \approx 6 \times 10^{10} \text{ ft}^3/\text{day} / (125 \times 10^9 \text{ ft}^3/\text{mile}^3)$$

$$\approx 60/125 \text{ mile}^3/\text{day}$$

$$\approx 1/2 \text{ mile}^3/\text{day}$$

The proximity of the two estimates to one another, and especially to the almanac's answer, is a fine example of sheer dumb luck.

Quick Checks. Polya devotes three pages of his *How to Solve It* to "Test by Dimension", which he describes as a "well-known, quick and efficient means to check geometrical or physical formulas". The first rule is that the dimensions in a sum must be the same, which is in turn the dimension of the sum — you can add feet together to get feet, but you can't add seconds to pounds. The second rule is that the dimension of a product is the product of the dimensions. The examples above obey both rules; multiplying

$$(\text{miles} + \text{miles}) \times \text{miles} \times \text{miles/day} = \text{miles}^3/\text{day}$$

has the right form, apart from any constants.

A simple table can help you keep track of dimensions in complicated expressions like those above. To perform Weinberger's calculation, we first write down the three original factors.

1000	miles	1000	miles	1	mile
				5000	year

Next we simplify the expression by cancelling terms, which shows that the output is 200 miles^3/year.

$$\frac{1000 \text{ miles}}{} \left| \frac{1000 \text{ miles}}{} \right| \frac{1 \text{ mile}}{5000 \text{ year}} \left| \begin{array}{c} 200 \quad \text{mile}^3 \end{array} \right.$$

Now we multiply by the identity (well, almost) that there are 400 days per year.

$$\frac{1000 \text{ miles}}{} \left| \frac{1000 \text{ miles}}{} \right| \frac{1 \text{ mile}}{5000 \text{ year}} \left| 200 \quad \text{mile}^3 \right| \frac{\text{year}}{400 \text{ days}}$$

Cancellation yields the (by now familiar) answer of half a cubic mile per day.

$$\frac{1000 \text{ miles}}{} \left| \frac{1000 \text{ miles}}{} \right| \frac{1 \text{ mile}}{5000 \text{ year}} \left| \frac{200 \text{ mile}^3}{} \right| \frac{\text{year}}{400 \text{ days}} \left| \frac{1}{2} \right.$$

These tabular calculations help you keep track of dimensions.

Dimension tests check the form of equations. Check your multiplications and divisions with an old trick from slide rule days: independently compute the leading digit and the exponent. One can make several quick checks for addition.

3142	3142	3142
2718	2718	2718
+1123	+1123	+1123
983	6982	6973

The first sum has too few digits and the second sum errs in the least significant digit. The technique of "casting out nines" reveals the error in the third example: the digits in the summands sum to 8 modulo 9, while those in the answer sum to 7 modulo 9. In a correct addition, the sums of the digits are equal after "casting out" groups of digits that sum to nine.

Above all, don't forget common sense: be suspicious of any calculations that show that the Mississippi River discharges 100 gallons of water per day.

Rules of Thumb. I first learned the "Rule of 72" in a course on accounting. Assume that you invest a sum of money for y years at an interest rate of r percent per year. The financial version of the rule says that if $r \times y = 72$, then your money will roughly double. The approximation is quite accurate: investing $1000 at 6 percent interest for 12 years gives $2012, and $1000 at 8 percent for 9 years gives $1999.

The Rule of 72 is handy for estimating the growth of any exponential process. If a bacterial colony in a dish grows at the rate of three percent per hour, then it doubles in size every day. And doubling brings programmers back to familiar rules of thumb: because $2^{10} = 1024$, ten doublings is about a thousand, twenty doublings is about a million, and thirty doublings is about a billion.

Suppose that an exponential program takes ten seconds to solve a problem of size $n = 40$, and that increasing n by one increases the run time by 12 percent (we probably learned this by plotting its growth on a logarithmic scale). The Rule of 72 tells us that the run time doubles when n increases by 6, or goes up by a factor of about 1000 when n increases by 60. When $n = 100$, the program should therefore take about 10,000 seconds, or a few hours. But what happens when n increases to 160, and the time rises to 10^7 seconds? How much time is that?

You might find it hard to memorize that there are 3.155×10^7 seconds in a year. On the other hand, it is hard to forget Tom Duff's handy rule of thumb that, to within half a percent,

> π *seconds is a nanocentury.*

Because the exponential program takes 10^7 seconds, we should be prepared to wait about four months.

Practice. As with many activities, your estimation skills can only be improved with practice. Try the problems at the end of this column, and the estimation quiz in Appendix 2 (a similar quiz once gave me a much-needed dose of humility about my estimation prowess). Section 7.8 describes quick calculations in everyday life. Most workplaces provide ample opportunities for back-of-the-envelope estimates. How many foam "packing peanuts" came in that box? How much time do people at your facility spend waiting in line every day, for morning coffee, lunch, photocopiers and the like? How much does that cost the company in (loaded) salary? And the next time you're *really* bored at the lunch table, ask your colleagues how much water flows out of the Mississippi River each day.

7.2 Performance Estimates

Let's turn now to a quick calculation in computing. Nodes in your data structure (it might be a linked list or a hash table) hold an integer and a pointer to a node:

```
struct node { int i; struct node *p; };
```

Back-of-the-envelope quiz: will two million such nodes fit in the main memory of your 128-megabyte computer?

Looking at my system performance monitor shows that my 128-megabyte machine typically has about 85 megabytes free. (I've verified that by running the vector rotation code from Column 2 to see when the disk starts thrashing.) But how much memory will a node take? In the old days of 16-bit machines, a pointer and an integer would take four bytes. As I write this edition of the book, 32-bit integers and pointers are most common, so I would expect the answer to be eight bytes. Every now and then I compile in 64-bit mode, so it might take sixteen bytes. We can find out the answer for any particular system with a single line of C:

```
printf("sizeof(struct node)=%d\n", sizeof(struct node));
```

My system represented each record in eight bytes, as I expected. The 16 megabytes should fit comfortably into the 85 megabytes of free memory.

So when I used two million of those eight-byte records, why did my 128-megabyte machine start thrashing like crazy? The key is that I allocated them dynamically, using the C *malloc* function (similar to the C++ *new* operator). I had assumed that the eight-byte records might have another 8 bytes of overhead; I expected the nodes to take a total of about 32 megabytes. In fact, each node had 40 bytes of overhead to consume a total of 48 bytes per record. The two million records therefore used a total of 96 megabytes. (On other systems and compilers, though, the records had just 8 bytes of overhead each.)

Appendix 3 describes a program that explores the memory cost of several common structures. The first lines it produces are made with the *sizeof* operator:

```
sizeof(char)=1  sizeof(short)=2  sizeof(int)=4
sizeof(float)=4  sizeof(struct *)=4  sizeof(long)=4
sizeof(double)=8
```

I expected precisely those values from my 32-bit compiler. Further experiments measured the differences between successive pointers returned by the storage allocator; this is a plausible guess at record size. (One should always verify such rough guesses with other tools.) I now understand that, with this space-hogging allocator, records between 1 and 12 bytes will consume 48 bytes of memory, records between 13 and 28 bytes will consume 64 bytes, and so forth. We will return to this space model in Columns 10 and 13.

Let's try one more quick computing quiz. You know that the run time of your numerical algorithm is dominated by its n^3 square root operations, and $n = 1000$ in this application. About how long will your program take to compute the one billion square roots?

To find the answer on my system, I started with this little C program:

```
#include <math.h>
int main(void)
{    int i, n = 1000000;
     float fa;
     for (i = 0; i < n; i++)
          fa = sqrt(10.0);
     return 0;
}
```

I ran the program with a command to report how much time it takes. (I check such times with an old digital watch that I keep next to my computer; it has a broken band but a working stopwatch.) I found that the program took about 0.2 seconds to compute one million square roots, 2 seconds to compute ten million, and 20 seconds to compute 100 million. I would guess that it will take about 200 seconds to compute a billion square roots.

But will a square root in a real program take 200 nanoseconds? It might be much slower: perhaps the square root function cached the most recent argument as a starting value. Calling such a function repeatedly with the same argument might give it an unrealistic advantage. Then again, in practice the function might be much faster: I compiled the program with optimization disabled (optimization removed the main loop, so it always ran in zero time). Appendix 3 describes how to expand this tiny program to produce a one-page description of the time costs of primitive C operations for a given system.

How fast is networking? To find out, I type *ping machine-name*. It takes a few milliseconds to *ping* a machine in the same building, so that represents the startup time. On a good day, I can *ping* a machine on the other coast of the United States in about 70 milliseconds (traversing the 5000 miles of the round-trip voyage at the speed of light accounts for about 27 of those milliseconds); on a bad day, I get timed out after waiting 1000 milliseconds. Measuring the time to copy a large file shows that a ten-megabit Ethernet moves about a megabyte a second (that is, it achieves about 80 percent of its potential bandwidth). Similarly, a hundred-megabit Ethernet with the wind at its back moves ten megabytes a second.

Little experiments can put key parameters at your fingertips. Database designers should know the times for reading and writing records, and for joins of various forms. Graphics programmers should know the cost of key screen operations. The short time required to do such little experiments today will be more than paid in the time you save by making wise decisions tomorrow.

7.3 Safety Factors

The output of any calculation is only as good as its input. With good data, simple calculations can yield accurate answers that are sometimes quite useful. Don Knuth once wrote a disk sorting package, only to find that it took twice the time predicted by his calculations. Diligent checking uncovered the flaw: due to a software bug, the system's one-year-old disks had run at only half their advertised speed for their entire lives. When the bug was fixed, Knuth's sorting package behaved as predicted and every other disk-bound program also ran faster.

Often, though, sloppy input is enough to get into the right ballpark. (The estimation quiz in Appendix 2 may help you to judge the quality of your guesses.) If you guess about twenty percent here and fifty percent there and still find that a design is a hundred times above or below specification, additional accuracy isn't needed. But before placing too much confidence in a twenty percent margin of error, consider Vic Vyssotsky's advice from a talk he has given on several occasions.

"Most of you", says Vyssotsky, "probably recall pictures of 'Galloping Gertie', the Tacoma Narrows Bridge which tore itself apart in a windstorm in 1940. Well, suspension bridges had been ripping themselves apart that way for eighty years or so before Galloping Gertie. It's an aerodynamic lift phenomenon, and to do a proper engineering calculation of the forces, which involve drastic nonlinearities, you have to use the mathematics and concepts of Kolmogorov to model the eddy spectrum. Nobody really knew how to do this correctly in detail until the 1950's or thereabouts. So, why hasn't the Brooklyn Bridge torn itself apart, like Galloping Gertie?

"It's because John Roebling had sense enough to know what he *didn't* know. His notes and letters on the design of the Brooklyn Bridge still exist, and they are a fascinating example of a good engineer recognizing the limits of his knowledge. He knew about aerodynamic lift on suspension bridges; he had watched it. And he knew he didn't know enough to model it. So he designed the stiffness of the truss on the Brooklyn Bridge roadway to be *six times* what a normal calculation based on known static and dynamic loads would have called for. And, he specified a network of diagonal stays running down to the roadway, to stiffen the entire bridge structure. Go look at those sometime; they're almost unique.

"When Roebling was asked whether his proposed bridge wouldn't collapse like so many others, he said, 'No, because I designed it six times as strong as it needs to be, to prevent that from happening.'

"Roebling was a good engineer, and he built a good bridge, by employing a huge safety factor to compensate for his ignorance. Do we do that? I submit to you that in calculating performance of our real-time software systems we ought to derate them by a factor of two, or four, or six, to compensate for our ignorance. In making reliability/availability commitments, we ought to stay back from the objectives we *think* we can meet by a factor of ten, to compensate for our ignorance. In estimating size and cost and schedule, we should be conservative by a factor of two or four to compensate for our ignorance. We should design the way John Roebling did, and not the way his contemporaries did — so far as I know, none of the suspension bridges built by Roebling's contemporaries in the United States still stands, and a quarter of all the bridges of any type built in the U.S. in the 1870's collapsed within ten years of their construction.

"Are we engineers, like John Roebling? I wonder."

7.4 Little's Law

Most back-of-the-envelope calculations use obvious rules: total cost is unit cost times number of units. Sometimes, though, one needs a more subtle insight. Bruce Weide wrote the following note about a surprisingly versatile rule.

"The 'operational analysis' introduced by Denning and Buzen (see *Computing Surveys 10*, 3, November 1978, 225–261) is much more general than queueing network models of computer systems. Their exposition is excellent, but because of the article's limited focus, they didn't explore the generality of Little's Law. The proof methods have nothing to do with queues or with computer systems. Imagine *any* system in which things enter and leave. Little's Law states that 'The average number of things in the system is the product of the average rate at which things leave the system and the average time each one spends in the system.' (And if there is a gross 'flow balance' of things entering and leaving, the exit rate is also the entry rate.)

"I teach this technique of performance analysis in my computer architecture classes at Ohio State University. But I try to emphasize that the result is a general law of systems theory, and can be applied to many other kinds of systems. For instance, if you're in line waiting to get into a popular nightspot, you might figure out how long you'll have to wait by standing there for a while and trying to estimate the rate at which people are entering. With Little's Law, though, you could reason, 'This place holds about 60 people, and the average Joe will be in there about 3 hours, so we're entering at the rate of about 20 people an hour. The line has 20 people in it, so that means we'll wait about an hour. Let's go home and read *Programming Pearls* instead.' You get the picture.''

Peter Denning succinctly phrases this rule as ''The average number of objects in a queue is the product of the entry rate and the average holding time.'' He applies it to his wine cellar: ''I have 150 cases of wine in my basement and I consume (and purchase) 25 cases per year. How long do I hold each case? Little's Law tells me to divide 150 cases by 25 cases/year, which gives 6 years.''

He then turns to more serious applications. ''The response-time formula for a multi-user system can be proved using Little's Law and flow balance. Assume n users of average think time z are connected to an arbitrary system with response time r. Each user cycles between thinking and waiting-for-response, so the total number of jobs in the meta-system (consisting of users and the computer system) is fixed at n. If you cut the path from the system's output to the users, you see a meta-system with average load n, average response time $z + r$, and throughput x (measured in jobs per time unit). Little's Law says $n = x \times (z + r)$, and solving for r gives $r = n/x - z$.''

7.5 Principles

When you use back-of-the-envelope calculations, be sure to recall Einstein's famous advice.

Everything should be made as simple as possible, but no simpler.

We know that simple calculations aren't too simple by including safety factors to compensate for our mistakes in estimating parameters and our ignorance of the problem at hand.

7.6 Problems

The quiz in Appendix 2 contains additional problems.

1. While Bell Labs is about a thousand miles from the mighty Mississippi, we are only a couple of miles from the usually peaceful Passaic River. After a particularly heavy week of rains, the June 10, 1992, edition of the *Star-Ledger* quoted an engineer as saying that ''the river was traveling about 200 miles per hour, about five times faster than average''. Any comments?

2. At what distances can a courier on a bicycle with removable media be a more rapid carrier of information than a high-speed data line?

3. How long would it take you to fill a floppy disk by typing?

4. Suppose the world is slowed down by a factor of a million. How long does it take for your computer to execute an instruction? Your disk to rotate once? Your disk arm to seek across the disk? You to type your name?

5. Prove why ''casting out nines'' correctly tests addition. How can you further test the Rule of 72? What can you prove about it?

6. A United Nations estimate put the 1998 world population at 5.9 billion and the

annual growth rate at 1.33 percent. Were this rate to continue, what would the population be in 2050?

7. Appendix 3 describes programs to produce models of the time and space costs of your system. After reading about the models, write down your guesses for the costs on your system. Retrieve the programs from the book's web site, run them on your system, and compare those estimates to your guesses.

8. Use quick calculations to estimate the run time of designs sketched in this book.

   a. Evaluate programs and designs for their time and space requirements.

   b. Big-oh arithmetic can be viewed as a formalization of quick calculations — it captures the growth rate but ignores constant factors. Use the big-oh run times of the algorithms in Columns 6, 8, 11, 12, 13, 14 and 15 to estimate the run time of their implementation as programs. Compare your estimates to the experiments reported in the columns.

9. Suppose that a system makes 100 disk accesses to process a transaction (although some systems need fewer, some systems require several hundred disk accesses per transaction). How many transactions per hour per disk can the system handle?

10. Estimate your city's death rate, measured in percent of population per year.

11. [P. J. Denning] Sketch a proof of Little's Law.

12. You read in a newspaper article that a United States quarter-dollar coin has ''an average life of 30 years''. How can you check that claim?

7.7 Further Reading

My all-time favorite book on common sense in mathematics is Darrell Huff's 1954 classic *How To Lie With Statistics*; it was reissued by Norton in 1993. The examples are now quaint (some of those rich folks make a whopping twenty-five thousand dollars per year!), but the principles are timeless. John Allen Paulos's *Innumeracy: Mathematical Illiteracy and Its Consequences* is a 1990 approach to similar problems (published by Farrar, Straus and Giroux).

Physicists are well aware of this topic. After this column appeared in *Communications of the ACM*, Jan Wolitzky wrote

> I've often heard ''back-of-the-envelope'' calculations referred to as ''Fermi approximations'', after the physicist. The story is that Enrico Fermi, Robert Oppenheimer, and the other Manhattan Project brass were behind a low blast wall awaiting the detonation of the first nuclear device from a few thousand yards away. Fermi was tearing up sheets of paper into little pieces, which he tossed into the air when he saw the flash. After the shock wave passed, he paced off the distance travelled by the paper shreds, performed a quick ''back-of-the-envelope'' calculation, and arrived at a figure for the explosive yield of the bomb, which was confirmed much later by expensive monitoring equipment.

A number of relevant web pages can be found by searching for strings like ''back of the envelope'' and ''Fermi problems''.

7.8 Quick Calculations in Everyday Life *[Sidebar]*

The publication of this column in *Communications of the ACM* provoked many interesting letters. One reader told of hearing an advertisement state that a salesperson had driven a new car 100,000 miles in one year, and then asking his son to examine the validity of the claim. Here's one quick answer: there are 2000 working hours per year (50 weeks times 40 hours per week), and a salesperson might average 50 miles per hour; that ignores time spent actually selling, but it does multiply to the claim. The statement is therefore at the outer limits of believability.

Everyday life presents us with many opportunities to hone our skills at quick calculations. For instance, how much money have you spent in the past year eating in restaurants? I was once horrified to hear a New Yorker quickly compute that he and his wife spend more money each month on taxicabs than they spend on rent. And for California readers (who may not know what a taxicab is), how long does it take to fill a swimming pool with a garden hose?

Several readers commented that quick calculations are appropriately taught at an early age. Roger Pinkham wrote

> I am a teacher and have tried for years to teach ''back-of-the-envelope'' calculations to anyone who would listen. I have been marvelously unsuccessful. It seems to require a doubting-Thomas turn of mind.
>
> My father beat it into me. I come from the coast of Maine, and as a small child I was privy to a conversation between my father and his friend Homer Potter. Homer maintained that two ladies from Connecticut were pulling 200 pounds of lobsters a day. My father said, ''Let's see. If you pull a pot every fifteen minutes, and say you get three legal per pot, that's 12 an hour or about 100 per day. I don't believe it!''
>
> ''Well it is true!'' swore Homer. ''You never believe anything!''
>
> Father wouldn't believe it, and that was that. Two weeks later Homer said, ''You know those two ladies, Fred? They were only pulling 20 pounds a day.''
>
> Gracious to a fault, father grunted, ''Now that I believe.''

Several other readers discussed teaching this attitude to children, from the viewpoints of both parent and child. Popular questions for children were of the form ''How long would it take you to walk to Washington, D.C.?'' and ''How many leaves did we rake this year?'' Administered properly, such questions seem to encourage a life-long inquisitiveness in children, at the cost of bugging the heck out of the poor kids at the time.

COLUMN 8: **ALGORITHM DESIGN TECHNIQUES**

Column 2 describes the everyday effect of algorithm design on programmers: algorithmic insights can make a program simpler. In this column we'll see a less frequent but more dramatic contribution of the field: sophisticated algorithms sometimes give extreme performance improvements.

This column studies four different algorithms for one small problem, with an emphasis on the techniques used to design them. Some of the algorithms are a little complicated, but with justification. While the first program we'll study takes fifteen days to solve a problem of size 100,000, the final program solves the same problem in five milliseconds.

8.1 The Problem and a Simple Algorithm

The problem arose in one-dimensional pattern recognition; we'll see its history later. The input is a vector x of n floating-point numbers; the output is the maximum sum found in any *contiguous* subvector of the input. For instance, if the input vector contains these ten elements

then the program returns the sum of $x[2..6]$, or 187. The problem is easy when all the numbers are positive; the maximum subvector is the entire input vector. The rub comes when some of the numbers are negative: should we include a negative number in hopes that positive numbers on either side will compensate for it? To complete the problem definition, we'll say that when all inputs are negative the maximum-sum subvector is the empty vector, which has sum zero.

The obvious program for this task iterates over all pairs of integers i and j satisfying $0 \le i \le j < n$; for each pair it computes the sum of $x[i..j]$ and checks whether that sum is greater than the maximum sum so far. The pseudocode for Algorithm 1 is

```
maxsofar = 0
for i = [0, n)
    for j = [i, n)
        sum = 0
        for k = [i, j]
            sum += x[k]
        /* sum is sum of x[i..j] */
        maxsofar = max(maxsofar, sum)
```

This code is short, straightforward and easy to understand. Unfortunately, it is also slow. On my computer, for instance, the program takes about 22 minutes if n is 10,000 and fifteen days if n is 100,000; we'll see the timing details in Section 8.5.

Those times are anecdotal; we get a different kind of feeling for the algorithm's efficiency using the big-oh notation described in Section 6.1. The outermost loop is executed exactly n times, and the middle loop is executed at most n times in each execution of the outer loop. Multiplying those two factors of n shows that the code in the middle loop is executed $O(n^2)$ times. The innermost loop within the middle loop is never executed more than n times, so its cost is $O(n)$. Multiplying the cost per inner loop times its number of executions shows that the cost of the entire program is proportional to n cubed. We'll therefore refer to this as a cubic algorithm.

This example illustrates the technique of big-oh analysis and many of its strengths and weaknesses. Its primary weakness is that we still don't really know the amount of time the program will take for any particular input; we just know that the number of steps is $O(n^3)$. That weakness is often compensated for by two strong points of the method. Big-oh analyses are usually easy to perform (as above), and the asymptotic run time is often sufficient for a back-of-the-envelope calculation to decide whether a program is sufficient for a given application.

The next several sections use asymptotic run time as the only measure of program efficiency. If that makes you uncomfortable, peek ahead to Section 8.5, which shows that such analyses are extremely informative for this problem. Before you read further, though, take a minute to try to find a faster algorithm.

8.2 Two Quadratic Algorithms

Most programmers have the same response to Algorithm 1: "There's an obvious way to make it a lot faster." There are two obvious ways, however, and if one is obvious to a given programmer then the other often isn't. Both algorithms are quadratic — they take $O(n^2)$ steps on an input of size n — and both achieve their run time by computing the sum of $x[i..j]$ in a constant number of steps rather than in the $j-i+1$ additions of Algorithm 1. But the two quadratic algorithms use very different methods to compute the sum in constant time.

The first quadratic algorithm computes the sum quickly by noticing that the sum of $x[i..j]$ is intimately related to the sum previously computed (that of $x[i..j-1]$). Exploiting that relationship leads to Algorithm 2.

```
maxsofar = 0
for i = [0, n)
    sum = 0
    for j = [i, n)
        sum += x[j]
        /* sum is sum of x[i..j] */
        maxsofar = max(maxsofar, sum)
```

The statements inside the first loop are executed n times, and those inside the second loop are executed at most n times on each execution of the outer loop, so the total run time is $O(n^2)$.

An alternative quadratic algorithm computes the sum in the inner loop by accessing a data structure built before the outer loop is ever executed. The ith element of _cumarr_ contains the cumulative sum of the values in $x[0..i]$, so the sum of the values in $x[i..j]$ can be found by computing $cumarr[j] - cumarr[i-1]$. This results in the following code for Algorithm 2b.

```
cumarr[-1] = 0
for i = [0, n)
    cumarr[i] = cumarr[i-1] + x[i]
maxsofar = 0
for i = [0, n)
    for j = [i, n)
        sum = cumarr[j] - cumarr[i-1]
        /* sum is sum of x[i..j] */
        maxsofar = max(maxsofar, sum)
```

(Problem 5 addresses how we might access $cumarr[-1]$.) This code takes $O(n^2)$ time; the analysis is exactly the same as that of Algorithm 2.

The algorithms we've seen so far inspect all possible pairs of starting and ending values of subvectors and evaluate the sum of the numbers in that subvector. Because there are $O(n^2)$ subvectors, any algorithm that inspects all those values must take at least quadratic time. Can you think of a way to sidestep this problem and achieve an algorithm that runs in less time?

8.3 A Divide-and-Conquer Algorithm

Our first subquadratic algorithm is complicated; if you get bogged down in its details, you won't lose much by skipping to the next section. It is based on the following divide-and-conquer recipe:

> To solve a problem of size n, recursively solve two subproblems of size approximately n/2, and combine their solutions to yield a solution to the complete problem.

In this case the original problem deals with a vector of size n, so the most natural way to divide it into subproblems is to create two subvectors of approximately equal size, which we'll call a and b.

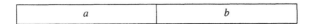

We then recursively find the maximum-sum subvectors in a and b, which we'll call m_a and m_b.

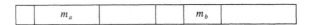

It is tempting to think that we have now solved the problem because the maximum-sum subvector of the entire vector must be either m_a or m_b. That is almost right. In fact, the maximum is either entirely in a, entirely in b, or it crosses the border between a and b; we'll call that m_c for the maximum *crossing* the border.

Thus our divide-and-conquer algorithm will compute m_a and m_b recursively, compute m_c by some other means, and then return the maximum of the three.

That description is almost enough to write code. All we have left to describe is how we'll handle small vectors and how we'll compute m_c. The former is easy: the maximum of a one-element vector is the only value in the vector (or zero if that number is negative), and the maximum of a zero-element vector was defined to be zero. To compute m_c we observe that its left side is the largest subvector starting at the boundary and reaching into a, and similarly for its right side in b. Putting these facts together leads to the following code for Algorithm 3:

```
float maxsum3(1, u)
    if (1 > u)  /* zero elements */
        return 0
    if (1 == u)  /* one element */
        return max(0, x[1])

    m = (1 + u) / 2
    /* find max crossing to left */
    lmax = sum = 0
    for (i = m; i >= 1; i--)
        sum += x[i]
        lmax = max(lmax, sum)
    /* find max crossing to right */
    rmax = sum = 0
    for i = (m, u]
        sum += x[i]
        rmax = max(rmax, sum)

    return max(lmax+rmax, maxsum3(1, m), maxsum3(m+1, u))
```

Algorithm 3 is originally invoked by the call

```
answer = maxsum3(0, n-1)
```

The code is subtle and easy to get wrong, but it solves the problem in $O(n \log n)$ time. We can prove that fact in several ways. An informal argument observes that the algorithm does $O(n)$ work on each of $O(\log n)$ levels of recursion. The argument can be made more precise by the use of recurrence relations. If $T(n)$ denotes the time to solve a problem of size n, then $T(1) = O(1)$ and

$$T(n) = 2T(n/2) + O(n).$$

Problem 15 shows that this recurrence has the solution $T(n) = O(n \log n)$.

8.4 A Scanning Algorithm

We'll now use the simplest kind of algorithm that operates on arrays: it starts at the left end (element $x[0]$) and scans through to the right end (element $x[n-1]$), keeping track of the maximum-sum subvector seen so far. The maximum is initially zero. Suppose that we've solved the problem for $x[0..i-1]$; how can we extend that to include $x[i]$? We use reasoning similar to that of the divide-and-conquer algorithm: the maximum-sum subarray in the first i elements is either in the first $i-1$ elements (which we'll store in *maxsofar*), or it ends in position i (which we'll store in *maxendinghere*).

	maxsofar		*maxendinghere*

Recomputing *maxendinghere* from scratch using code like that in Algorithm 3 yields yet another quadratic algorithm. We can get around this by using the technique that led to Algorithm 2: instead of computing the maximum subvector ending in position i from scratch, we'll use the maximum subvector that ends in position $i-1$. This results in Algorithm 4.

Kadanes Algo Wikipedia

```
maxsofar = 0
maxendinghere = 0
for i = [0, n)
    /* invariant: maxendinghere and maxsofar
       are accurate for x[0..i-1] */
    maxendinghere = max(maxendinghere + x[i], 0)
    maxsofar = max(maxsofar, maxendinghere)
```

The key to understanding this program is the variable *maxendinghere*. Before the first assignment statement in the loop, *maxendinghere* contains the value of the maximum subvector ending in position $i-1$; the assignment statement modifies it to contain the value of the maximum subvector ending in position i. The statement increases it by the value $x[i]$ so long as doing so keeps it positive; when it goes negative, it is reset to zero (because the maximum subvector ending at i is now the empty vector). Although the code is subtle, it is short and fast: its run time is $O(n)$, so we'll refer to it as a linear algorithm.

8.5 What Does It Matter?

So far we've played fast and loose with big-ohs; it's time to come clean and study the run times of the programs. I implemented the four primary algorithms in C on a 400MHz Pentium II, timed them, and extrapolated the observed run times to produce the following table. (The run time of Algorithm 2b was typically within ten percent of Algorithm 2, so it is not included.)

ALGORITHM		1	2	3	4
Run time in nanoseconds		$1.3n^3$	$10n^2$	$47n \log_2 n$	$48n$
Time to solve a problem of size	10^3	1.3 secs	10 msecs	.4 msecs	.05 msecs
	10^4	22 mins	1 sec	6 msecs	.5 msecs
	10^5	15 days	1.7 min	78 msecs	5 msecs
	10^6	41 yrs	2.8 hrs	.94 secs	48 msecs
	10^7	41 millennia	1.7 wks	11 secs	.48 secs
Max size problem solved in one	sec	920	10,000	1.0×10^6	2.1×10^7
	min	3600	77,000	4.9×10^7	1.3×10^9
	hr	14,000	6.0×10^5	2.4×10^9	7.6×10^{10}
	day	41,000	2.9×10^6	5.0×10^{10}	1.8×10^{12}
If n multiplies by 10, time multiplies by		1000	100	10+	10
If time multiplies by 10, n multiplies by		2.15	3.16	10−	10

This table makes a number of points. The most important is that proper algorithm design can make a big difference in run time; that point is underscored by the middle rows. The last two rows show how increases in problem size are related to increases in run time.

Another important point is that when we're comparing cubic, quadratic and linear algorithms with one another, the constant factors of the programs don't matter much. (The discussion of the $O(n!)$ algorithm in Section 2.4 shows that constant factors matter even less in functions that grow faster than polynomially.) To underscore this point, I conducted an experiment to make the constant factors of two algorithms differ by as much as possible. To achieve a huge constant factor I implemented Algorithm 4 on a Radio Shack TRS-80 Model III (a 1980 personal computer with a Z-80 processor running at 2.03MHz). To slow that poor old beast even further, I used an interpreted Basic that is an order or two of magnitude slower than compiled code. For the other end of the spectrum, I implemented Algorithm 1 on an Alpha 21164 running at 533MHz. I got the disparity I wanted: the run time of the cubic algorithm was measured as $0.58n^3$ nanoseconds, while the run time of the linear algorithm was $19.5n$ milliseconds, or $19,500,000n$ nanoseconds (that is, it processes about 50 elements per second). This table shows how those expressions translate to times for various problem sizes.

n	Alpha 21164A, C, Cubic Algorithm	TRS-80, Basic, Linear Algorithm
10	0.6 microsecs	200 millisecs
100	0.6 millisecs	2.0 secs
1000	0.6 secs	20 secs
10,000	10 mins	3.2 mins
100,000	7 days	32 mins
1,000,000	19 yrs	5.4 hrs

The difference in constant factors of thirty-three million allowed the cubic algorithm to start off faster, but the linear algorithm was bound to catch up. The break-even point for the two algorithms is around 5,800, where each takes just under two minutes of run time.

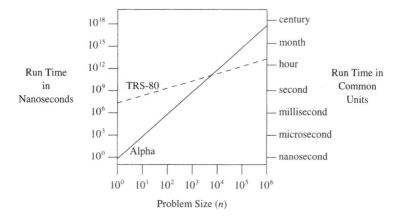

8.6 Principles

The history of the problem sheds light on the algorithm design techniques. The problem arose in a pattern-matching problem faced by Ulf Grenander at Brown University; the original problem was in the two-dimensional form described in Problem 13. In that version, the maximum-sum subarray was the maximum likelihood estimator of a certain kind of pattern in a digitized picture. Because the two-dimensional problem required too much time to solve, Grenander simplified it to one dimension to gain insight into its structure.

Grenander observed that the cubic time of Algorithm 1 was prohibitively slow, and derived Algorithm 2. In 1977 he described the problem to Michael Shamos, who overnight designed Algorithm 3. When Shamos showed me the problem shortly thereafter, we thought that it was probably the best possible; researchers had just shown that several similar problems require time proportional to $n \log n$. A few days later Shamos described the problem and its history at a Carnegie Mellon seminar attended by statistician Jay Kadane, who sketched Algorithm 4 within a minute.

Fortunately, we know that there is no faster algorithm: any correct algorithm must take $O(n)$ time (see Problem 6).

Even though the one-dimensional problem is completely solved, Grenander's original two-dimensional problem remains open two decades after it was posed, as the second edition of this book goes to press. Because of the computational expense of all known algorithms, Grenander had to abandon that approach to his pattern-matching problem. Readers who feel that the linear-time algorithm for the one-dimensional problem is "obvious" are therefore urged to find an "obvious" algorithm for Problem 13!

The algorithms in this story illustrate important algorithm design techniques.

Save state to avoid recomputation. This simple form of dynamic programming was used in Algorithms 2 and 4. By using space to store results, we avoid using time to recompute them.

Preprocess information into data structures. The *cumarr* structure in Algorithm 2b allows the sum of a subvector to be quickly computed.

Divide-and-conquer algorithms. Algorithm 3 uses a simple form of divide-and-conquer; textbooks on algorithm design describe more advanced forms.

Scanning algorithms. Problems on arrays can often be solved by asking "how can I extend a solution for $x[0..i-1]$ to a solution for $x[0..i]$?" Algorithm 4 stores both the old answer and some auxiliary data to compute the new answer.

Cumulatives. Algorithm 2b uses a cumulative table in which the ith element contains the sum of the first I values of x; such tables are common when dealing with ranges. Business analysts, for instance, find the sales from March to October by subtracting the February year-to-date sales from the October year-to-date sales.

Lower bounds. Algorithm designers sleep peacefully only when they know their algorithms are the best possible; for this assurance, they must prove a matching lower bound. The linear lower bound for this problem is the subject of Problem 6; more complex lower bounds can be quite difficult.

8.7 Problems

1. Algorithms 3 and 4 use subtle code that is easy to get wrong. Use the program verification techniques of Column 4 to argue the correctness of the code; specify the loop invariants carefully.

2. Time the four algorithms on your machine to build a table like that in Section 8.5.

3. Our analysis of the four algorithms was done only at the big-oh level of detail. Analyze the number of *max* functions used by each algorithm as exactly as possible; does this exercise give any insight into the running times of the programs? How much space does each algorithm require?

4. If the elements in the input array are random real numbers chosen uniformly from $[-1, 1]$, what is the expected value of the maximum subvector?

5. For simplicity, Algorithm 2b accessed *cumarr*$[-1]$. How would you deal with that issue in C?

6. Prove that any correct algorithm for computing maximum subvectors must inspect all n inputs. (Algorithms for some problems may correctly ignore some inputs; consider Saxe's algorithm in Solution 2.2 and Boyer and Moore's substring searching algorithm.)

7. When I first implemented the algorithms, my scaffolding always compared the answer produced by the various algorithms to that produced by Algorithm 4. I was distraught to see the scaffolding report errors in Algorithms 2b and 3, but when I looked closely at the numerical answers, I found that although not identical, they were very close. What was going on?

8. Modify Algorithm 3 (the divide-and-conquer algorithm) to run in linear worst-case time.

9. We defined the maximum subvector of an array of negative numbers to be zero, the sum of the empty subvector. Suppose that we had instead defined the maximum subvector to be the value of the largest element; how would you change the various programs?

10. Suppose that we wished to find the subvector with the sum closest to zero rather than that with maximum sum. What is the most efficient algorithm you can design for this task? What algorithm design techniques are applicable? What if we wished to find the subvector with the sum closest to a given real number t?

11. A turnpike consists of $n - 1$ stretches of road between n toll stations; each stretch has an associated cost of travel. It is trivial to tell the cost of going between any two stations in $O(n)$ time using only an array of the costs or in constant time using a table with $O(n^2)$ entries. Describe a data structure that requires $O(n)$ space but allows the cost of any route to be computed in constant time.

12. After the array $x[0..n-1]$ is initialized so that every element is zero, n of the following operations are performed

```
for i = [l, u]
    x[i] += v
```

where l, u and v are parameters of each operation (l and u are integers satisfying $0 \le l \le u < n$, and v is a real number). After the n operations, the values of $x[0..n-1]$ are reported in order. The method just sketched requires $O(n^2)$ time. Can you find a faster algorithm?

13. In the maximum subarray problem we are given an $n \times n$ array of reals, and we must find the maximum sum contained in any rectangular subarray. What is the complexity of this problem?

14. Given integers m and n and the real vector $x[n]$, find the integer i ($0 \le i < n - m$) such that the sum $x[i] + ... + x[i + m]$ is nearest zero.

15. What is the solution of the recurrence $T(n) = 2T(n/2) + cn$ when $T(1)=0$ and n is a power of two? Prove your result by mathematical induction. What if $T(1)=c$?

8.8 Further Reading

Only extensive study and practice can put algorithm design techniques at your fingertips; most programmers will get this only from a course or textbook on algorithms. *Data Structures and Algorithms* by Aho, Hopcroft and Ullman (published by Addison-Wesley in 1983) is an excellent undergraduate text. Chapter 10 on "Algorithm Design Techniques" is especially relevant to this column.

Cormen, Leiserson and Rivest's *Introduction to Algorithms* was published by MIT Press in 1990. This thousand-page volume provides a thorough overview of the field. Parts I, II and III cover foundations, sorting and searching. Part IV on "Advanced Design and Analysis Techniques" is particularly relevant to the theme of this column. Parts V, VI and VII survey advanced data structures, graph algorithms and other selected topics.

Those books and seven others were collected onto a CD-ROM as *Dr. Dobb's Essential Books on Algorithms and Data Structures*. The CD was published in 1999 by Miller Freeman, Inc. It is an invaluable reference work for any programmer interested in algorithms and data structures. As this book goes to press, the complete electronic set could be ordered from the Dr. Dobb's web site at *www.ddj.com* for about the price of one physical book.

CODE TUNING

Some programmers pay too much attention to efficiency; by worrying too soon about little "optimizations" they create ruthlessly clever programs that are insidiously difficult to maintain. Others pay too little attention; they end up with beautifully structured programs that are utterly inefficient and therefore useless. Good programmers keep efficiency in context: it is just one of many problems in software, but it is sometimes very important.

Previous columns have discussed high-level approaches to efficiency: problem definition, system structure, algorithm design and data structure selection. This column is about a low-level approach. "Code tuning" locates the expensive parts of an existing program and then makes little changes to improve its speed. It's not always the right approach to follow and it's rarely glamorous, but it can sometimes make a big difference in a program's performance.

9.1 A Typical Story

Chris Van Wyk and I chatted about code tuning early one afternoon; he then wandered off to improve a C program. A few hours later, he had halved the run time of a three-thousand line graphics program.

Although the run time for typical images was much shorter, the program took ten minutes to process some complicated pictures. Van Wyk's first step was to *profile* the program to find how much time was spent in each function (a profile of a similar, but smaller, program is shown on the next page). Running the program on ten typical test pictures showed that it spent almost seventy percent of its time in the memory allocation function *malloc*.

Van Wyk's next step was to study the memory allocator. Because his program accessed *malloc* through a single function that provided error checking, he was able to modify that function without examining the source code of *malloc*. He inserted a few lines of accounting code, which showed that the most popular kind of record was allocated thirty times more frequently than the runner-up. If you knew that the majority of the program's time was spent looking through storage for a single type of record, how would you modify it to make it faster?

Van Wyk solved his problem by applying the principle of *caching*: data that is accessed most often should be the cheapest to access. He modified his program by caching free records of the most common type in a linked list. He could then handle the common request by a quick access to that list rather than by invoking the general storage allocator; this reduced the total run time of his program to 45 percent of what it had been previously (so the storage allocator now took 30 percent of the total time). An additional benefit was that the reduced fragmentation of the modified allocator made more efficient use of main memory than the original allocator. Solution 2 shows an alternative implementation of this ancient technique; we'll use a similar approach several times in Column 13.

This story illustrates the art of code tuning at its best. By spending a few hours measuring and adding about twenty lines to a 3000-line program, Van Wyk doubled its speed without altering the users' view of the program or increasing the difficulty of maintenance. He used general tools to achieve the speedup: profiling identified the "hot spot" of his program and caching reduced the time spent there.

This profile of a typical little C program is similar, in both form and content, to Van Wyk's profile:

Func Time	%	Func+Child Time	%	Hit Count	Function
1413.406	52.8	1413.406	52.8	200002	malloc
474.441	17.7	2109.506	78.8	200180	insert
285.298	10.7	1635.065	61.1	250614	rinsert
174.205	6.5	2675.624	100.0	1	main
157.135	5.9	157.135	5.9	1	report
143.285	5.4	143.285	5.4	200180	bigrand
27.854	1.0	91.493	3.4	1	initbins

On this run, the majority of the time went to *malloc*. Problem 2 encourages you to reduce the run time of this program by caching nodes.

9.2 A First Aid Sampler

We'll turn now from a large program to several small functions. Each describes a problem that I've seen in various contexts. The problems consumed most of the run time in their applications, and the solutions use general principles.

Problem One — Integer Remainders. Section 2.3 sketches three algorithms for rotating a vector. Solution 2.3 implements a "juggling" algorithm with this operation in the inner loop:

```
k = (j + rotdist) % n;
```

The cost model in Appendix 3 shows that the C remainder operator % can be very expensive: while most arithmetic operations take about ten nanoseconds, the % operator takes close to 100 nanoseconds. We might be able to reduce the time of the program by implementing the operation with this code:

```
k = j + rotdist;
if (k >= n)
    k -= n;
```

This replaces the expensive % operator with a comparison and (rarely) a subtraction. But will that make any difference in the complete function?

My first experiment ran the program with the rotation distance *rotdist* set to 1, and the run time dropped from $119n$ nanoseconds to $57n$ nanoseconds. The program was almost twice as fast, and the 62 nanoseconds observed in the speedup was close to what was predicted by the cost model.

My next experiment set *rotdist* to 10, and I was shocked to see that the run time of both methods was identical at $206n$ nanoseconds. Experiments like the graph in Solution 2.4 soon led me to conjecture the cause: At *rotdist* = 1, the algorithm accessed memory sequentially, and the remainder operator dominated the time. When *rotdist* = 10, though, the code accessed every tenth word of memory, and fetching RAM into caches became dominant.

In the old days, programmers learned that it was futile to try to speed up the computations in programs that spend their time doing input and output. On modern architectures, it is equally futile to try to reduce computation time when so many of the cycles are spent accessing memory.

Problem Two — Functions, Macros and Inline Code. Throughout Column 8, we had to compute the maximum of two values. In Section 8.4, for instance, we used code like this:

```
maxendinghere = max(maxendinghere, 0);
maxsofar = max(maxsofar, maxendinghere);
```

The *max* function returns the maximum of its two arguments:

```
float max(float a, float b)
{   return a > b ? a : b; }
```

The run time of this program is about $89n$ nanoseconds.

Old C programmers might have the knee-jerk reaction to replace this particular function with a macro:

```
#define max(a, b) ((a) > (b) ? (a) : (b))
```

This is certainly uglier and more error-prone. With many optimizing compilers, it will make no difference at all (such compilers write small functions in line). On my system, however, this change reduced the run time of Algorithm 4 from $89n$ nanoseconds to $47n$ nanoseconds, for a speedup factor of almost two.

My delight with this speedup evaporated when I measured the effect of changing Algorithm 3 in Section 8.3 to use a macro: for $n = 10,000$, its run time increased from ten milliseconds to a hundred seconds, for a slowdown factor of 10,000. The macro appeared to have increased the run time of Algorithm 3 from its previous $O(n \log n)$ to something closer to $O(n^2)$. I soon discovered that the call-by-name semantics of macros caused Algorithm 3 to call itself recursively more than twice, and therefore increased its asymptotic running time. Problem 4 gives a more extreme example of such a slowdown.

While C programmers have to fret about tradeoffs between performance and correctness, C++ programmers enjoy the best of both worlds. C++ allows one to request that a function be compiled inline, which combines the clean semantics of functions with the low overhead of macros.

Out of curiosity, I avoided both macros and functions, and wrote out the computation in *if* statements:

```
if (maxendinghere < 0)
    maxendinghere = 0;
if (maxsofar < maxendinghere)
    maxsofar = maxendinghere;
```

The run time was essentially unchanged.

Problem Three — Sequential Search. We'll turn now to sequentially searching a (potentially unsorted) table:

```
int ssearch1(t)
    for i = [0, n)
        if x[i] == t
            return i
    return -1
```

This succinct code takes $4.06n$ nanoseconds, on the average, to look up an element that is in the array x. Because it looks at only half the elements in the array in a typical successful search, it spends about 8.1 nanoseconds at each table element.

The loop is svelte, but a tiny bit of fat may be trimmed. The inner loop has two tests: the first tests whether i is at the end of the array, and the second tests whether $x[i]$ is the desired element. We can replace the first test with the second by placing a *sentinel* value at the end of the array:

```
int ssearch2(t)
    hold = x[n]
    x[n] = t
    for (i = 0; ; i++)
        if x[i] == t
            break
    x[n] = hold
    if i == n
        return -1
    else
        return i
```

This drops the run time to $3.87n$ nanoseconds, for a speedup of about five percent. This code assumes that the array has been allocated so that $x[n]$ may be temporarily overwritten. It is careful to save $x[n]$ and to restore it after the search; that is unnecessary in most applications, and will be deleted from the next version.

The innermost loop now contains just an increment, an array access, and a test. Is there any way to reduce that further? Our final sequential search unrolls the loop eight times to remove the increment; further unrolling did not make it faster.

```
int ssearch3(t)
    x[n] = t
    for (i = 0; ; i += 8)
        if (x[i  ] == t) {           break }
        if (x[i+1] == t) { i += 1;  break }
        if (x[i+2] == t) { i += 2;  break }
        if (x[i+3] == t) { i += 3;  break }
        if (x[i+4] == t) { i += 4;  break }
        if (x[i+5] == t) { i += 5;  break }
        if (x[i+6] == t) { i += 6;  break }
        if (x[i+7] == t) { i += 7;  break }
    if i == n
        return -1
    else
        return i
```

This drops the time to $1.70n$ nanoseconds, for a reduction of about 56 percent. On old machines, reducing the overhead might have given a speedup of ten or twenty percent. On modern machines, though, loop unrolling can help to avoid pipeline stalls, to reduce branches, and to increase instruction-level parallelism.

Problem Four — Computing Spherical Distances. The final problem is typical of applications that deal with geographic or geometric data. The first part of the input is a set S of five thousand points on the surface of a globe; each point is represented by its latitude and longitude. After those points are stored in a data structure of our choice, the program reads the second part of the input: a sequence of twenty thousand points, each represented by latitude and longitude. For every point in that sequence, the program must tell which point in S is closest to it, where distance is measured as the angle between the rays from the center of the globe to the two points.

Margaret Wright encountered a similar problem at Stanford University in the early 1980's as she computed maps to summarize data on the global distribution of certain genetic traits. Her straightforward solution represented the set S by an array of latitude and longitude values. The nearest neighbor to each point in the sequence was found by calculating its distance to every point in S using a complicated trigonometric formula involving ten sine and cosine functions. While the program was simple to code and produced fine maps for small data sets, each large map required several hours of mainframe time, which was well beyond the project's budget.

Because I had previously worked on geometric problems, Wright asked me to try my hand at this one. After spending much of a weekend on it, I developed several fancy algorithms and data structures for solving it. Fortunately (in retrospect), each would have required many hundreds of lines of code, so I didn't try to code any of them. When I described the data structures to Andrew Appel, he had a key insight: Rather than approach the problem at the level of data structures, why not use the simple data structure of keeping the points in an array, but tune the code to reduce the cost of computing the distances between points? How would you exploit this idea?

The cost can be greatly reduced by changing the representation of points: rather than using latitudes and longitudes, we'll represent a point's location on the surface of the globe by its x, y and z coordinates. Thus the data structure is an array that holds each point's latitude and longitude (which may be needed for other operations) as well as its three Cartesian coordinates. As each point in the sequence is processed, a few trigonometric functions translate its latitude and longitude into x, y and z coordinates, and we then compute its distance to every point in S. Its distance to a point in S is computed as the sum of the squares of the differences in the three dimensions, which is usually much cheaper than computing one trigonometric function, let alone ten. (The cost model of run times in Appendix 3 gives details for one system.) This method computes the correct answer because the angle between two points increases monotonically with the square of their Euclidean distance.

Although this approach does require additional storage, it yields substantial benefits: when Wright incorporated the change into her program, the run time for complicated maps was reduced from several hours to half a minute. In this case, code tuning solved the problem with a couple of dozen lines of code, while algorithmic and data structure changes would have required many hundreds of lines.

9.3 Major Surgery — Binary Search

We'll turn now to one of the most extreme examples I know of code tuning. The details are from Problem 4.8: we are to perform a binary search in a table of one thousand integers. As we go through the process, keep in mind that tuning is usually not needed in binary search — the algorithm is so efficient that code tuning is often superfluous. In Column 4, we therefore ignored microscopic efficiency and concentrated on achieving a simple, correct and maintainable program. Sometimes, though, the tuned search can make a big difference in a system.

We'll develop the fast binary search in a sequence of four programs. They are subtle, but there is good reason to follow them closely: the final program is usually two or three times faster than the binary search of Section 4.2. Before reading on, can you spot any obvious waste in that code?

```
l = 0; u = n-1
loop
    /* invariant: if t is present, it is in x[l..u] */
    if l > u
        p = -1; break
    m = (l + u) / 2
    case
        x[m] <  t:   l = m+1
        x[m] == t:   p = m; break
        x[m] >  t:   u = m-1
```

Our development of the fast binary search will start with the modified problem of locating the *first occurrence* of the integer *t* in the integer array $x[0..n-1]$; the above code might return any one of multiple occurrences of *t* (we need just such a search in Section 15.3). The main loop of the program is similar to the one above; we'll keep indices *l* and *u* into the array that bracket the position of *t*, but we'll use the invariant relation that $x[l] < t \le x[u]$ and $l < u$. We'll assume that $n \ge 0$, that $x[-1] < t$ and that $x[n] \ge t$ (but the program will never access the two fictitious elements). The binary search code is now

```
l = -1; u = n
while l+1 != u
      /* invariant: x[l] < t && x[u] >= t && l < u */
      m = (l + u) / 2
      if x[m] < t
            l = m          not m+1
      else
            u = m          not m-1
/* assert l+1 = u && x[l] < t && x[u] >= t */
p = u
if p >= n || x[p] != t
      p = -1
```

The first line initializes the invariant. As the loop is repeated, the invariant is maintained by the *if* statement; it's easy to check that both branches maintain the invariant. Upon termination we know that if *t* is anywhere in the array, then its first occurrence is in position *u*; that fact is stated more formally in the *assert* comment. The final two statements set *p* to the index of the first occurrence of *t* in *x* if it is present, and to -1 if it is not present.

While this binary search solves a more difficult problem than the previous program, it is potentially more efficient: it makes only one comparison of *t* to an element of *x* in each iteration of the loop. The previous program sometimes had to test two such outcomes.

The next version of the program is the first to exploit the fact that we know that *n* is 1000. It uses a different representation of a range: instead of representing $l..u$ by its lower and upper values, we'll represent it by its lower value *l* and an increment *i* such that $l+i=u$. The code will ensure that *i* is at all times a power of two; this property is easy to keep once we have it, but it is hard to get originally (because the array is of size $n = 1000$). The program is therefore preceded by an assignment and *if* statement to ensure that the range being searched is initially of size 512, the largest power of two less than 1000. Thus *l* and $l+i$ together represent either $-1..511$ or $488..1000$. Translating the previous binary search program to this new representation of a range yields this code:

```
i = 512
l = -1
if x[511] < t
     l = 1000 - 512
while i != 1
     /* invariant: x[l] < t && x[l+i] >= t && i = 2^j */
     nexti = i / 2
     if x[l+nexti] < t
          l = l + nexti
          i = nexti
     else
          i = nexti
/* assert i == 1 && x[l] < t && x[l+i] >= t */
p = l+1
if p > 1000 || x[p] != t
     p = -1
```

The correctness proof of this program has exactly the same flow as the proof of the previous program. This code is usually slower than its predecessor, but it opens the door for future speedups.

The next program is a simplification of the above, incorporating some optimizations that a smart compiler might perform. The first *if* statement is simplified, the variable *nexti* is removed, and the assignments to *nexti* are removed from the inner *if* statement.

```
i = 512
l = -1
if x[511] < t
     l = 1000 - 512
while i != 1
     /* invariant: x[l] < t && x[l+i] >= t && i = 2^j */
     i = i / 2
     if x[l+i] < t
          l = l + i
/* assert i == 1 && x[l] < t && x[l+i] >= t */
p = l+1
if p > 1000 || x[p] != t
     p = -1
```

Although the correctness argument for the code still has the same structure, we can now understand its operation on a more intuitive level. When the first test fails and l stays zero, the program computes the bits of p in order, most significant bit first.

The final version of the code is not for the faint of heart. It removes the overhead of loop control and the division of i by two by unrolling the entire loop. Because i assumes only ten distinct values in this program, we can write them all down in the code, and thereby avoid computing them over and over again at run time.

```
l = -1
if (x[511]    < t) l = 1000 - 512
     /* assert x[l] < t && x[l+512] >= t */
if (x[l+256] < t) l += 256
     /* assert x[l] < t && x[l+256] >= t */
if (x[l+128] < t) l += 128
if (x[l+64 ] < t) l += 64
if (x[l+32 ] < t) l += 32
if (x[l+16 ] < t) l += 16
if (x[l+8  ] < t) l += 8
if (x[l+4  ] < t) l += 4
if (x[l+2  ] < t) l += 2
     /* assert x[l] < t && x[l+2  ] >= t */
if (x[l+1  ] < t) l += 1
     /* assert x[l] < t && x[l+1  ] >= t */
p = l+1
if p > 1000 || x[p] != t
     p = -1
```

We can understand this code by inserting the complete string of assertions like those surrounding the test of $x[l+256]$. Once you do the two-case analysis to see how that *if* statement behaves, all the other *if* statements fall into line.

I've compared the clean binary search of Section 4.2 with this fine-tuned binary search on a variety of systems. The first edition of this book reported the run times across four machines, five programming languages, and several levels of optimizations; the speedups ranged from a 38 percent reduction to a factor of five (an 80 percent reduction). When I measured it on my current machine, I was shocked and delighted to see a reduction in search time for $n = 1000$ from 350 nanoseconds to 125 nanoseconds per search (a reduction of 64 percent).

The speedup seemed too good to be true, and it was. Close inspection showed that my timing scaffolding was searching for each array element in order: first $x[0]$, then $x[1]$, and so forth. This gave binary search particularly favorable memory access patterns and wonderful branch prediction. I therefore changed the scaffolding to search for the elements in random order. The clean binary search took 418 nanoseconds, while the loop-unrolled version took 266 nanoseconds, for a speedup of 36 percent.

This derivation is an idealized account of code tuning at its most extreme. We replaced the obvious binary search program (which doesn't appear to have much fat on it) with a super-lean version that is substantially faster. (This function has been known in the computing underground since the early 1960's. I learned it from Guy Steele in the early 1980's; he learned it at MIT, where it had been known since the late 1960's. Vic Vyssotsky used this code at Bell Labs in 1961; each *if* statement in the pseudocode was implemented in three IBM 7090 instructions.)

The program verification tools of Column 4 played a crucial role in the task. Because we used them, we can believe that the final program is correct; when I first saw the final code presented with neither derivation nor verification, I looked upon it as magic.

9.4 Principles

The most important principle about code tuning is that it should be done rarely. That sweeping generalization is explained by the following points.

The Role of Efficiency. Many other properties of software are as important as efficiency, if not more so. Don Knuth has observed that premature optimization is the root of much programming evil; it can compromise the correctness, functionality and maintainability of programs. Save concern for efficiency for when it matters.

Measurement Tools. When efficiency is important, the first step is to profile the system to find out where it spends its time. Profiling a program usually shows that most of the time is going to a few hot spots and that the rest of the code is rarely executed (in Section 6.1, for instance, a single function accounted for 98 percent of the run time). Profiling points to the critical areas; for the other parts we follow the wise maxim of, "If it ain't broke, don't fix it." A cost model for run times like that in Appendix 3 can help a programmer to understand why certain operations and functions are expensive.

Design Levels. We saw in Column 6 that efficiency problems can be attacked in many ways. Before tuning code, we should make sure that other approaches don't provide a more effective solution.

When Speedups Are Slowdowns. Replacing the % remainder operator with an *if* statement sometimes gave a factor-of-two speedup and other times made no difference in run time. Converting a function to a macro sped up one function by a factor of two, and slowed down another by ten thousand. After making an "improvement", it is critical to measure its effect on representative input. Because of these stories and dozens more like them, we must be careful to heed Jurg Nievergelt's warning to code tuners: people who play with bits should expect to get bitten.

The discussion above considers whether and when to tune code; once we decide to do so, that still leaves the question of how. Appendix 4 contains a list of general rules for code tuning. All the examples we've seen can be explained in terms of those principles; I'll do that now with the names of the rules in *italics*.

Van Wyk's Graphics Program. The general strategy of Van Wyk's solution was to *Exploit Common Cases*; his particular exploitation involved *Caching* a list of the most common kind of record.

Problem One — Integer Remainders. The solution *Exploited an Algebraic Identity* to replace an expensive remainder operation with a cheap comparison.

Problem Two — Functions, Macros and Inline Code. *Collapsing a Procedure Hierarchy* by replacing a function with a macro gave a speedup of almost a factor of two, but writing the code inline made no further difference.

Problem Three — Sequential Search. Using a *sentinel* to *Combine Tests* gave a speedup of about five percent. *Loop Unrolling* gave an additional speedup of about 56 percent.

Problem Four — Computing Spherical Distances. Storing Cartesian coordinates along with latitudes and longitudes is an example of *Data Structure*

Augmentation; using the cheaper Euclidean distance rather than the angular distance *Exploits an Algebraic Identity*.

Binary Search. *Combining Tests* reduced the number of array comparisons per inner loop from two to one, *Exploiting an Algebraic Identity* changed representations from a lower and upper bound to a lower bound and an increment, and *Loop Unrolling* expanded the program to remove all loop overhead.

So far we've tuned code to reduce CPU time. One can tune code for other purposes, such as reducing paging or increasing a cache hit ratio. Perhaps the most common use of code tuning beyond reducing run time is to reduce the space required by a program; the next column is devoted to the topic.

9.5 Problems

1. Profile one of your own programs, and then try to use the approach described in this column to reduce the run time of its hot spots.

2. This book's web site contains the C program profiled in the introduction; it implements a small subset of a C++ program that we'll see in Column 13. Try profiling it on your system. Unless you have a particularly efficient *malloc* function, it will probably spend most of its time in *malloc*. Try to reduce that time by implementing a node cache like Van Wyk's.

3. What special properties of the "juggling" rotation algorithm allowed us to replace the % remainder operator with an *if* statement, and not a more costly *while* statement? Experiment to determine when it is worth replacing a % remainder operator with a *while* statement.

4. When n is a positive integer at most the size of the array, this recursive C function returns the maximum value in the array $x[0..n-1]$:

```
float arrmax(int n)
{   if (n == 1)
         return x[0];
     else
         return max(x[n-1], arrmax(n-1));
}
```

When *max* is a function, it finds the maximum element of a vector with $n = 10,000$ elements in a few milliseconds. When *max* is the C macro

```
#define max(a, b) ((a) > (b) ? (a) : (b))
```

this algorithm takes 6 seconds to find the maximum of $n = 27$ elements and 12 seconds to find the maximum of $n = 28$ elements. Give an input that tickles this dreadful behavior, and analyze the run time mathematically.

5. How do the various binary search algorithms behave if they are (against specification) applied to unsorted arrays?

6. C and C++ libraries provide character classification functions such as *isdigit, isup-per* and *islower* to determine the types of characters. How would you implement those functions?

7. Given a very long sequence (say, billions or trillions) of bytes, how would you efficiently count the total number of one bits? (That is, how many bits are turned on in the entire sequence?)

8. How can sentinels be used in a program to find the maximum element in an array?

9. Because sequential search is simpler than binary search, it is usually more efficient for small tables. On the other hand, the logarithmic number of comparisons made by binary search implies that it will be faster than the linear time of sequential search for large tables. The break-even point is a function of how much each program is tuned. How low and how high can you make that break-even point? What is it on your machine when both programs are equally tuned?

10. D. B. Lomet observes that hashing may solve the 1000-integer search problem more efficiently than the tuned binary search. Implement a fast hashing program and compare it to the tuned binary search; how do they compare in terms of speed and space?

11. In the early 1960's, Vic Berecz found that most of the time in a simulation program at Sikorsky Aircraft was devoted to computing trigonometric functions. Further investigation showed that the functions were computed only at integral multiples of five degrees. How did he reduce the run time?

12. One sometimes tunes programs by thinking about mathematics rather than code. To evaluate the polynomial

$$y = a_n x^n + a_{n-1} x^{n-1} + \cdots + a_1 x^1 + a_0$$

the following code uses $2n$ multiplications. Give a faster function.

```
y = a[0]
xi = 1
for i = [1, n]
    xi = x * xi
    y = y + a[i]*xi
```

9.6 Further Reading

Section 3.8 describes Steve McConnell's *Code Complete*. Chapter 28 of his book describes "Code-Tuning Strategy"; it gives an overview of performance in general, and describes the approach of code-tuning in detail. Chapter 29 is an excellent collection of rules for code tuning.

Appendix 4 of this book presents a related collection of code-tuning rules, together with descriptions of how they have been applied in this book.

If you're like several people I know, your first thought on reading the title of this column is, "How quaint!" In the bad old days of computing, so the story goes, programmers were constrained by small machines, but those days are long gone. The new philosophy is, "A gigabyte here, a gigabyte there, pretty soon you're talking about real memory." And there is truth in that view — many programmers use big machines and rarely have to worry about squeezing space from their programs.

But every now and then, thinking hard about compact programs can be profitable. Sometimes the thought gives new insight that makes the program simpler. Reducing space often has desirable side-effects on run time: smaller programs are faster to load and fit more easily into a cache, and less data to manipulate usually means less time to manipulate it. The time required to transmit data across a network is usually directly proportional to the size of the data. Even with cheap memories, space can be critical. Tiny machines (such as those found in toys and household appliances) still have tiny memories. When huge machines are used to solve huge problems, we must still be careful with memory.

Keeping perspective on its importance, let's survey a few important techniques for reducing space.

10.1 The Key — Simplicity

Simplicity can yield functionality, robustness, speed and space. Dennis Ritchie and Ken Thompson originally developed the Unix operating system on a machine with 8192 18-bit words. In their paper about the system, they remark that "there have always been fairly severe size constraints on the system and its software. Given the partially antagonistic desires for reasonable efficiency and expressive power, the size constraint has encouraged not only economy but a certain elegance of design."

Fred Brooks observed the power of simplification when he wrote a payroll program for a national company in the mid 1950's. The bottleneck of the program was the representation of the Kentucky state income tax. The tax was specified in the law by a two-dimensional table with income as one dimension, and number of exemptions as the other. Storing the table explicitly required thousands of words of memory, more than the capacity of the machine.

The first approach Brooks tried was to fit a mathematical function through the tax table, but it was so jagged that no simple function would come close. Knowing that it was made by legislators with no predisposition to crazy mathematical functions, Brooks consulted the minutes of the Kentucky legislature to see what arguments had led to the bizarre table. He found that the Kentucky tax was a simple function of the income that remained *after* federal tax was deducted. His program therefore calculated federal tax from existing tables, and then used the remaining income and a table of just a few dozen words of memory to find the Kentucky tax.

By studying the context in which the problem arose, Brooks was able to replace the original problem to be solved with a simpler problem. While the original problem appeared to require thousands of words of data space, the modified problem was solved with a negligible amount of memory.

Simplicity can also reduce code space. Column 3 describes several large programs that were replaced by small programs with more appropriate data structures. In those cases, a simpler view of the program reduced the source code from thousands to hundreds of lines and probably also shrank the size of the object code by an order of magnitude.

10.2 An Illustrative Problem

In the early 1980's, I consulted on a system that stored neighborhoods in a geographical database. Each of the two thousand neighborhoods had a number in the range 0..1999, and was depicted on a map as a point. The system allowed the user to access any one of the points by touching an input pad. The program converted the physical location selected to a pair of integers with x and y both in the range 0..199 — the board was roughly four feet square and the program used quarter-inch resolution. It then used that (x, y) pair to tell which, if any, of the two thousand points the user had chosen. Because no two points could be in the same (x, y) location, the programmer responsible for the module represented the map by a 200×200 array of point identifiers (an integer in the range 0..1999, or -1 if no point was at that location). The bottom left corner of that array might look like this, where empty squares represent cells that do not hold a point.

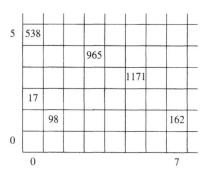

In the corresponding map, point 17 is in location (0, 2), point 538 is in (0, 5), and the four other visible locations in the first column are empty.

The array was easy to implement and gave rapid access time. The programmer had the choice of implementing each integer in 16 or 32 bits. Had he chosen 32-bit integers, the $200 \times 200 = 40,000$ elements would have consumed 160 kilobytes. He therefore chose the shorter representation, and the array used 80 kilobytes, or one-sixth of the half-megabyte memory. Early in the life of the system that was no problem. As the system grew, though, it started to run out of space. The programmer asked me how we might reduce the storage devoted to this structure. How would you advise the programmer?

This is a classic opportunity for using a sparse data structure. This example is old, but I've seen the same story recently in representing a $10,000 \times 10,000$ matrix with a million active entries on a hundred-megabyte computer.

An obvious representation of sparse matrices uses an array to represent all columns, and linked lists to represent the active elements in a given column. This picture has been rotated 90 degrees clockwise for a prettier layout:

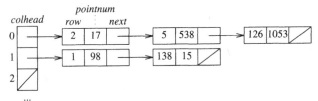

This picture shows three points in the first column: point 17 is in (0, 2), point 538 is in (0, 5), and point 1053 is in (0,126). Two points are in column 2, and none are in column 3. We search for the point (i, j) with this code:

```
for (p = colhead[i]; p != NULL; p = p->next)
    if p->row == j
        return p->pointnum
return -1
```

Looking up an array element visits at most 200 nodes in the worst case, but only about ten nodes on the average.

This structure uses an array of 200 pointers and also 2000 records, each with an integer and two pointers. The model of space costs in Appendix 3 tells us that the pointers will occupy 800 bytes. If we allocate the records as a 2000-element array, they will occupy 12 bytes each, for a total of 24,800 bytes. (If we were to use the default *malloc* described in that appendix, though, each record would consume 48 bytes, and the overall structure would in fact increase from the original 80 kilobytes to 96.8 kilobytes.)

The programmer had to implement the structure in a version of Fortran that did not support pointers and structures. We therefore used an array of 201 elements to represent the columns, and two parallel arrays of 2000 elements to represent the points. Here are those three arrays, with the integer indices in the bottom array also depicted as arrows. (The 1-indexed Fortran arrays have been changed to use 0-indexing for consistency with the other arrays in this book.)

The points in column i are represented in the *row* and *pointnum* arrays between locations *firstincol*[i] and *firstincol*[$i+1$] -1; even though there are only 200 columns, *firstincol*[200] is defined to make this condition hold. To determine what point is stored in position (i, j) we use this pseudocode:

```
for k = [firstincol[i], firstincol[i+1])
    if row[k] == j
        return pointnum[k]
return -1
```

This version uses two 2000-element arrays and one 201-element array. The programmer implemented exactly this structure, using 16-bit integers for a total of 8402 bytes. It is a little slower than using the complete matrix (about ten node visits on the average). Even so, the program had no trouble keeping up with the user. Because of the good module structure of the system, this approach was incorporated in a few hours by changing a few functions. We observed no degradation in run time and gained 70 sorely needed kilobytes.

Had the structure still been a space hog, we could have reduced its space even further. Because the elements of the *row* array are all less than 200, they can each be stored in a single-byte unsigned *char*; this reduces the space to 6400 bytes. We could even remove the *row* array altogether, if the row is already stored with the point itself:

```
for k - [firstincol[i], firstincol[i+1])
    if point[pointnum[k]].row == j
        return pointnum[k]
return -1
```

This reduces the space to 4400 bytes.

In the real system, rapid lookup time was critical both for user interaction and because other functions looked up points through the same interface. If run time had not been important and if the points had *row* and *col* fields, then we could have achieved the ultimate space reduction to zero bytes by sequentially searching through the array of points. Even if the points did not have those fields, the space for the structure could be reduced to 4000 bytes by "key indexing": we scan through an array in which the ith element contains two one-byte fields that give the *row* and *col* values of point i.

This problem illustrates several general points about data structures. The problem is classic: sparse array representation (a sparse array is one in which most entries have the same value, usually zero). The solution is conceptually simple and easy to implement. We used a number of space-saving measures along the way. We need no *lastincol* array to go with *firstincol*; we instead use the fact that the last point in this column is immediately before the first point in the next column. This is a trivial example of recomputing rather than storing. Similarly, there is no *col* array to go with *row*; because we only access *row* through the *firstincol* array, we always know the current column. Although *row* started with 32 bits, we reduced its representation to 16 and finally 8 bits. We started with records, but eventually went to arrays to squeeze out a few kilobytes here and there.

10.3 Techniques for Data Space

Although simplification is usually the easiest way to solve a problem, some hard problems just won't yield to it. In this section we'll study techniques that reduce the space required to store the data accessed by a program; in the next section we'll consider reducing the memory used to store the program during execution.

Don't Store, Recompute. The space required to store a given object can be dramatically reduced if we don't store it but rather recompute it whenever it is needed. This is exactly the idea behind doing away with the matrix of points, and performing a sequential search each time from scratch. A table of the prime numbers might be replaced by a function for testing primality. This method trades more run time for less space, and it is applicable only if the objects to be "stored" can be recomputed from their description.

Such "generator programs" are often used in executing several programs on identical random inputs, for such purposes as performance comparisons or regression tests of correctness. Depending on the application, the random object might be a file of randomly generated lines of text or a graph with randomly generated edges. Rather than storing the entire object, we store just its generator program and the random seed that defines the particular object. By taking a little more time to access them, huge objects can be represented in a few bytes.

Users of PC software may face such a choice when they install software from a CD-ROM or DVD-ROM. A "typical" installation might store hundreds of megabytes of data on the system's hard drive, where it can be read quickly. A "minimal" installation, on the other hand, will keep those files on the slower device, but will not use the disk space. Such an installation conserves magnetic disk space by using more time to read the data each time the program is invoked.

For many programs that run across networks, the most pressing concern about data size is the time it will take to transmit it. We can sometimes decrease the amount of data transmitted by caching it locally, following the dual advice of "Store, don't retransmit."

Sparse Data Structures. Section 10.2 introduced these structures. In Section 3.1 we saved space by storing a "ragged" three-dimensional table in a two-dimensional array. If we use a key to be stored as an index into a table, then we need not store the key itself; rather, we store only its relevant attributes, such as a count of how many times it has been seen. Applications of this *key indexing* technique are described in the catalog of algorithms in Appendix 1. In the sparse matrix example above, key indexing through the *firstincol* array allowed us to do without a *col* array.

Storing pointers to shared large objects (such as long text strings) removes the cost of storing many copies of the same object, although one has to be careful when modifying a shared object that all its owners desire the modification. This technique is used in my desk almanac to provide calendars for the years 1821 through 2080; rather than listing 260 distinct calendars it gives fourteen canonical calendars (seven days of the week for January 1 times leap year or non-leap year) and a table giving a calendar number for each of the 260 years.

Some telephone systems conserve communication bandwidth by viewing voice conversations as a sparse structure. When the volume in one direction falls below a critical level, silence is transmitted using a succinct representation, and the bandwidth thus saved is used to transmit other conversations.

Data Compression. Insights from information theory reduce space by encoding objects compactly. In the sparse matrix example, for instance, we compressed the representation of a row number from 32 to 16 to 8 bits. In the early days of personal computers, I built a program that spent much of its time reading and writing long strings of decimal digits. I changed it to encode the two decimal digits a and b in one byte (instead of the obvious two) by the integer $c = 10 \times a + b$. The information was decoded by the two statements

```
a = c / 10
b = c % 10
```

This simple scheme reduced the input/output time by half, and also squeezed a file of numeric data onto one floppy disk instead of two. Such encodings can reduce the space required by individual records, but the small records might take more time to encode and decode (see Problem 6).

Information theory can also compress a stream of records being transmitted over a channel such as a disk file or a network. Sound can be recorded at CD-quality by recording two channels (stereo) at 16-bit accuracy at 44,100 samples per second. One second of sound requires 176,400 bytes using this representation. The MP3 standard compresses typical sound files (especially music) to a small fraction of that size. Problem 10.10 asks you to measure the effectiveness of several common formats for representing text, images, sounds and the like. Some programmers build special-purpose compression algorithms for their software; Section 13.8 sketches how a file of 75,000 English words was squeezed into 52 kilobytes.

Allocation Policies. Sometimes how much space you use isn't as important as how you use it. Suppose, for instance, that your program uses three different types of records, x, y and z, all of the same size. In some languages your first impulse might be to declare, say, 10,000 objects of each of the three types. But what if you used 10,001 x's and no y's or z's? The program could run out of space after using 10,001 records, even though 20,000 others were completely unused. *Dynamic allocation* of records avoids such obvious waste by allocating records as they are needed.

Dynamic allocation says that we shouldn't ask for something until we need it; the policy of *variable-length records* says that when we do ask for something, we should ask for only as much as we need. In the old punched-card days of eighty-column records it was common for more than half the bytes on a disk to be trailing blanks. Variable-length files denote the end of lines by a newline character and thereby double the storage capacity of such disks. I once tripled the speed of an input/output-bound program by using records of variable length: the maximum record length was 250, but only about 80 bytes were used on the average.

Garbage collection recycles discarded storage so that the old bits are as good as new. The Heapsort algorithm in Section 14.4 *overlays* two logical data structures used at separate times in the same physical storage locations.

In another approach to *sharing* storage, Brian Kernighan wrote a traveling sales-man program in the early 1970's in which the lion's share of the space was devoted to two 150×150 matrices. The two matrices, which I'll call a and b to protect their anonymity, represented distances between points. Kernighan therefore knew that they had zero diagonals ($a[i,i] = 0$) and that they were symmetric ($a[i, j] = a[j, i]$). He therefore let the two triangular matrices share space in one square matrix, c, one corner of which looked like

0	$b[0,1]$	$b[0,2]$	$b[0,3]$
$a[1,0]$	0	$b[1,2]$	$b[1,3]$
$a[2,0]$	$a[2,1]$	0	$b[2,3]$
$a[3,0]$	$a[3,1]$	$a[3,2]$	0

Kernighan could then refer to $a[i,j]$ by the code

```
c[max(i, j), min(i, j)]
```

and similarly for b, but with the *min* and *max* swapped. This representation has been used in various programs since the dawn of time. The technique made Kernighan's program somewhat more difficult to write and slightly slower, but the reduction from two 22,500-word matrices to just one was significant on a 30,000-word machine. And if the matrices were 30,000×30,000, the same change would have the same effect today on a gigabyte machine.

On modern computing systems, it may be critical to use *cache-sensitive memory layouts*. Although I had studied this theory for many years, I gained a visceral appre-ciation the first time I used some multi-disk CD software. National telephone directories and national maps were a delight to use; I had to replace CDs only rarely, when my browsing moved from one part of the country to another. When I used my first two-disk encyclopedia, though, I found myself swapping CDs so often that I went back to the prior year's version on one CD; the memory layout was not sensitive to my access pattern. Solution 2.4 graphs the performance of three algorithms with very different memory access patterns. We'll see in Section 13.2 an application in which even though arrays touch more data than linked lists, they are faster because their sequential memory accesses interact efficiently with the system's cache.

10.4 Techniques for Code Space

Sometimes the space bottleneck is not in the data but rather in the size of the program itself. In the bad old days, I saw graphics programs with pages of code like

```
for i = [17, 43] set(i, 68)
for i = [18, 42] set(i, 69)
for j = [81, 91] set(30, j)
for j = [82, 92] set(31, j)
```

where $set(i, j)$ turns on the picture element at screen position (i, j). Appropriate functions, say *hor* and *vert* for drawing horizontal and vertical lines, would allow that code to be replaced by

```
hor(17, 43, 68)
hor(18, 42, 69)
vert(81, 91, 30)
vert(82, 92, 31)
```

This code could in turn be replaced by an interpreter that read commands from an array like

```
h 17 43 68
h 18 42 69
v 81 91 30
v 82 92 31
```

If that still took too much space, each of the lines could be represented in a 32-bit word by allocating two bits for the command (h, v, or two others) and ten bits for each of the three numbers, which are integers in the range 0..1023. (The translation would, of course, be done by a program.) This hypothetical case illustrates several general techniques for reducing code space.

Function Definition. Replacing a common pattern in the code by a function simplified the above program and thereby reduced its space requirements and increased its clarity. This is a trivial instance of "bottom-up" design. Although one can't ignore the many merits of "top-down" methods, the homogeneous world view given by good primitive objects, components and functions can make a system easier to maintain and simultaneously reduce space.

Microsoft removed seldom-used functions to shrink its full Windows system down to the more compact Windows CE to run in the smaller memories found in "mobile computing platforms". The smaller User Interface (UI) runs nicely on little machines with cramped screens ranging from embedded systems to handheld computers; the familiar interface is a great benefit to users. The smaller Application Programmer Interface (API) makes the system familiar to Windows API programmers (and tantalizingly close, if not already compatible, for many programs).

Interpreters. In the graphics program we replaced a long line of program text with a four-byte command to an interpreter. Section 3.2 describes an interpreter for form-letter programming; although its main purpose is to make a program simpler to build and to maintain, it incidentally reduces the program's space.

In their *Practice of Programming* (described in Section 5.9 of this book), Kernighan and Pike devote Section 9.4 to "Interpreters, Compilers and Virtual Machines". Their examples support their conclusion: "Virtual machines are a lovely old idea, recently made fashionable again by Java and the Java Virtual Machine (JVM); they give an easy way to produce portable, efficient representations of programs written in a high-level language."

Translation to Machine Language. One aspect of space reduction over which most programmers have relatively little control is the translation from the source language into the machine language. Some minor compiler changes reduced the code space of early versions of the Unix system by as much as five percent. As a last resort, a programmer might consider coding key parts of a large system into assembly language by hand. This expensive, error-prone process usually yields only small dividends; nevertheless, it is used often in some memory-critical systems such as digital signal processors.

The Apple Macintosh was an amazing machine when it was introduced in 1984. The little computer (128 kilobytes of RAM) had a startling user interface and a powerful collection of software. The design team anticipated shipping millions of copies, and could afford only a 64 kilobyte Read-Only Memory. The team put an incredible amount of system functionality into the tiny ROM by careful function definition (involving generalizing operators, merging functions and deleting features) and hand coding the entire ROM in assembly language. They estimated that their extremely tuned code, with careful register allocation and choice of instructions, is half the size of equivalent code compiled from a high-level language (although compilers have improved a great deal since then). The tight assembly code was also very fast.

10.5 Principles

The Cost of Space. What happens if a program uses ten percent more memory? On some systems such an increase will have no cost: previously wasted bits are now put to good use. On very small systems the program might not work at all: it runs out of memory. If the data is being transported across a network, it will probably take ten percent longer to arrive. On some caching and paging systems the run time might increase dramatically because the data that was previously close to the CPU now thrashes to Level-2 cache, RAM or disk (see Section 13.2 and Solution 2.4). Know the cost of space before you set out to reduce that cost.

The "Hot Spots" of Space. Section 9.4 described how the run time of programs is usually clustered in hot spots: a few percent of the code frequently accounts for most of the run time. The opposite is true in the memory required by code: whether an instruction is executed a billion times or not at all, it requires the same space to store (except when large portions of code are never swapped into main memory or small caches). Data can indeed have hot spots: a few common types of records frequently account for most of the storage. In the sparse matrix example, for instance, a single data structure accounted for fifteen percent of the storage on a half-megabyte machine. Replacing it with a structure one-tenth the size had a substantial impact on the system; reducing a one-kilobyte structure by a factor of a hundred would have had negligible impact.

Measuring Space. Most systems provide performance monitors that allow a programmer to observe the memory used by a running program. Appendix 3 describes a model of the cost of space in C++; it is particularly helpful when used in conjunction with a performance monitor. Special-purpose tools are sometimes helpful. When a program started growing uncomfortably large, Doug McIlroy merged the linker output with the source file to show how many bytes each line consumed (some macros expanded to hundreds of lines of code); that allowed him to trim down the object code. I once found a memory leak in a program by watching a movie (an "algorithm animation") of the blocks of memory returned by the storage allocator.

Tradeoffs. Sometimes a programmer must trade away performance, functionality or maintainability to gain memory; such engineering decisions should be made only after all alternatives are studied. Several examples in this column showed how reducing space may have a positive impact on the other dimensions. In Section 1.4, a bitmap data structure allowed a set of records to be stored in internal memory rather than on disk and thereby reduced the run time from minutes to seconds and the code from hundreds to dozens of lines. This happened only because the original solution was far from optimal, but we programmers who are not yet perfect often find our code in exactly that state. We should always look for techniques that improve all aspects of our solutions before we trade away any desirable properties.

Work with the Environment. The programming environment can have a substantial impact on the space efficiency of a program. Important issues include the representations used by a compiler and run-time system, memory allocation policies, and paging policies. Space cost models like that in Appendix 3 can help you to ensure that you aren't working against your system.

Use the Right Tool for the Job. We've seen four techniques that reduce data space (Recomputing, Sparse Structures, Information Theory and Allocation Policies), three techniques that reduce code space (Function Definition, Interpreters and Translation) and one overriding principle (Simplicity). When memory is critical, be sure to consider all your options.

10.6 Problems

1. In the late 1970's Stu Feldman built a Fortran 77 compiler that barely fit in a 64-kilobyte code space. To save space he had packed some integers in critical records into four-bit fields. When he removed the packing and stored the fields in eight bits, he found that although the data space increased by a few hundred bytes, the overall size of the program went down by several thousand bytes. Why?

2. How would you write a program to build the sparse-matrix data structure described in Section 10.2? Can you find other simple but space-efficient data structures for the task?

3. How much total disk space does your system have? How much is currently available? How much RAM? How much RAM is typically available? Can you measure the sizes of the various caches on your system?

4. Study data in non-computer applications such as almanacs and other reference books for examples of squeezing space.

5. In the early days of programming, Fred Brooks faced yet another problem of representing a large table on a small computer (beyond that in Section 10.1). He couldn't store the entire table in an array because there was room for only a few bits for each table entry (actually, there was one decimal digit available for each entry — I said that it was in the early days!). His second approach was to use numerical analysis to fit a function through the table. That resulted in a function that was quite close to the true table (no entry was more than a couple of units off the true entry) and required an unnoticeably small amount of memory, but legal constraints meant that the approximation wasn't good enough. How could Brooks get the required accuracy in the limited space?

6. The discussion of Data Compression in Section 10.3 mentioned decoding $10 \times a + b$ with / and % operations. Discuss the time and space tradeoffs involved in replacing those operations by logical operations or table lookups.

7. In a common type of profiler, the value of the program counter is sampled on a regular basis; see, for instance, Section 9.1. Design a data structure for storing those values that is efficient in time and space and also provides useful output.

8. Obvious data representations allocate eight bytes for a date (MMDDYYYY), nine bytes for a social security number (DDD-DD-DDDD), and 25 bytes for a name (14 for last, 10 for first, and 1 for middle initial). If space is critical, how far can you reduce those requirements?

9. Compress an online dictionary of English to be as small as possible. When counting space, measure both the data file and the program that interprets the data.

10. Raw sound files (such as .wav) can be compressed to .mp3 files; raw image files (such as .bmp) can be compressed to .gif or .jpg files; raw motion picture files (such as .avi) can be compressed to .mpg files. Experiment with these file formats to estimate their compression effectiveness. How effective are these special-purpose compression formats when compared to general-purpose schemes (such as gzip)?

11. A reader observes, "With modern programs, it's often not the code that you write, but the code that you *use* that's large." Study your programs to see how large they are after linking. How can you reduce that space?

10.7 Further Reading

The *20th Anniversary Edition* of Fred Brooks's *Mythical Man Month* was published by Addison-Wesley in 1995. It reprints the delightful essays of the original book, and also adds several new essays, including his influential "No Silver Bullet— Essence and Accident in Software Engineering". Chapter 9 of the book is entitled "Ten pounds in a five-pound sack"; it concentrates on managerial control of space in large projects. He raises such important issues as size budgets, function specification, and trading space for function or time.

Many of the books cited in Section 8.8 describe the science and technology underlying space-efficient algorithms and data structures.

10.8 A Big Squeeze *[Sidebar]*

In the early 1980's, Ken Thompson built a two-phase program that solves chess endgames for given configurations such as a King and two Bishops matched against a King and a Knight. (This program is distinct from the former world-computer-champion Belle chess machine developed by Thompson and Joe Condon.) The learning phase of the program computed the distance to checkmate for all possible chessboards (over the given set of four or five pieces) by working backwards from all possible checkmates; computer scientists will recognize this technique as dynamic programming, while chess experts know it as retrograde analysis. The resulting database made the program omniscient with respect to the given pieces, so in the game-playing phase it played perfect endgames. The game it played was described by chess experts with phrases like "complex, fluid, lengthy and difficult" and "excruciating slowness and mystery", and it upset established chess dogma.

Explicitly storing all possible chessboards was prohibitively expensive in space. Thompson therefore used an encoding of the chessboard as a key to index a disk file of board information; each record in the file contained 12 bits, including the distance to checkmate from that position. Because there are 64 squares on a chessboard, the positions of five fixed pieces can be encoded by five integers in the range 0..63 that give the location of each piece. The resulting key of 30 bits implied a table of 2^{30} or about 1.07 billion 12-bit records in the database, which exceeded the capacity of the disk available at the time.

Thompson's key insight was that chessboards that are mirror images around any of the dotted lines in the following figure have the same value and need not be duplicated in the database.

His program therefore assumed that the White King was in one of the ten numbered squares; an arbitrary chessboard can be put into this form by a sequence of at most three reflections. This normalization reduced the disk file to 10×64^4 or 10×2^{24} 12-bit records. Thompson further observed that because the Black King cannot be adjacent to the White King, there are only 454 legal board positions for the two Kings in which the White King is in one of the ten squares marked above. Exploiting that fact, his database shrunk to 454×64^3 or about 121 million 12-bit records, which fit comfortably on a single (dedicated) disk.

Even though Thompson knew there would be just one copy of his program, he had to squeeze the file onto one disk. Thompson exploited symmetry in data structures to reduce disk space by a factor of eight, which was critical for the success of his entire system. Squeezing space also reduced its run time: decreasing the number of positions examined in the endgame program reduced the time of its learning phase from many months to a few weeks.

PART III: **THE PRODUCT**

Now comes the fun. Parts I and II laid a foundation; the next five columns use that material to build interesting programs. The problems are important in themselves, and they provide focal points where the techniques of previous columns converge in real applications.

Column 11 describes several general-purpose sorting algorithms. Column 12 describes a particular problem from a real application (generating a random sample of integers), and shows how it can be attacked in a variety of ways. One approach is to view it as a problem in set representation, which is the subject of Column 13. Column 14 introduces the heap data structure, and shows how it yields efficient algorithms for sorting and for priority queues. Column 15 tackles several problems that involve searching for words or phrases in very long text strings.

How should you sort a sequence of records into order? The answer is usually easy: *Use a library sort function.* We took this approach in Solution 1.1 and twice in the anagram program in Section 2.8. Unfortunately, this plan doesn't always work. Existing sorts may be cumbersome to employ or too slow to solve a particular problem (as we saw in Section 1.1). In such cases, a programmer has no choice but to write a sort function.

11.1 Insertion Sort

Insertion Sort is the method most card players use to sort their cards. They keep the cards dealt so far in sorted order, and as each new card arrives they insert it into its proper relative position. To sort the array $x[n]$ into increasing order, start with the first element as the sorted subarray $x[0..0]$ and then insert the elements $x[1]$, ..., $x[n-1]$, as in this pseudocode.

```
for i = [1, n)
    /* invariant: x[0..i-1] is sorted */
    /* goal: sift x[i] down to its
            proper place in x[0..i] */
```

The following four lines show the progress of the algorithm on a four-element array. The "|" represents the variable i; elements to its left are sorted, while elements to its right are in their original order.

```
3|1 4 2
1 3|4 2
1 3 4|2
1 2 3 4|
```

The sifting is accomplished by a right-to-left loop that uses the variable j to keep track of the element being sifted. The loop swaps the element with its predecessor in the array as long as there is a predecessor (that is, $j > 0$) and the element hasn't reached its final position (that is, it is out of order with its predecessor). Thus the entire sort is *isort*1:

115

```
for i = [1, n)
    for (j = i; j > 0 && x[j-1] > x[j]; j--)
        swap(j-1, j)
```

For those rare times when I need to write my own sort, that's the first function I try;
it's just three straightforward lines.

Programmers inclined to tuning code might be uncomfortable with the *swap* function call in the inner loop. We can perhaps speed up the code by writing the function
body inline, though many optimizing compilers will do this for us. We replace the
function with this code, which uses the variable t to exchange $x[j]$ and $x[j-1]$.

```
t = x[j];  x[j] = x[j-1];  x[j-1] = t
```

On my machine, *isort*2 takes about one third the time of *isort*1.

This change opens the door for another speedup. Because the variable t is
assigned the same value over and over (the value originally in $x[i]$), we can move the
assignments to and from t out of the loop, and change the comparison to yield *isort*3:

```
for i = [1, n)
    t = x[i]
    for (j = i; j > 0 && x[j-1] > t; j--)
        x[j] = x[j-1]
    x[j] = t
```

This code shifts elements right by one position so long as t is less than the array value,
and finally moves t into its correct position. This five-line function is a little more
subtle than its predecessors, but on my system it runs about fifteen percent faster than
the *isort*2 function.

On random data as well as in the worst case, the run time of Insertion Sort is proportional to n^2. Here are the run times of the three programs when their inputs are n
random integers:

PROGRAM	LINES OF C	NANOSECONDS
Insertion Sort 1	3	$11.9n^2$
Insertion Sort 2	5	$3.8n^2$
Insertion Sort 3	5	$3.2n^2$

The third sort takes a few milliseconds to sort $n = 1000$ integers, a third of a second to
sort $n = 10,000$ integers, and almost an hour to sort a million integers. We'll soon see
code to sort a million integers in under a second. If the input array is already almost
sorted, though, Insertion Sort is much faster because each element sifts down just a
short distance. An algorithm in Section 11.3 exploits exactly this property.

11.2 A Simple Quicksort

This algorithm was described by C. A. R. Hoare in his classic paper "Quicksort"
in the *Computer Journal 5*, 1, April 1962, pp. 10-15. It uses the *divide-and-conquer*
approach of Section 8.3: to sort an array we divide it into two smaller pieces and sort
those recursively. For instance, to sort the eight-element array

we *partition* it around the first element (55) so that all elements less than 55 are to the left of it, while all greater elements are to its right

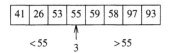

If we then recursively sort the subarray from 0 to 2 and the subarray from 4 to 7, independently, the entire array is sorted.

The average run time of this algorithm is much less than the $O(n^2)$ time of Insertion Sort, because a partitioning operation goes a long way towards sorting the sequence. After a typical partitioning of n elements, about half the elements are above the partition value and half the elements are below it. In a similar amount of run time, the sift operation of Insertion Sort manages to get just one more element into the right place.

We now have a sketch of a recursive function. We represent the active portion of the array by the two indices l and u, for the lower and upper limits. The recursion stops when we come to an array with fewer than two elements. The code is

```
void qsort(l, u)
    if l >= u then
        /* at most one element, do nothing */
        return
    /* goal: partition array around a particular value,
       which is eventually placed in its correct position p
    */
    qsort(l, p-1)
    qsort(p+1, u)
```

To partition the array around the value t we'll start with a simple scheme that I learned from Nico Lomuto. We will see a faster program for this job in the next section†, but this function is so easy to understand that it's hard to get wrong, and it is by no means slow. Given the value t, we are to rearrange $x[a..b]$ and compute the index m (for "middle") such that all elements less than t are to one side of m, while all other elements are on the other side. We'll accomplish the job with a simple *for* loop that scans the array from left to right, using the variables i and m to maintain the

---

† Most presentations of Quicksort use the two-sided partitioning in the next section. Although the basic idea of that code is simple, I have always found the details tricky — I once spent the better part of two days chasing down a bug hiding in a short partitioning loop. A reader of a draft of this column complained that the standard method is in fact simpler than Lomuto's, and sketched some code to make his point; I stopped looking after I found two bugs.

following invariant in array x.

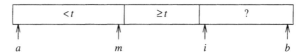

When the code inspects the ith element it must consider two cases. If $x[i] \geq t$ then all is fine; the invariant is still true. On the other hand, when $x[i] < t$, we can regain the invariant by incrementing m (which will index the new location of the small element), and then swapping $x[i]$ and $x[m]$. The complete partitioning code is

```
m = a-1
for i = [a, b]
    if x[i] < t
        swap(++m, i)
```

In Quicksort we'll partition the array $x[l..u]$ around the value $t = x[l]$; a will therefore be $l + 1$ and b will be u. Thus the invariant of the partitioning loop is depicted as

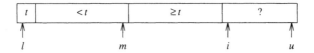

When the loop terminates we have

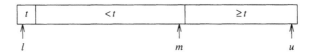

We then swap $x[l]$ with $x[m]$ to give†

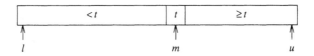

We can now recursively call the function twice with the parameters $(l, m-1)$ and $(m+1, u)$.

The final code is our first complete Quicksort, $qsort1$. To sort the array $x[n]$, we call the function $qsort1(0, n-1)$.

---

† It is tempting to ignore this step and to recur with parameters (l, m) and $(m+1, u)$; unfortunately, this gives an infinite loop when t is the strictly greatest element in the subarray. I would have caught the bug had I tried to verify termination, but the reader can probably guess how I really discovered it. Miriam Jacob gave an elegant proof of incorrectness: since $x[l]$ is never moved, the sort can only work if the minimum element in the array starts in $x[0]$.

```
void qsort1(l, u)
    if (l >= u)
        return
    m = l
    for i = [l+1, u]
        /* invariant: x[l+1..m]    <  x[l] &&
                        x[m+1..i-1] >= x[l] */
        if (x[i] < x[l])
            swap(++m, i)
    swap(l, m)
    /* x[l..m-1] < x[m] <= x[m+1..u] */
    qsort1(l, m-1)
    qsort1(m+1, u)
```

Problem 2 describes Bob Sedgewick's modification to this partitioning code, which results in the slightly faster *qsort2*.

Most of the proof of correctness of this program was given in its derivation (which is, of course, its proper place). The proof proceeds by induction: the outer *if* statement correctly handles empty and single-element arrays, and the partitioning code correctly sets up larger arrays for the recursive calls. The program can't make an infinite sequence of recursive calls because the element $x[m]$ is excluded at each invocation; this is exactly the same argument that we used in Section 4.3 to show that binary search terminates.

This Quicksort runs in $O(n \log n)$ time and $O(\log n)$ stack space on the average, for an input array that is a random permutation of distinct elements. The mathematical arguments are similar to those in Section 8.3. Most algorithms texts analyze Quicksort's run time, and also prove the lower bound that any comparison-based sort must use $O(n \log n)$ comparisons; Quicksort is therefore close to optimal.

The *qsort1* function is the simplest Quicksort I know, and it illustrates many important attributes of the algorithm. The first is that it is indeed quick: on my system, this function sorts a million random integers in just over a second, about twice as fast as the finely-tuned C library *qsort*. (That function has an expensive general-purpose interface.) This sort may be appropriate for a few well-behaved applications, but it has another property of many Quicksorts: it can degrade to quadratic time on some common inputs. The next section studies more robust Quicksorts.

11.3 Better Quicksorts

The *qsort1* function quickly sorts an array of random integers, but how does it perform on nonrandom inputs? As we saw in Section 2.4, programmers often sort to bring together equal elements. We should therefore consider an extreme case: an array of *n* identical elements. Insertion sort performs very well on this input: each element is sifted down zero positions, so the total run time is $O(n)$. The *qsort1* function, on the other hand, blows this case badly. Each of $n - 1$ partitioning passes uses $O(n)$ time to peel off a single element, so the total run time is $O(n^2)$. The run time for $n = 1,000,000$ jumps from a second to two hours.

We can avoid this problem with careful two-sided partitioning code, using this loop invariant:

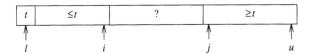

The indices i and j are initialized to the two extremes of the array to be partitioned. The main loop has two inner loops. The first inner loop moves i up over small elements and stops on a large element; the second inner loop moves j down over large elements and stops on a small element. The main loop then tests the indices for crossing and swaps the two values.

But how does the code respond to equal elements? The first temptation is to scan right over them to avoid doing excess work, but this leads to quadratic behavior when all inputs are equal. We will instead stop each scan on equal elements, and swap them. Although this approach performs more swaps than necessary, it transforms the worst case of all equal elements into a best case that requires almost exactly $n \log_2 n$ comparisons. This code implements that partitioning:

```
void qsort3(1, u)
    if 1 >= u
        return
    t = x[1]; i = 1; j = u+1
    loop
        do i++ while i <= u && x[i] < t
        do j-- while x[j] > t
        if i > j
            break
        swap(i, j)
    swap(1, j)
    qsort3(1, j-1)
    qsort3(j+1, u)
```

In addition to taming the degenerate case of all equal elements, this code also performs fewer swaps on the average than *qsort*1.

The Quicksorts that we have seen so far always partition around the first element in the array. This is fine for random inputs, but it can require excessive time and space for some common inputs. If the array is already sorted in increasing order, for instance, it will partition around the smallest element, then the second smallest, and so on through the entire array in order, in $O(n^2)$ time. We do far better to choose a partitioning element at random; we accomplish this by swapping $x[l]$ with a random entry in $x[l..u]$:

```
swap(1, randint(1, u));
```

If you don't have the *randint* function handy, Problem 12.1 investigates how you might make your own. But whatever code you use, be careful that *randint* returns a value in the range $[l, u]$ — a value out of range is an insidious bug. Combining the random partition element and the two-way partitioning code, the expected run time of the Quicksort is now proportional to $n \log n$, for any input array of n elements. The random performance bound is a result of calling the random number generator, rather than an assumption about the distribution of inputs.

Our Quicksorts spend a great deal of time sorting very small subarrays. It would be faster to sort those using a simple method like Insertion Sort rather than firing up all the machinery of Quicksort. Bob Sedgewick developed a particularly clever implementation of this idea. When Quicksort is called on a small subarray (that is, when l and u are near), we do nothing. We implement this by changing the first *if* statement in the function to

```
if u-l > cutoff
    return
```

where *cutoff* is a small integer. When the program finishes, the array will not be sorted, but it will be grouped into small clumps of randomly ordered values such that the elements in one clump are less than elements in any clump to its right. We must clean up within the clumps by another sort method. Because the array is almost sorted, Insertion Sort is just right for the job. We sort the entire array by the code

```
qsort4(0, n-1)
isort3()
```

Problem 3 investigates the best choice for *cutoff*.

As a final piece of code tuning, we may expand the code for the *swap* function in the inner loop (because the other two calls to *swap* aren't in the inner loop, writing them in line would have a negligible impact on the speed). Here is our final Quicksort, *qsort4*:

```
void qsort4(1, u)
    if u - 1 < cutoff
        return
    swap(1, randint(1, u))
    t = x[1]; i = 1; j = u+1
    loop
        do i++; while i <= u && x[i] < t
        do j--; while x[j] > t
        if i > j
            break
        temp = x[i]; x[i] = x[j]; x[j] = temp
    swap(1, j)
    qsort4(1, j-1)
    qsort4(j+1, u)
```

Problems 4 and 11 mention further ways of improving Quicksort's performance.

The versions of Quicksort are summarized in this table. The right column gives the *average* run time in nanoseconds to sort n random integers; many of the functions can degrade to quadratic behavior on some inputs.

PROGRAM	LINES OF CODE	NANOSECONDS
C Library *qsort*	3	$137n \log_2 n$
Quicksort 1	9	$60n \log_2 n$
Quicksort 2	9	$56n \log_2 n$
Quicksort 3	14	$44n \log_2 n$
Quicksort 4	15+5	$36n \log_2 n$
C++ Library *sort*	1	$30n \log_2 n$

The *qsort*4 function uses 15 lines of C, and also the 5 lines of *isort*3. For a million random integers, the run times range from 0.6 seconds for the C++ *sort* to 2.7 seconds for the C *qsort*. In Column 14, we'll see an algorithm that is guaranteed to sort n integers in $O(n \log n)$ time, even in the worst case.

11.4 Principles

This exercise teaches several important lessons about both sorting in particular and programming in general.

The C library *qsort* is easy and relatively fast; it is slower than the hand-made Quicksorts only because its general and flexible interface uses a function call for each comparison. The C++ library *sort* has the simplest interface: we sort the array x with the call $sort(x, x+n)$; it also has a particularly efficient implementation. If a system sort can meet your needs, don't even consider writing your own code.

Insertion Sort is simple to code and may be fast enough for small sorting jobs. Sorting 10,000 integers with *isort*3 requires just a third of a second on my system.

For large n, the $O(n \log n)$ run time of Quicksort is crucial. The algorithm design techniques of Column 8 gave us the basic idea for the divide-and-conquer algorithm, and the program verification techniques of Column 4 helped us implement the idea in succinct and efficient code.

Even though the big speedups are achieved by changing algorithms, the code tuning techniques of Column 9 speed up Insertion Sort by a factor of 4 and Quicksort by a factor of 2.

11.5 Problems

1. Like any other powerful tool, sorting is often used when it shouldn't be and not used when it should be. Explain how sorting could be overused or underused when calculating the following statistics of an array of n floating point numbers: minimum, maximum, mean, median and mode.

2. [R. Sedgewick] Speed up Lomuto's partitioning scheme by using $x[l]$ as a sentinel. Show how this scheme allows you to remove the *swap* after the loop.

3. How could you experiment to find the best value of *cutoff* on a particular system?

4. Although Quicksort uses only $O(\log n)$ stack space on the average, it can use linear space in the worst case. Explain why, then modify the program to use only logarithmic space in the worst case.

5. [M. D. McIlroy] Show how to use Lomuto's partitioning scheme to sort varying-length bit strings in time proportional to the sum of their lengths.

6. Use the techniques of this column to implement other sorting algorithms. Selection sort first places the smallest value in $x[0]$, then the smallest remaining value in $x[1]$, and so forth. Shell sort (or ''diminishing increment sort'') is like Insertion Sort, but moves elements down h positions rather than just one position. The value of h starts large, and shrinks.

7. Implementations of the sorting programs in this column can be found on this book's web site. Time them on your system and summarize them in a table like that in Section 11.3.

8. Sketch a one-page guide to show a user of your system how to select a sort. Make sure that your method considers the importance of run time, space, programmer time (development and maintenance), generality (what if I want to sort character strings that represent Roman numerals?), stability (items with equal keys should retain their relative order), special properties of the input data, etc. As an extreme test of your method, try feeding it the sorting problem described in Column 1.

9. Write a program for finding the kth-smallest element in the array $x[0..n-1]$ in $O(n)$ expected time. Your algorithm may permute the elements of x.

10. Gather and display empirical data on the run time of a Quicksort program.

11. Write a ''fat pivot'' partitioning function with the postcondition

How would you incorporate the function into a Quicksort program?

12. Study sorting methods used in non-computer applications (such as mail rooms and change sorters).

13. The Quicksort programs in this column choose a partitioning element at random. Study better choices, such as the median element of a sample from the array.

14. The Quicksorts in this column represented a subarray with two integer indices; this is necessary in a language like Java, which does not have pointers into arrays. In C or C++, though, it is possible to sort an array of integers using a function like

```
void qsort(int x[], int n)
```

for the original call and for all recursive calls. Modify the algorithms in this column to use this interface.

11.6 Further Reading

Since the first edition was published by Addison-Wesley in 1973, Don Knuth's *Art of Computer Programming, Volume 3: Sorting and Searching* has been the definitive reference on the topic. He describes all important algorithms in detail, analyzes their run times mathematically, and implements them in assembly code. The exercises and references describe many important variations of the primary algorithms. Knuth updated and revised the book for a second edition in 1998. The MIX assembly language that he uses shows its age, but the principles revealed in the code are timeless.

Bob Sedgewick gives a more modern treatment of sorting and searching in the monumental third edition of his *Algorithms*. Parts 1 through 4 cover Fundamentals, Data Structures, Sorting and Searching. *Algorithms in C* was published by Addison-Wesley in 1997, *Algorithms in C++* (with C++ consulting by Chris Van Wyk) appeared in 1998, and *Algorithms in Java* (with Java consulting by Tim Lindholm) appeared in 1999. He emphasizes the implementation of useful algorithms (in the language of your choice), and intuitively explains their performance.

These two books are the primary references for this column on sorting, for Column 13 on searching, and for Column 14 on heaps.

COLUMN 12: **A SAMPLE PROBLEM**

Small computer programs are often educational and entertaining. This column tells the story of a tiny program that, in addition to those qualities, proved useful to a company.

12.1 The Problem

It was the early 1980's, and the company had just purchased their first personal computers. After I got their primary system up and running, I encouraged people to keep an eye open for tasks around the office that could be done by a program. The firm's business was public opinion polling, and an alert employee suggested automating the task of drawing a random sample from a printed list of precincts. Because doing the job by hand required a boring hour with a table of random numbers, she proposed the following program.

> The input consists of a list of precinct names and an integer m. The output is a list of m of the precincts chosen at random. There are usually a few hundred precinct names (each a string of at most a dozen characters), and m is typically between 20 and 40.

That's the user's idea for a program. Do you have any suggestions about the problem definition before we dive into coding?

My primary response was that it was a great idea; the task was ripe for automation. I then pointed out that typing several hundred names, while perhaps easier than dealing with long columns of random numbers, was still a tedious and error-prone task. In general, it's foolish to prepare a lot of input when the program is going to ignore the bulk of it anyway. I therefore suggested an alternative program.

> The input consists of two integers m and n, with $m < n$. The output is a sorted list of m random integers in the range $0..n-1$ in which no integer occurs more than once.† For probability buffs, we desire a sorted

---

† The real program produced m integers in the range $1..n$; I have changed to a zero-based range in this column for consistency with the other ranges in the book, and so that we can use the programs to produce random samples of C arrays. Programmers may count from zero, but pollsters start at one.

125

selection without replacement in which each selection occurs with equal probability.

When $m = 20$ and $n = 200$, the program might produce a 20-element sequence that starts 4, 15, 17, ... The user then draws a sample of size 20 from 200 precincts by counting through the list and marking the 4th, 15th, and 17th names, and so on. (The output is required to be sorted because the hardcopy list isn't numbered.)

That specification met with the enthusiastic approval of its potential users. After the program was implemented, the task that previously required an hour could be accomplished in a few minutes.

Now look at the problem from the other side: how would you implement the program? Assume that you have a function *bigrand*() that returns a large random integer (much larger than m and n), and a function *randint*(i, j) that returns a random integer chosen uniformly in the range $i..j$. Problem 1 looks inside the implementation of such functions.

12.2 One Solution

As soon as we settled on the problem to be solved, I ran to my nearest copy of Knuth's *Seminumerical Algorithms* (having copies of Knuth's three volumes both at home and at work has been well worth the investment). Because I had studied the book carefully a decade earlier, I vaguely recalled that it contained several algorithms for problems like this. After spending a few minutes considering several possible designs that we'll study shortly, I realized that Algorithm S in Knuth's Section 3.4.2 was the ideal solution to my problem.

The algorithm considers the integers 0, 1, 2, ..., $n - 1$ in order, and selects each one by an appropriate random test. By visiting the integers in order, we guarantee that the output will be sorted.

To understand the selection criterion, let's consider the example that $m = 2$ and $n = 5$. We should select the first integer 0 with probability 2/5; a program implements that by a statement like

```
if (bigrand() % 5) < 2
```

Unfortunately, we can't select 1 with the same probability. doing so might or might not give us a total of 2 out of the 5 integers. We will therefore bias the decision and select 1 with probability 1/4 if 0 was chosen but with probability 2/4 if 0 was not chosen. In general, to select s numbers out of r remaining, we'll select the next number with probability s/r. Here is the pseudocode:

```
select = m
remaining = n
for i = [0, n)
    if (bigrand() % remaining) < select
        print i
        select--
    remaining--
```

As long as $m \le n$, the program selects exactly m integers: it can't select more because when *select* goes to zero no integer is selected, and it can't select fewer because when *select/remaining* goes to one an integer is always selected. The *for* statement ensures that the integers are printed in sorted order. The above description should help you believe that each subset is equally likely to be picked; Knuth gives a probabilistic proof of that fact.

Knuth's second volume made the program easy to write. Even including titles, input, output, range checking and the like, the final program required only thirteen lines of Basic. It was finished half an hour after the problem was defined, and was used for years without problems. Here is an implementation in C++:

```
void genknuth(int m, int n)
{    for (int i = 0; i < n; i++)
        /* select m of remaining n-i */
        if ((bigrand() % (n-i)) < m) {
            cout << i << "\n";
            m--;
        }
}
```

The program used only a few dozen bytes of memory, and was lightning fast for the company's problems. This code can be slow, however, when n is very large. Using this algorithm to generate a few random 32-bit positive integers (that is, $n = 2^{32}$), for instance, requires about twelve minutes on my computer. Back-of-the-envelope quiz: how long would it take to generate one random 48- or 64-bit integer with this code?

12.3 The Design Space

One part of a programmer's job is solving today's problem. Another, and perhaps more important, part of the job is to prepare for solving tomorrow's problems. Sometimes that preparation involves taking classes or studying books like Knuth's. More often, though, programmers learn by the mental exercise of asking how we might have solved a problem differently. Let's do that now by exploring the space of possible designs for the sampling problem.

When I talked about the problem to a seminar at West Point, I asked for a better approach than the original problem statement (typing all 200 names to the program). One student suggested photocopying the precinct list, cutting the copy with a paper slicer, shaking the slips in a paper bag, and then pulling out the required number of slips. That cadet showed the "conceptual blockbusting" that is the subject of Adams's book cited in Section 1.7.†

From now on we'll confine our search to a program to write m sorted integers at

---

† Page 57 of that book sketches Arthur Koestler's views on three kinds of creativity. *Ah!* insights are his name for originality, and *aha!* insights are acts of discovery. He would call this cadet's solution a *haha!* insight: the low-tech answer to a high-tech question is an act of comic inspiration (as in Solutions 1.10, 1.11 and 1.12).

random from $0..n-1$. We'll start by evaluating Program 1. The algorithmic idea is straightforward, the code is short, it uses just a few words of space, and the run time is fine for this application. The run time is proportional to n, though, which might be prohibitive for some applications. It's worth a few minutes to study other ways of solving the problem. Sketch as many high-level designs as you can before reading on; don't worry about implementation details yet.

One solution inserts random integers into an initially empty set until there are enough. In pseudocode, it can be sketched as

```
initialize set S to empty
size = 0
while size < m do
    t = bigrand() % n
    if t is not in S
        insert t into S
        size++
print the elements of S in sorted order
```

The algorithm is not biased towards any particular element; its output is random. We are still left with the problem of implementing the set S; think about an appropriate data structure.

In the old days, I would have worried about the relative merits of sorted linked lists, binary search trees, and all the other usual data structure suspects. Today, though, I can exploit the work put into the C++ Standard Template Library and call a set a *set*:

```
void gensets(int m, int n)
{   set<int> S;
    while (S.size() < m)
        S.insert(bigrand() % n);
    set<int>::iterator i;
    for (i = S.begin(); i != S.end(); ++i)
        cout << *i << "\n";
}
```

I was delighted that the real code is the same length as the pseudocode. This program generates and prints a million sorted, distinct 31-bit random integers in about 20 seconds on my machine. Since it takes about 12.5 seconds just to generate and to print a million unsorted integers without worrying about duplicates, the set operations consume just 7.5 seconds.

The C++ STL specification guarantees that each insertion will run in $O(\log m)$ time, and iterating through the set will take $O(m)$ time, so the complete program will take $O(m \log m)$ time (when m is small compared to n). The data structure is, however, expensive in terms of space: my 128-megabyte machine starts thrashing around $m = 1,700,000$. The next column considers possible implementations of the set.

Another way to generate a sorted subset of random integers is to shuffle an n-element array that contains the numbers $0..n-1$, and then sort the first m for the output. Knuth's Algorithm P in Section 3.4.2 shuffles the array $x[0..n-1]$.

```
for i = [0, n)
    swap(i, randint(i, n-1))
```

Ashley Shepherd and Alex Woronow observed that in this problem we need shuffle only the first m elements of the array, which gives this C++ program:

```
void genshuf(int m, int n)
{   int i, j;
    int *x = new int[n];
    for (i = 0; i < n; i++)
        x[i] = i;
    for (i = 0; i < m; i++) {
        j = randint(i, n-1);
        int t = x[i]; x[i] = x[j]; x[j] = t;
    }
    sort(x, x+m);
    for (i = 0; i < m; i++)
        cout << x[i] << "\n";
}
```

(handwritten annotation: shuffle m ints.)

(handwritten annotation: → sort them)

The algorithm uses n words of memory and $O(n + m \log m)$ time, but the technique of Problem 1.9 reduces the time to $O(m \log m)$. We can view this algorithm as an alternative to Program 2 in which we represent the set of selected elements in $x[0..i-1]$ and the set of unselected elements in $x[i..n-1]$. By explicitly representing the unselected elements we avoid testing whether the new element was previously chosen. Unfortunately, because this method uses $O(n)$ time and memory, it is usually dominated by the algorithm from Knuth.

The functions we have seen so far offer several different solutions to the problem, but they by no means cover the design space. Suppose, for instance, that n is a million and m is $n - 10$. We might generate a sorted random sample of 10 elements, and then report the integers that aren't there. Next, suppose that n is ten million and m is 2^{31}. We could generate eleven million integers, sort them, scan through to remove duplicates, and then generate a ten-million-element sorted sample of that. Solution 9 describes a particularly clever algorithm based on searching due to Bob Floyd.

12.4 Principles

This column illustrates several important steps in the programming process. Although the following discussion presents the stages in one natural order, the design process is more active: we hop from one activity to another, usually iterating through each many times before arriving at an acceptable solution.

Understand the Perceived Problem. Talk with the user about the context in which the problem arises. Problem statements often include ideas about solutions; like all early ideas, they should be considered but not to the exclusion of others.

Specify an Abstract Problem. A clean, crisp problem statement helps us first to solve this problem and then to see how this solution can be applied to other problems.

Explore the Design Space. Too many programmers jump too quickly to "the" solution to their problem; they think for a minute and code for a day rather than thinking for an hour and coding for an hour. Using informal high-level languages helps us to describe designs: pseudocode represents control flow and abstract data types represent the crucial data structures. Knowledge of the literature is invaluable at this stage of the design process.

Implement One Solution. On lucky days our exploration of the design space shows that one program is far superior to the rest; at other times we have to prototype the top few to choose the best. We should strive to implement the chosen design in straightforward code, using the most powerful operations available.†

Retrospect. Polya's delightful *How to Solve It* can help any programmer become a better problem solver. On page 15 he observes that "There remains always something to do; with sufficient study and penetration, we could improve any solution, and, in any case, we can always improve our understanding of the solution." His hints are particularly helpful for looking back at programming problems.

12.5 Problems

1. The C library *rand()* function typically returns about fifteen random bits. Use that function to implement a function *bigrand()* to return at least 30 random bits, and a function *randint(l, u)* to return a random integer in the range [*l*, *u*].

2. Section 12.1 specified that all *m*-element subsets be chosen with equal probability, which is a stronger requirement than choosing each integer with probability *m/n*. Describe an algorithm that chooses each element equiprobably, but chooses some subsets with greater probability than others.

3. Show that when *m* < *n*/2, the expected number of *member* tests made by the set-based algorithm before finding a number not in the set is less than 2.

4. Counting the *member* tests in the set-based program leads to many interesting problems in combinatorics and probability theory. How many *member* tests does the program make on the average as a function of *m* and *n*? How many does it make when *m* = *n*? When is it likely to make more than *m* tests?

5. This column described several algorithms for one problem; all are available at this book's web site. Measure their performance on your system, and describe when each is appropriate as a function of constraints on run time, space, etc.

6. [Class Exercise] I assigned the problem of generating sorted subsets twice in an

---

† Problem 6 describes a class exercise that I graded on programming style. Most students turned in one-page solutions and received mediocre grades. Two students who had spent the previous summer on a large software development project turned in beautifully documented five-page programs, broken into a dozen functions, each with an elaborate heading. They received failing grades. The best programs worked in five lines of code, and the inflation factor of sixty was too much for a passing grade. When the pair complained that they were employing standard software engineering tools, I should have quoted Pamela Zave: "The purpose of software engineering is to control complexity, not to create it." A few more minutes spent looking for a simple program might have spared them hours documenting their complex program.

undergraduate course on algorithms. Before the unit on sorting and searching, students had to write a program for $m = 20$ and $n = 400$; the primary grading criterion was a short, clean program — run time was not an issue. After the unit on sorting and searching they had to solve the problem again with $m = 5,000,000$ and $n = 1,000,000,000$, and the grade was based primarily on run time.

7. [V. A. Vyssotsky] Algorithms for generating combinatorial objects are often profitably expressed as recursive functions. Knuth's algorithm can be written as

```
void randselect(m, n)
        pre    0 <= m <= n
        post   m distinct integers from 0..n-1 are
               printed in decreasing order
    if m > 0
        if (bigrand() % n) < m
            print n-1
            randselect(m-1, n-1)
        else
            randselect(m, n-1)
```

This program prints the random integers in decreasing order; how could you make them appear in increasing order? Argue the correctness of the resulting program. How could you use the basic recursive structure of this program to generate all m-element subsets of $0..n-1$?

8. How would you generate a random selection of m integers from $0..n-1$ with the constraint that the final output must appear in random order? How would you generate a sorted list if duplicate integers were allowed in the list? What if both duplicates and random order were desired?

9. [R. W. Floyd] When m is near n, the set-based algorithm generates many random numbers that are discarded because they are already present in the set. Can you find an algorithm that uses only m random numbers, even in the worst case?

10. How could you select one of n objects at random, where you see the objects sequentially but you don't know the value of n beforehand? For concreteness, how would you read a text file, and select and print one random line, when you don't know the number of lines in advance?

11. [M. I. Shamos] A promotional game consists of a card containing 16 spots, which hide a random permutation of the integers $1..16$. The player rubs the dots off the card to expose the hidden integers. If the integer 3 is ever exposed then the card loses; if 1 and 2 (in either order) are both revealed then the card wins. Describe the steps you would take to compute the probability that randomly choosing a sequence of spots wins the game; assume that you may use at most one hour of CPU time.

12. My first version of one of the programs in this column had a nasty bug that caused the program to die when $m = 0$. For other values of m, it produced output that looked random but wasn't. How would you test a program that produces a sample to ensure that its output is indeed random?

12.6 Further Reading

Volume 2 of Don Knuth's *Art of Computer Programming* is *Seminumerical Algorithms*. The third edition was published by Addison-Wesley in 1998. Chapter 3 (the first half of the book) is about random numbers, and Chapter 4 (the second half) is about arithmetic. Section 3.4.2 on "Random Sampling and Shuffling" is especially relevant to this column. If you need to build a random number generator or functions that perform advanced arithmetic, then you need this book.

COLUMN 13: **SEARCHING**

Searching problems come in many varieties. A compiler looks up a variable name to find its type and address. A spelling checker looks up a word in a dictionary to ensure that it is spelled correctly. A directory program looks up a subscriber name to find a telephone number. An Internet domain name server looks up a name to find an IP address. These applications, and thousands like them, all need to search a set of data to find the information associated with a particular item.

This column studies in detail one searching problem: how do we store a set of integers, with no other associated data? Though tiny, this problem raises many of the key issues that arise in implementing any data structure. We'll start with the precise definition of the task, and use that to investigate the most common set representations.

13.1 The Interface

We'll continue with the problem of the last column: generating a sorted sequence of *m* random integers in the range [0, *maxval*), chosen without duplicates. Our job is to implement this pseudocode:

```
initialize set S to empty
size = 0
while size < m do
    t = bigrand() % maxval
    if t is not in S
        insert t into S
        size++
print the elements of S in sorted order
```

We'll call our data structure an *IntSet*, for set of integers. We'll define the interface to be a C++ class with these public members:

```
class IntSetImp {
public:
    IntSetImp(int maxelements, int maxval);
    void insert(int t);
    int size();
    void report(int *v);
};
```

The constructor *IntSetImp* initializes the set to be empty. The function has two arguments describing the maximum number of elements in the set and (one greater than) the maximum size of any element; a particular implementation may ignore one or both of those parameters. The *insert* function adds a new integer to the set, if it is not already present. The *size* function tells the current number of elements, and *report* writes the elements (in sorted order) into the vector *v*.

This little interface is clearly for instructional use only. It lacks many components critical for an industrial-strength class, such as error handling and a destructor. An expert C++ programmer would probably use an abstract class with virtual functions to specify this interface, and then write each implementation as a derived class. We will instead take the simpler (and sometimes more efficient) approach of using names such as *IntSetArr* for the array implementation, *IntSetList* for the list implementation, and so forth. We'll use the name *IntSetImp* to represent an arbitrary implementation.

This C++ code uses such a data structure in this function to generate a sorted set of random integers:

```
void gensets(int m, int maxval)
{   int *v = new int[m];
    IntSetImp S(m, maxval);
    while (S.size() < m)
        S.insert(bigrand() % maxval);
    S.report(v);
    for (int i = 0; i < m; i++)
        cout << v[i] << "\n";
}
```

Because the *insert* function does not put duplicate elements into the set, we need not test whether the element is in the set before we insert it.

The easiest implementation of an *IntSet* uses the powerful and general *set* template from the C++ Standard Template Library:

```
class IntSetSTL {
private:
    set<int> S;
public:
    IntSetSTL(int maxelements, int maxval) { }
    int size() { return S.size(); }
    void insert(int t) { S.insert(t); }
    void report(int *v)
    {   int j = 0;
        set<int>::iterator i;
        for (i = S.begin(); i != S.end(); ++i)
            v[j++] = *i;
    }
};
```

The constructor ignores its two arguments. Our *IntSet*, *size* and *insert* functions correspond exactly to their STL counterparts. The *report* function uses the standard iterator to write the elements of the set into the array, in sorted order. This general-purpose structure is good but not perfect: we'll soon see implementations that are a factor of five more efficient for this particular task in both time and space.

13.2 Linear Structures

We'll build our first set implementation with the simplest structure: an array of integers. Our class keeps the current number of elements in the integer n, and the integers themselves in the vector x:

```
private:
    int n, *x;
```

(The complete implementation of all classes can be found in Appendix 5.) This pseudocode version of the C++ constructor allocates the array (with one extra element for a sentinel) and sets n to zero:

```
IntSetArray(maxelements, maxval)
    x = new int[1 + maxelements]
    n = 0
    x[0] = maxval
```

Because we have to report the elements in sorted order, we'll store them that way at all times. (Unsorted arrays are superior in some other applications.) We'll also keep the sentinel element *maxval* at the end of the sorted elements; *maxval* is larger than any element in the set. This replaces the test for running off the end of the list with a test for finding a greater element (which we already need). That will make our insertion code simpler, and will incidentally make it faster:

```
void insert(t)
    for (i = 0; x[i] < t; i++)
        ;
    if x[i] == t
        return
    for (j = n; j >= i; j--)
        x[j+1] = x[j]
    x[i] = t
    n++
```

The first loop scans over array elements that are less than the insertion value t. If the new element is equal to t, then it is already in the set so we return immediately. Otherwise, we slide the greater elements (including the sentinel) up by one, insert t into the resulting hole, and increment n. This takes $O(n)$ time.

The *size* function is identical in all of our implementations:

```
int size()
    return n
```

The *report* function copies all of the elements (except the sentinel) to the output array in $O(n)$ time:

```
void report(v)
    for i = [0, n)
        v[i] = x[i]
```

Arrays are an excellent structure for sets when the size is known in advance. Because our arrays are sorted, we could use binary search to build a *member* function that runs in $O(\log n)$ time. We'll see details on the run times of arrays at the end of this section.

If the size of a set is not known in advance, linked lists are a prime candidate for set representation; lists also remove the cost of sliding over elements in an insertion.

Our class *IntSetList* will use this private data:

```
private:
    int n;
    struct node {
        int val;
        node *next;
        node(int v, node *p) { val = v; next = p; }
    };
    node *head, *sentinel;
```

Each node in a linked list has an integer value and a pointer to the next node in the list. The *node* constructor assigns its two parameters to the two fields.

For the same reasons that we used sorted arrays, we'll keep our linked lists in sorted order. Just as in arrays, our lists will use a sentinel node with a value larger than any real value. The constructor builds such a node and sets *head* to point to it.

```
IntSetList(maxelements, maxval)
    sentinel = head = new node(maxval, 0)
    n = 0
```

The *report* function walks the list, putting the sorted elements into the output vector:

```
void report(int *v)
    j = 0
    for (p = head; p != sentinel; p = p->next)
        v[j++] = p->val
```

To insert an item into a sorted linked list we walk along the list until we either find the element (and immediately return), or find a greater value, and insert it at that point. Unfortunately, the variety of cases usually leads to complicated code; see Solution 4. The simplest code I know for the task is a recursive function that is originally called as

```
void insert(t)
    head = rinsert(head, t)
```

The recursive part is clean:

```
node *rinsert(p, t)
    if p->val < t
        p->next = rinsert(p->next, t)
    else if p->val > t
        p = new node(t, p)
        n++
    return p
```

When a programming problem is hidden under a pile of special cases, recursion often leads to code as straightforward as this.

When we use either structure to generate m random integers, each of the m searches runs in time proportional to m, on the average. Each structure will therefore take total time proportional to m^2. I suspected that the list version would be slightly faster than the array version: it uses extra space (for the pointers) to avoid moving over the upper values in the array. Here are the run times with n held fixed at 1,000,000 and m varying from 10,000 to 40,000:

STRUCTURE	SET SIZE (m)		
	10,000	20,000	40,000
Arrays	0.6	2.6	11.1
Simple Lists	5.7	31.2	170.0
Lists (Remove Recursion)	1.8	12.6	73.8
Lists (Group Allocation)	1.2	5.7	25.4

The run time of arrays grew quadratically, just as I expected, with very reasonable constants. My first implementation of lists, though, started out an order of magnitude slower than arrays, and grew faster than n^2. Something was wrong.

My first response was to blame the recursion. In addition to the overhead of the recursive call, the recursion depth of the *rinsert* function is the position in which the element is found, which is $O(n)$. And after recurring all the way down the list, the code assigns the original value back into almost every pointer. When I changed the recursive function to the iterative version described in Solution 4, the run time dropped by a factor of almost three.

My next response was to change the storage allocation to use the technique in Problem 5: rather than allocating a *new* node for every insertion, the constructor allocates a single block of m nodes, and *insert* passes them out as they are needed. This was an improvement in two distinct ways:

The cost model for run time in Appendix 3 shows that storage allocation is about two orders of magnitude more time-consuming than most simple operations. We have replaced m of those expensive operations with just one.

The cost model for space in Appendix 3 suggests that if we allocate nodes as a block, each node consumes just eight bytes (four for the integer and four for the pointer); 40,000 nodes consume 320 kilobytes and fit comfortably in my machine's Level-2 cache. If we allocate the nodes individually, however, then each consumes 48 bytes, and collectively their 1.92 megabytes overflows the Level-2 cache.

On a different system with a more efficient allocator, removing recursion gave a factor of five speedup, while changing to a single allocation gave just ten percent. Like most code-tuning techniques, caching and recursion removal sometimes yield great benefit, and other times have no effect.

The array insertion algorithm searches down the sequence to find the place to insert the target value, then pushes over the greater values. The list insertion algorithm does the first part, but not the second. So if lists do half the work, why do they take twice the time? Part of the reason is that they take twice as much memory: large lists must read 8-byte nodes into a cache to access the 4-byte integer. Another part of the reason is that arrays access data with perfect predictability, while access patterns for lists bounce all around memory.

13.3 Binary Search Trees

We'll turn now from linear structures to structures that support fast search and insertion. This picture shows a binary search tree after inserting the integers 31, 41, 59 and 26, in that order:

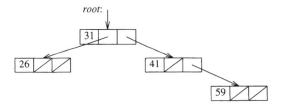

The *IntSetBST* class defines nodes and a root:

```
private:
    int n, *v, vn;
    struct node {
        int val;
        node *left, *right;
        node(int i) { val = i; left = right = 0; }
    };
    node *root;
```

We initialize the tree by setting the root to be empty, and perform the other actions by calling recursive functions.

```
IntSetBST(int maxelements, int maxval) { root = 0; n = 0; }
void insert(int t) { root = rinsert(root, t); }
void report(int *x) { v = x; vn = 0; traverse(root); }
```

The insertion function walks down the tree until either the value is found (and the search terminates), or the search falls out of the tree (and the node is inserted):

```
node *rinsert(p, t)
    if p == 0
        p = new node(t)
        n++
    else if t < p->val
        p->left = rinsert(p->left, t)
    else if t > p->val
        p->right = rinsert(p->right, t)
    // do nothing if p->val == t
    return p
```

Because the elements in our application are inserted in a random order, we will not worry about sophisticated balancing schemes. (Problem 1 shows that other algorithms on random sets can lead to highly unbalanced trees.)

The *inorder* traversal† first processes the left subtree, then reports the node itself, and then processes the right subtree:

```
void traverse(p)
    if p == 0
        return
    traverse(p->left)
    v[vn++] = p->val
    traverse(p->right)
```

It uses the variable *vn* to index the next available element in the vector *v*.

This table gives the run time for the STL *set* structure that we saw in Section 13.1 (as it is implemented on my system), for binary search trees and for several structures that we'll see in the next section. The maximum integer size is held fixed at $n = 10^8$, and *m* goes as high as possible until the system runs out of RAM and starts thrashing to disk.

STRUCTURE	SET SIZE (m)					
	1,000,000		5,000,000		10,000,000	
	Secs	Mbytes	Secs	Mbytes	Secs	Mbytes
STL	9.38	72				
BST	7.30	56				
BST*	3.71	16	25.26	80		
Bins	2.36	60				
Bins*	1.02	16	5.55	80		
BitVec	3.72	16	5.70	32	8.36	52

These times do not include the time required to print the output, which is slightly

---

† My first version of this program led to a bizarre bug: the compiler reported an internal inconsistency and died. I turned off optimization, the ''bug'' went away, and I blamed the compiler writers. I later realized that the problem was that when I quickly wrote the traversal code, I forgot to include the *if* test for *p* being null. The optimizer tried to convert the tail recursion into a loop, and died when it could not find a test to terminate the loop.

greater than the time of the STL implementation. Our simple binary search trees avoid the complex balancing scheme used by the STL (the STL specification guarantees good worst-case performance), and is therefore slightly faster and uses less space. The STL started thrashing at about $m = 1,600,000$, while our first BST thrashes at about $m = 1,900,000$. The row marked "BST*" describes a binary search tree incorporating several optimizations. The most important is that it allocates the nodes all at once (as in Problem 5). That greatly reduces the tree's space requirements, which reduces the run time by about a third. The code also converts recursion to iteration (as in Problem 4) and uses the sentinel node described in Problem 7, for an additional speedup of about 25 percent.

13.4 Structures for Integers

We'll turn now to two final structures that exploit the fact that our sets represent integers. Bit vectors are an old friend from Column 1. Here are their private data and functions:

```
enum { BITSPERWORD = 32, SHIFT = 5, MASK = 0x1F };
int n, hi, *x;
void set(int i)  {           x[i>>SHIFT] |=  (1<<(i & MASK)); }
void clr(int i)  {           x[i>>SHIFT] &= ~(1<<(i & MASK)); }
int  test(int i) { return x[i>>SHIFT] &   (1<<(i & MASK)); }
```

The constructor allocates the arrays and turns off all bits:

```
IntSetBitVec(maxelements, maxval)
    hi = maxval
    x = new int[1 + hi/BITSPERWORD]
    for i = [0, hi)
        clr(i)
    n = 0
```

i % 32 ≡ i & (2^5 − 1)

divide by 2^5 = right shift by 5

Problem 8 suggests how we might speed this up by operating on a word of data at a time. Similar speedups apply to the *report* function:

```
void report(v)
    j - 0
    for i = [0, hi)
        if test(i)
            v[j++] = i
```

Finally, the *insert* function turns on the bit and increments n, but only if the bit was previously off:

```
void insert(t)
    if test(t)
        return
    set(t)
    n++
```

The table in the previous section shows that if the maximum value n is small enough so the bit vector fits in main memory, then the structure is remarkably efficient (and Problem 8 shows how to make it even more so). Unfortunately, if n is 2^{32}, a bit vector requires half a gigabyte of main memory.

Our final data structure combines the strengths of lists and bit vectors. It places the integers into a sequence of "buckets" or "bins". If we have four integers in the range 0..99, we place them into four bins. Bin 0 contains integers in the range 0..24, bin 1 represents 25..49, bin 2 represents 50..74, and bin 3 represents 75..99:

```
              41
        | 26 | 31 | 59 |    |
```

The m bins can be viewed as a kind of hashing. The integers in each bin are represented by a sorted linked list. Because the integers are uniformly distributed, each linked list has expected length one.

The structure has this private data:

```
private:
    int n, bins, maxval;
    struct node {
        int val;
        node *next;
        node(int v, node *p) { val = v; next = p; }
    };
    node **bin, *sentinel;
```

The constructor allocates the array of bins and a sentinel element with a large value, and initializes each bin to point to the sentinel:

```
IntSetBins(maxelements, pmaxval)
    bins = maxelements
    maxval = pmaxval
    bin = new node*[bins]
    sentinel = new node(maxval, 0)
    for i = [0, bins)
        bin[i] = sentinel
    n = 0
```

The *insert* function needs to place the integer t into its proper bin. The obvious mapping of $t*bins/maxval$ can lead to numerical overflow (and some nasty debugging, as I can state from bitter personal experience). We will instead use the safer mapping in this code:

```
void insert(t)
    i = t / (1 + maxval/bins)
    bin[i] = rinsert(bin[i], t)
```

The *rinsert* is the same as for linked lists. Similarly, the *report* function is essentially the linked list code applied to every bin, in order:

```
void report(v)
    j = 0
    for i = [0, bins)
        for (node *p = bin[i]; p != sentinel; p = p->next)
            v[j++] = p->val
```

The table in the last section shows that bins are fast. The row marked "Bins*" describes the run time of bins that are modified to allocate all nodes during initialization (as in Problem 5); the modified structures use about one quarter the space and half the time of the original. Removing recursion dropped the run time by an additional ten percent.

13.5 Principles

We've skimmed five important data structures for representing sets. The average performance of those structures, when m is small compared to n, is described in this table (b denotes the number of bits per word):

SET REPRESENTATION	O(TIME PER OPERATION)			TOTAL TIME	SPACE IN WORDS
	Init	*insert*	*report*		
Sorted Array	1	m	m	$O(m^2)$	m
Sorted List	1	m	m	$O(m^2)$	$2m$
Binary Tree	1	log m	m	$O(m \log m)$	$3m$
Bins	m	1	m	$O(m)$	$3m$
Bit Vector	n	1	n	$O(n)$	n/b

This table barely scratches the surface of set representations for problems like this; Solution 10 mentions other possibilities. Section 15.1 describes data structures for searching sets of words.

Although we've concentrated on data structures for set representations, we've learned several principles that apply to many programming tasks.

The Role of Libraries. The C++ Standard Template Library provided a general-purpose solution that was easy to implement and should prove simple to maintain and to extend. When you face a problem with data structures, your first inclination should be to search for a general tool that solves the problem. In this case, though, special-purpose code could exploit properties of the particular problem to be much faster.

The Importance of Space. In Section 13.2 we saw that finely tuned linked lists do half the work of arrays but take twice the time. Why? Arrays use half as much memory per element, and access memory sequentially. In Section 13.3 we saw that using custom memory allocation for binary search trees reduced space by a factor of three and time by a factor of two. Time increased substantially as we overflowed memory at magic boundaries (on my machine) at a half-megabyte (the Level-2 cache size) and near 80 megabytes (the amount of free RAM).

Code Tuning Techniques. The most substantial improvement we saw was replacing general-purpose memory allocation with a single allocation of a large block. This eliminated many expensive calls, and also used space more efficiently. Rewriting a recursive function to be iterative sped up linked lists by a whopping factor of three, but gave only a ten percent speedup for bins. Sentinels gave clean, simple code for most structures, and incidentally decreased the run time.

13.6 Problems

1. Solution 12.9 describes Bob Floyd's algorithm for generating a sorted set of random integers. Can you implement his algorithm using the *IntSets* in this section? How do these structures perform on the nonrandom distributions generated by Floyd's algorithm?

2. How would you change the toy *IntSet* interface to make it more robust?

3. Augment the set classes with a *find* function that tells whether a given element is in the set. Can you implement that function to be more efficient than *insert*?

4. Rewrite the recursive insertion functions for lists, bins and binary search trees to use iteration, and measure the difference in run times.

5. Section 9.1 and Solution 9.2 describe how Chris Van Wyk avoided many calls to a storage allocator by keeping a collection of available nodes in his own structure. Show how that same idea applies to *IntSets* implemented by lists, bins and binary search trees.

6. What can you learn by timing this fragment on the various implementations of *IntSet*?

```
IntSetImp S(m, n);
for (int i = 0; i < m; i++)
    S.insert(i);
```

7. Our arrays, linked lists and bins all employ sentinels. Show how to apply the same technique to binary search trees.

8. Show how to speed up the initialization and reporting operations on bit vectors by using parallelism to operate on many bits at a time. Is it most efficient to operate on a *char, short, int, long* or some other unit?

9. Show how to speed up bins by replacing the expensive division operator with a cheaper logical shift.

10. What other data structures might be used to represent sets of integers in contexts similar to generating random numbers?

11. Build the fastest possible complete function to generate a sorted array of random integers without duplicates. (You need not feel constrained to use any prescribed interface for set representation.)

13.7 Further Reading

The excellent algorithms texts by Knuth and Sedgewick are described in Section 11.6. Searching is the topic of Chapter 6 (the second half) of Knuth's *Sorting and Searching*, and is Part 4 (the final quarter) of Sedgewick's *Algorithms*.

13.8 A Real Searching Problem *[Sidebar]*

The toy structures in the body of this column have laid the groundwork for us to study an industrial-strength data structure. This sidebar surveys the remarkable structure that Doug McIlroy used to represent a dictionary in the *spell* program that he wrote in 1978. When I wrote the original columns in this book in the 1980's, I spell-checked them all with McIlroy's program. I used *spell* once again for this edition, and found that it is still a useful tool. Details of McIlroy's program can be found in his paper "Development of a spelling list" in *IEEE Transactions on Communications COM-30*, 1 (January 1982, pp. 91-99). My dictionary defines a pearl as something "very choice or precious"; this program qualifies.

The first problem McIlroy faced was assembling the word list. He started by intersecting an unabridged dictionary (for validity) with the million-word Brown University corpus (for currency). That was a reasonable beginning, but there was much work left to do.

McIlroy's approach is illustrated in his quest for proper nouns, which are omitted from most dictionaries. First came people: the 1000 most common last names in a large telephone directory, a list of boys' and girls' names, famous names (like Dijkstra and Nixon), and mythological names from an index to Bulfinch. After observing "misspellings" like *Xerox* and *Texaco*, he added companies on the Fortune 500 list. Publishing companies are rampant in bibliographies, so they're in. Next came geography: the nations and their capitals, the states and theirs, the hundred largest cities in the United States and in the world, and don't forget oceans, planets and stars.

He also added common names of animals and plants, and terms from chemistry, anatomy and (for local consumption) computing. But he was careful not to add too much: he kept out valid words that tend to be real-life misspellings (like the geological term *cwm*) and included only one of several alternative spellings (hence *traveling* but not *travelling*).

McIlroy's trick was to examine *spell*'s output from real runs; for some time, *spell* automatically mailed a copy of the output to him (tradeoffs between privacy and efficacy were viewed differently in bygone days). When he spotted a problem, he would apply the broadest possible solution. The result is a fine list of 75,000 words: it includes most of the words I use in my documents, yet still finds my spelling errors.

The program uses affix analysis to peel prefixes and suffixes off words; that is both necessary and convenient. It's necessary because there is no such thing as a word list for English; a spelling checker must either guess at the derivation of words like *misrepresented* or report as errors a lot of valid English words. Affix analysis has the convenient side effect of reducing the size of the dictionary.

The goal of affix analysis is to reduce *misrepresented* down to *sent*, stripping off *mis-*, *re-*, *pre-*, and *-ed*. (Even though *represent* doesn't mean "to present again" and *present* doesn't mean "sent beforehand", *spell* uses coincidences to reduce dictionary size.) The program's tables contain 40 prefix rules and 30 suffix rules. A "stop list" of 1300 exceptions halts good but incorrect guesses like reducing *entend* (a misspelling of *intend*) to *en-* + *tend*. This analysis reduces the 75,000 word list to 30,000 words. McIlroy's program loops on each word, stripping affixes and looking up the result until it either finds a match or no affixes remain (and the word is declared to be an error).

Back-of-the-envelope analysis showed the importance of keeping the dictionary in main memory. This was particularly hard for McIlroy, who originally wrote the program on a PDP-11 that had a 64-kilobyte address space. The abstract of his paper summarizes his space squeezing: "Stripping prefixes and suffixes reduces the list below one third of its original size, hashing discards 60 percent of the bits that remain, and data compression halves it once again." Thus a list of 75,000 English words (and roughly as many inflected forms) was represented in 26,000 16-bit computer words.

McIlroy used hashing to represent 30,000 English words in 27 bits each (we'll see soon why 27 is a good choice). We'll study a progression of schemes illustrated on the toy word list

a list of five words

The first hashing method uses an n-element hash table roughly the size of the list and a hash function that maps a string into an integer in the range $[0, n)$. (We'll see a hash function for strings in Section 15.1.) The ith entry of the table points to a linked list that contains all strings that hash to i. If null lists are represented by empty cells and the hash function yields $h(a) = 2$, $h(list) = 1$, etc., then a five-element table might look like

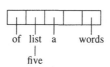

To look up the word w we perform a sequential search in the list pointed to by the $h(w)^{th}$ cell.

The next scheme uses a much larger table. Choosing $n = 23$ makes it likely that most hash cells contain just one element. In this example, $h(a) = 13$ and $h(list) = 5$.

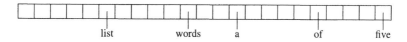

The *spell* program uses $n = 2^{27}$ (roughly 134 million), and all but a few of the non-empty lists contain just a single element.

The next step is daring: instead of a linked list of words, McIlroy stores just a single bit in each table entry. This reduces space dramatically, but introduces errors. This picture uses the same hash function as the previous example, and represents zero bits by empty cells.

					1					1			1					1				1

To look up word w, the program accesses the $h(w)^{th}$ bit in the table. If that bit is zero, then the program correctly reports that word w is not in the table. If the bit is one, then the program assumes that w is in the table. Sometimes a bad word happens to hash to a valid bit, but the probability of such an error is just $30,000/2^{27}$, or roughly $1/4,000$. On the average, therefore, one out of every 4000 bad words will sneak by as valid. McIlroy observed that typical rough drafts rarely contain more than 20 errors, so this defect hampers at most one run out of every hundred — that's why he chose 27.

Representing the hash table by a string of $n = 2^{27}$ bits would consume over sixteen million bytes. The program therefore represents just the one bits; in the above example, it stores these hash values:

$$5 \quad 10 \quad 13 \quad 18 \quad 22$$

The word w is declared to be in the table if $h(w)$ is present. The obvious representation of those values uses 30,000 27-bit words, but McIlroy's machine had only 32,000 16-bit words in its address space. He therefore sorted the list and used a variable-length code to represent the *differences* between successive hash values. Assuming a fictitious starting value of zero, the above list is compressed to

$$5 \; 5 \; 3 \; 5 \; 4$$

McIlroy's *spell* represents the differences in an average of 13.6 bits each. That left a few hundred extra words to point at useful starting points in the compressed list and thereby speed up the sequential search. The result is a 64-kilobyte dictionary that has fast access time and rarely makes mistakes.

We've already considered two aspects of *spell*'s performance: it produced useful output and it fit in a 64-kilobyte address space. It was also fast. Even on the ancient machines on which it was first built, it was able to spell-check a ten-page paper in half a minute, and a book the size of this one in about ten minutes (which seemed blazingly fast at the time). The spelling of a single word could be checked in a few seconds, because the small dictionary could be quickly read from disk.

COLUMN 14: **HEAPS**

This column is about "heaps", a data structure that we'll use to solve two important problems.

Sorting. Heapsort never takes more than $O(n \log n)$ time to sort an n-element
array, and uses just a few words of extra space.

Priority Queues. Heaps maintain a set of elements under the operations of inserting new elements and extracting the smallest element in the set; each operation
requires $O(\log n)$ time.

For both problems, heaps are simple to code and computationally efficient.

This column has a bottom-up organization: we start at the details and work up to
the big picture. The next two sections describe the heap data structure and two functions to operate on it. The two subsequent sections use those tools to solve the problems mentioned above.

14.1 The Data Structure

A heap is a data structure for representing a collection of items.† Our examples
will represent numbers, but the elements in a heap may be of any ordered type.
Here's a heap of twelve integers:

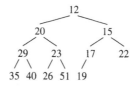

This binary tree is a heap by virtue of two properties. We'll call the first property
order: the value at any node is less than or equal to the values of the node's children.
This implies that the least element of the set is at the root of the tree (12 in the

---

† In other computing contexts, the word "heap" refers to a large segment of memory from which variable-
size nodes are allocated; we will ignore that interpretation in this column.

147

example), but it doesn't say anything about the relative order of left and right children. The second heap property is *shape*; the idea is captured by the picture

In words, a binary tree with the *shape* property has its terminal nodes on at most two levels, with those on the bottom level as far left as possible. There are no "holes" in the tree; if it contains n nodes, no node is at a distance more than $\log_2 n$ from the root. We'll soon see how the two properties together are restrictive enough to allow us to find the minimum element in a set, but lax enough so that we can efficiently reorganize the structure after inserting or deleting an element.

Let's turn now from the abstract properties of heaps to their implementation. The most common representation of binary trees employs records and pointers. We'll use an implementation that is suitable only for binary trees with the *shape* property, but is quite effective for that special case. A 12-element tree with *shape* is represented in the 12-element array $x[1..12]$ as

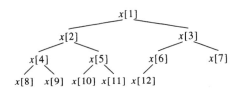

Notice that heaps use a one-based array; the easiest approach in C is to declare $x[n+1]$ and waste element $x[0]$. In this *implicit* representation of a binary tree, the root is in $x[1]$, its two children are in $x[2]$ and $x[3]$, and so on. The typical functions on the tree are defined as follows.

```
root = 1
value(i) = x[i]
leftchild(i) = 2*i
rightchild(i) = 2*i+1
parent(i) = i / 2
null(i) = (i < 1) or (i > n)
```

An n-element implicit tree necessarily has the *shape* property: it makes no provision for missing elements.

This picture shows a 12-element heap and its implementation as an implicit tree in a 12-element array.

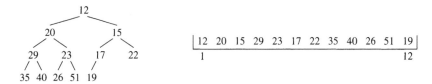

Because the *shape* property is guaranteed by the representation, from now on the name *heap* will mean that the value in any node is greater than or equal to the value in its parent. Phrased precisely, the array $x[1..n]$ has the *heap* property if

$$\forall_{2 \leq i \leq n} \; x[i / 2] \leq x[i]$$

Recall that the "/" integer division operator rounds down, so 4/2 and 5/2 are both 2. In the next section we will want to talk about the subarray $x[l..u]$ having the *heap* property (it already has a variant of the *shape* property); we may mathematically define $heap(l, u)$ as

$$\forall_{2l \leq i \leq u} \; x[i / 2] \leq x[i]$$

14.2 Two Critical Functions

In this section we will study two functions for fixing an array whose *heap* property has been broken at one end or the other. Both functions are efficient: they require roughly log n steps to re-organize a heap of n elements. In the bottom-up spirit of this column, we will define the functions here and then use them in the next sections.

Placing an arbitrary element in $x[n]$ when $x[1..n-1]$ is a heap will probably not yield $heap(1, n)$; re-establishing the property is the job of function *siftup*. Its name describes its strategy: it sifts the new element up the tree as far as it should go, swapping it with its parent along the way. (This section will use the typical heap definition of which way is up: the root of the heap is $x[1]$ at the top of the tree, and therefore $x[n]$ is at the bottom of the array.) The process is illustrated in the following pictures, which (left to right) show the new element 13 being sifted up the heap until it is at its proper position as the right child of the root.

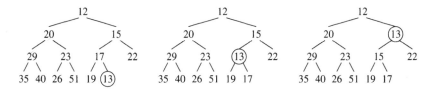

The process continues until the circled node is greater than or equal to its parent (as in this case) or it is at the root of the tree. If the process starts with $heap(1, n-1)$ true, it leaves $heap(1, n)$ true.

With that intuitive background, let's write the code. The sifting process calls for a loop, so we start with the loop invariant. In the picture above, the heap property holds everywhere in the tree except between the circled node and its parent. If we let i be the index of the circled node, then we can use the invariant

```
loop
    /* invariant: heap(1, n) except perhaps
                between i and its parent */
```

Because we originally have $heap(1, n-1)$, we may initialize the loop by the assignment $i = n$.

The loop must check whether we have finished yet (either by the circled node being at the top of the heap or greater than or equal to its parent) and, if not, make progress towards termination. The invariant says that the *heap* property holds everywhere except perhaps between i and its parent. If the test $i == 1$ is true, then i has no parent and the *heap* property thus holds everywhere; the loop may therefore terminate. When i does have a parent, we let p be the parent's index by assigning $p = i/2$. If $x[p] \leq x[i]$ then the heap property holds everywhere, and the loop may terminate.

If, on the other hand, i is out of order with its parent, then we swap $x[i]$ and $x[p]$. This step is illustrated in the following picture, in which the keys are single letters and node i is circled.

BEFORE:
a and b are
out of order

AFTER:
All nodes
are in order

After the swap, all five elements are in the proper order: $b < d$ and $b < e$ because b was originally higher in the heap†, $a < b$ because the test $x[p] \leq x[i]$ failed, and $a < c$ by combining $a < b$ and $b < c$. This gives the heap property everywhere in the array except possibly between p and its parent; we therefore regain the invariant by assigning $i = p$.

The pieces are assembled in this *siftup* code, which runs in time proportional to log n because the heap has that many levels.

---

† This important property is unstated in the loop invariant. Don Knuth observes that to be precise, the invariant should be strengthened to "*heap*$(1, n)$ holds if i has no parent; otherwise it would hold if $x[i]$ were replaced by $x[p]$, where p is the parent of i". Similar precision should also be used in the *siftdown* loop that we will study shortly.

```
void siftup(n)
        pre  n > 0 && heap(1, n-1)
        post heap(1, n)
    i = n
    loop
        /* invariant: heap(1, n) except perhaps
                    between i and its parent */
        if i == 1
            break
        p = i / 2
        if x[p] <= x[i]
            break
        swap(p, i)
        i = p
```

As in Column 4, the ''pre'' and ''post'' lines characterize the function: if the precondition is true before the function is called then the postcondition will be true after the function returns.

We'll turn now from *siftup* to *siftdown*. Assigning a new value to $x[1]$ when $x[1..n]$ is a heap leaves $heap(2, n)$; function *siftdown* makes $heap(1, n)$ true. It does so by sifting $x[1]$ down the array until either it has no children or it is less than or equal to the children it does have. These pictures show 18 being sifted down the heap until it is finally less than its single child, 19.

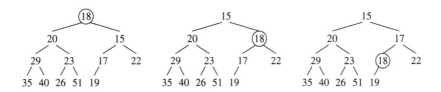

When an element is sifted up, it always goes towards the root. Sifting down is more complicated: an out-of-order element is swapped with its lesser child.

The pictures illustrate the invariant of the *siftdown* loop: the heap property holds everywhere except, possibly, between the circled node and its children.

```
    loop
        /* invariant: heap(1, n) except perhaps between
                    i and its (0, 1 or 2) children */
```

The loop is similar to *siftup*'s. We first check whether i has any children, and terminate the loop if it has none. Now comes the subtle part: if i does have children, then we set the variable c to index the lesser child of i. Finally, we either terminate the loop if $x[i] \leq x[c]$, or progress towards the bottom by swapping $x[i]$ and $x[c]$ and assigning $i = c$.

```
void siftdown(n)
        pre    heap(2, n) && n >= 0
        post   heap(1, n)
    i = 1
    loop
        /* invariant: heap(1, n) except perhaps between
                    i and its (0, 1 or 2) children */
        c = 2*i
        if c > n
            break
        /* c is the left child of i */
        if c+1 <= n
            /* c+1 is the right child of i */
            if x[c+1] < x[c]
                c++
        /* c is the lesser child of i */
        if x[i] <= x[c]
            break
        swap(c, i)
        i = c
```

A case analysis like that done for *siftup* shows that the swap operation leaves the heap property true everywhere except possibly between *c* and its children. Like *siftup*, this function takes time proportional to log *n*, because it does a fixed amount of work at each level of the heap.

14.3 Priority Queues

Every data structure has two sides. Looking from the outside, its *specification* tells what it does — a queue maintains a sequence of elements under the operations of *insert* and *extract*. On the inside, its *implementation* tells how it does it — a queue might use an array or a linked list. We'll start our study of priority queues by specifying their abstract properties, and then turn to implementations.

A priority queue manipulates an initially empty set† of elements, which we will call *S*. The *insert* function inserts a new element into the set; we can define that more precisely in terms of its pre- and postconditions.

```
void insert(t)
        pre    |S| < maxsize
        post   current S = original S ∪ {t}
```

Function *extractmin* deletes the smallest element in the set and returns that value in its single parameter *t*.

---

† Because the set can contain multiple copies of the same element, we might be more precise to call it a "multiset" or a "bag". The union operator is defined so that {2, 3} ∪ {2} = {2, 2, 3}.

```
int extractmin()
        pre   |S| > 0
        post  original S = current S ∪ {result}
              && result = min(original S)
```

This function could, of course, be modified to yield the maximum element, or any extreme element under a total ordering.

We can specify a C++ class for the job with a template that specifies the type *T* of elements in the queue:

```
template<class T>
class priqueue {
public:
    priqueue(int maxsize);  // init set S to empty
    void insert(T t);       // add t to S
    T extractmin();         // return smallest in S
};
```

Priority queues are useful in many applications. An operating system may use such a structure to represent a set of tasks; they are inserted in an arbitrary order, and the next task to be executed is extracted:

```
priqueue<Task> queue;
```

In discrete event simulation, the elements are times of events; the simulation loop extracts the next event and possibly adds more events to the queue:

```
priqueue<Event> eventqueue;
```

In both applications the basic priority queue must be augmented with additional information beyond the elements in the set; we will ignore that "implementation detail" in our discussion, but C++ classes usually handle it gracefully.

Sequential structures such as arrays or linked lists are obvious candidates for implementing priority queues. If the sequence is sorted it is easy to extract the minimum but hard to insert a new element; the situation is reversed for unsorted structures. This table shows the performance of the structures on an *n*-element set.

DATA STRUCTURE	RUN TIMES		
	1 *insert*	1 *extractmin*	*n* of each
Sorted Sequence	$O(n)$	$O(1)$	$O(n^2)$
Heaps	$O(\log n)$	$O(\log n)$	$O(n \log n)$
Unsorted Sequence	$O(1)$	$O(n)$	$O(n^2)$

Even though binary search can find the position of a new element in $O(\log n)$ time, moving the old elements to make way for the new may require $O(n)$ steps. If you've forgotten the difference between $O(n^2)$ and $O(n \log n)$ algorithms, review Section 8.5: when *n* is one million, the run times of those programs are three hours and one second.

The heap implementation of priority queues provides a middle ground between the two sequential extremes. It represents an *n*-element set in the array $x[1..n]$ with the heap property, where x is declared in C or C++ as $x[maxsize + 1]$ (we will not use $x[0]$). We initialize the set to be empty by the assignment $n = 0$. To insert a new element we increment n and place the new element in $x[n]$. That gives the situation that *siftup* was designed to fix: $heap(1, n-1)$. The insertion code is therefore

```
void insert(t)
    if n >= maxsize
        /* report error */
    n++
    x[n] = t
    /* heap(1, n-1) */
    siftup(n)
    /* heap(1, n) */
```

Function *extractmin* finds the minimum element in the set, deletes it, and restructures the array to have the heap property. Because the array is a heap, the minimum element is in $x[1]$. The $n-1$ elements remaining in the set are now in $x[2..n]$, which has the heap property. We regain $heap(1, n)$ in two steps. We first move $x[n]$ to $x[1]$ and decrement n; the elements of the set are now in $x[1..n]$, and $heap(2, n)$ is true. The second step calls *siftdown*. The code is straightforward.

```
int extractmin()
    if n < 1
        /* report error */
    t = x[1]
    x[1] = x[n--]
    /* heap(2, n) */
    siftdown(n)
    /* heap(1, n) */
    return t
```

Both *insert* and *extractmin* require $O(\log n)$ time when applied to heaps that contain n elements.

Here is a complete C++ implementation of priority queues:

```
template<class T>
class priqueue {
private:
    int n, maxsize;
    T *x;
    void swap(int i, int j)
    {   T t = x[i]; x[i] = x[j]; x[j] = t; }
```

```
public:
    priqueue(int m)
    {   maxsize = m;
        x = new T[maxsize+1];
        n = 0;
    }
    void insert(T t)
    {   int i, p;
        x[++n] = t;
        for (i = n; i > 1 && x[p=i/2] > x[i]; i = p)
            swap(p, i);
    }
    T extractmin()
    {   int i, c;
        T t = x[1];
        x[1] = x[n--];
        for (i = 1; (c = 2*i) <= n; i = c) {
            if (c+1 <= n && x[c+1] < x[c])
                c++;
            if (x[i] <= x[c])
                break;
            swap(c, i);
        }
        return t;
    }
};
```

This toy interface includes no error checking or destructor, but expresses the guts of the algorithm succinctly. While our pseudocode used a lengthy coding style, this dense code is at the other extreme.

14.4 A Sorting Algorithm

Priority queues provide a simple algorithm for sorting a vector: first insert each element in turn into the priority queue, then remove them in order. It is straightforward to code in C++ using the *priqueue* class:

```
template<class T>
void pqsort(T v[], int n)
{   priqueue<T> pq(n);
    int i;
    for (i = 0; i < n; i++)
        pq.insert(v[i]);
    for (i = 0; i < n; i++)
        v[i] = pq.extractmin();
}
```

The *n insert* and *extractmin* operations have a worst-case cost of $O(n \log n)$, which is superior to the $O(n^2)$ worst-case time of the Quicksorts we built in Column 11. Unfortunately, the array $x[0..n]$ used for heaps requires $n+1$ additional words of main memory.

We turn now to the Heapsort, which improves this approach. It uses less code, it uses less space because it doesn't require the auxiliary array, and it uses less time. For purposes of this algorithm we will assume that *siftup* and *siftdown* have been modified to operate on heaps in which the *largest* element is at the top; that is easy to accomplish by swapping "<" and ">" signs.

The simple algorithm uses two arrays, one for the priority queue and one for the elements to be sorted. Heapsort saves space by using just one. The single implementation array x represents two abstract structures: a heap at the left end and at the right end the sequence of elements, originally in arbitrary order and finally sorted. This picture shows the evolution of the array x; the array is drawn horizontally, while time marches down the vertical axis.

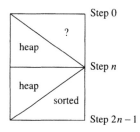

The Heapsort algorithm is a two-stage process: the first n steps build the array into a heap, and the next n steps extract the elements in decreasing order and build the final sorted sequence, right to left.

The first stage builds the heap. Its invariant can be drawn as

heap	?
1	i n

This code establishes *heap*(1, n), by sifting elements to move up front in the array.

```
for i = [2, n]
    /* invariant: heap(1, i-1) */
    siftup(i)
    /* heap(1, i) */
```

The second stage uses the heap to build the sorted sequence. Its invariant can be drawn as

heap, ≤	sorted, ≥
1	i n

The loop body maintains the invariant in two operations. Because $x[1]$ is the largest among the first i elements, swapping it with $x[i]$ extends the sorted sequence by one element. That swap compromises the heap property, which we regain by sifting down the new top element. The code for the second stage is

```
for (i = n; i >= 2; i--)
    /* heap(1, i)    && sorted(i+1, n) && x[1..i]   <= x[i+1..n] */
    swap(1, i)
    /* heap(2, i-1) && sorted(i, n)   && x[1..i-1] <= x[i..n]   */
    siftdown(i-1)
    /* heap(1, i-1) && sorted(i, n)   && x[1..i-1] <= x[i..n]   */
```

With the functions we've already built, the complete Heapsort algorithm requires just five lines of code.

```
for i = [2, n]
    siftup(i)
for (i = n; i >= 2; i--)
    swap(1, i)
    siftdown(i-1)
```

Because the algorithm uses $n - 1$ *siftup* and *siftdown* operations, each of cost at most $O(\log n)$, it runs in $O(n \log n)$ time, even in the worst case.

Solutions 2 and 3 describe several ways to speed up (and also simplify) the Heapsort algorithm. Although Heapsort guarantees worst-case $O(n \log n)$ performance, for typical input data, the fastest Heapsort is usually slower than the simple Quicksort in Section 11.2.

14.5 Principles

Efficiency. The *shape* property guarantees that all nodes in a heap are within $\log_2 n$ levels of the root; functions *siftup* and *siftdown* have efficient run times precisely because the trees are balanced. Heapsort avoids using extra space by overlaying two abstract structures (a heap and a sequence) in one implementation array.

Correctness. To write code for a loop we first state its invariant precisely; the loop then makes progress towards termination while preserving its invariant. The *shape* and *order* properties represent a different kind of invariant: they are invariant properties of the heap data structure. A function that operates on a heap may assume that the properties are true when it starts to work on the structure, and it must in turn make sure that they remain true when it finishes.

Abstraction. Good engineers distinguish between *what* a component does (the abstraction seen by the user) and *how* it does it (the implementation inside the black box). This column packages black boxes in two different ways: procedural abstraction and abstract data types.

Procedural Abstraction. You can use a sort function to sort an array without knowing its implementation: you view the sort as a single operation. Functions *siftup* and *siftdown* provide a similar level of abstraction: as we built priority queues and Heapsort, we didn't care *how* the functions worked, but we knew *what* they did (fixing an array with the *heap* property broken at one end or the other). Good engineering allowed us to define these black-box components once, and then use them to assemble two different kinds of tools.

Abstract Data Types. *What* a data type does is given by its methods and their specifications; *how* it does it is up to the implementation. We may employ the C++ *priqueue* class of this column or the C++ *IntSet* classes of the last column using only their specification to reason about their correctness. Their implementations may, of course, have an impact on the program's performance.

14.6 Problems

1. Implement heap-based priority queues to run as quickly as possible; at what values of n are they faster than sequential structures?

2. Modify *siftdown* to have the following specification.

   ```
   void siftdown(l, u)
           pre    heap(l+1, u)
           post   heap(l, u)
   ```

   What is the run time of the code? Show how it can be used to construct an n-element heap in $O(n)$ time and thereby a faster Heapsort that also uses less code.

3. Implement Heapsort to run as quickly as possible. How does it compare to the sorting algorithms tabulated in Section 11.3?

4. How might the heap implementation of priority queues be used to solve the following problems? How do your answers change when the inputs are sorted?

   a. Construct a Huffman code (such codes are discussed in most books on information theory and many books on data structures).

   b. Compute the sum of a large set of floating point numbers.

   c. Find the million largest of a billion numbers stored on a file.

   d. Merge many small sorted files into one large sorted file (this problem arises in implementing a disk-based merge sort program like that in Section 1.3).

5. The bin packing problem calls for assigning a set of n weights (each between zero and one) to a minimal number of unit-capacity bins. The first-fit heuristic for this problem considers the weights in the sequence in which they are presented, and places each weight into the first bin in which it fits, scanning the bins in increasing order. In his MIT thesis, David Johnson observed that a heap-like structure can implement this heuristic in $O(n \log n)$ time. Show how.

6. A common implementation of sequential files on disk has each block point to its successor, which may be any block on the disk. This method requires a constant amount of time to write a block (as the file is originally written), to read the first block in the file, and to read the ith block, once you have read the $i-1^{st}$ block. Reading the ith block from scratch therefore requires time proportional to i. When Ed McCreight was designing a disk controller at Xerox Palo Alto Research Center, he observed that by adding just one additional pointer per node, you can keep

all the other properties, but allow the ith block to be read in time proportional to log i. How would you implement that insight? Explain what the algorithm for reading the ith block has in common with the code in Problem 4.9 for raising a number to the ith power in time proportional to log i.

7. On some computers the most expensive part of a binary search program is the division by 2 to find the center of the current range. Show how to replace that division with a multiplication by two, assuming that the array to be searched has been constructed properly. Give algorithms for building and searching such a table.

8. What are appropriate implementations for a priority queue that represents integers in the range $[0, k)$, when the average size of the queue is much larger than k?

9. Prove that the simultaneous logarithmic run times of *insert* and *extractmin* in the heap implementation of priority queues are within a constant factor of optimal.

10. The basic idea of heaps is familiar to sports fans. Suppose that Brian beat Al and Lynn beat Peter in the semifinals, and that Lynn triumphed over Brian in the championship match. Those results are usually drawn as

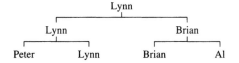

Such "tournament trees" are common in tennis tournaments and in post-season playoffs in football, baseball and basketball. Assuming that the results of matches are consistent (an assumption often invalid in athletics), what is the probability that the second-best player is in the championship match? Give an algorithm for "seeding" the players according to their pre-tournament rankings.

11. How are heaps, priority queues and Heapsort implemented in the C++ Standard Template Library?

14.7 Further Reading

The excellent algorithms texts by Knuth and Sedgewick are described in Section 11.6. Heaps and Heapsort are described in Section 5.2.3 of Knuth's *Sorting and Searching*. Priority queues and Heapsort are described in Chapter 9 of Sedgewick's *Algorithms*.

COLUMN 15: **STRINGS OF PEARLS**

We are surrounded by strings. Strings of bits make integers and floating-point numbers. Strings of digits make telephone numbers, and strings of characters make words. Long strings of characters make web pages, and longer strings yet make books. Extremely long strings represented by the letters A, C, G and T are in geneticists' databases and deep inside the cells of many readers of this book.

Programs perform a dazzling variety of operations on such strings. They sort them, count them, search them, and analyze them to discern patterns. This column introduces those topics by examining a few classic problems on strings.

15.1 Words

Our first problem is to produce a list of the words contained in a document. (Feed such a program a few hundred books, and you have a fine start at a word list for a dictionary.) But what exactly is a word? We'll use the trivial definition of a sequence of characters surrounded by white space, but this means that web pages will contain many "words" like "<html>", "<body>" and " ". Problem 1 asks how you might avoid such problems.

Our first C++ program uses the *sets* and *strings* of the Standard Template Library, in a slight modification of the program in Solution 1.1:

```
int main(void)
{   set<string> S;
    set<string>::iterator j;
    string t;
    while (cin >> t)
        S.insert(t);
    for (j = S.begin(); j != S.end(); ++j)
        cout << *j << "\n";
    return 0;
}
```

The *while* loop reads the input and *inserts* each word into the set *S* (by the STL specification, duplicates are ignored). The *for* loop then iterates through the set, and writes the words in sorted order. This program is elegant and fairly efficient (more on that topic soon).

161

Our next problem is to count the number of times each word occurs in the document. Here are the 21 most common words in the King James Bible, sorted in decreasing numeric order and aligned in three columns to save space:

the	62053	shall	9756	they	6890
and	38546	he	9506	be	6672
of	34375	unto	8929	is	6595
to	13352	I	8699	with	5949
And	12734	his	8352	not	5840
that	12428	a	7940	all	5238
in	12154	for	7139	thou	4629

Almost eight percent of the 789,616 words in the text were the word "the" (as opposed to 16 percent of the words in this sentence). By our definition of word, "and" and "And" have two separate counts.

These counts were produced by the following C++ program, which uses the Standard Template Library *map* to associate an integer count with each string:

```
int main(void)
{   map<string, int> M;
    map<string, int>::iterator j;
    string t;
    while (cin >> t)
        M[t]++;
    for (j = M.begin(); j != M.end(); ++j)
        cout << j->first << " " << j->second << "\n";
    return 0;
}
```

The *while* statement inserts each word *t* into the map *M* and increments the associated counter (which is initialized to zero at initialization). The *for* statement iterates through the words in sorted order and prints each word (*first*) and its count (*second*).

This C++ code is straightforward, succinct and surprisingly fast. On my machine, it takes 7.6 seconds to process the Bible. About 2.4 seconds go to reading, 4.9 seconds to the insertions, and 0.3 seconds to writing the ouput.

We can reduce the processing time by building our own hash table, using nodes that contain a pointer to a word, a count of how often the word has been seen, and a pointer to the next node in the table. Here is the hash table after inserting the strings "in", "the" and "in", in the unlikely event that both strings hash to 1:

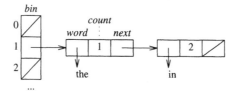

write on your own

We'll implement the hash table with this C structure:

```
typedef struct node *nodeptr;
typedef struct node {
    char *word;
    int count;
    nodeptr next;
} node;
```

Even by our loose definition of "word", the Bible has only 29,131 distinct words. We'll follow the old lore of using a prime number near that for our hash table size, and the popular multiplier of 31:

```
#define NHASH 29989
#define MULT 31
nodeptr bin[NHASH];
```

Our hash function maps a string to a positive integer less than *NHASH*:

```
unsigned int hash(char *p)
    unsigned int h = 0
    for ( ; *p; p++)
        h = MULT * h + *p
    return h % NHASH
```

$c \quad a \quad b$

$c * 31^2 + a * 31 + b$

$c * 31$

$(c * 31 + a) 31$

$(c * 31^2 + a 31) 31 + b$

Using *unsigned* integers ensures that *h* remains positive.

The *main* function initializes every bin to *NULL*, reads the word and increments the count of each, then iterates through the hash table to write the (unsorted) words and counts:

```
int main(void)
    for i = [0, NHASH)
        bin[i] = NULL
    while scanf("%s", buf) != EOF
        incword(buf)
    for i = [0, NHASH)
        for (p = bin[i]; p != NULL; p = p->next)
            print p->word, p->count
    return 0
```

The work is done by *incword*, which increments the count associated with the input word (and initializes it if it is not already there):

```
void incword(char *s)
    h = hash(s)
    for (p = bin[h]; p != NULL; p = p->next)
        if strcmp(s, p->word) == 0
            (p->count)++
            return
    p = malloc(sizeof(hashnode))
    p->count = 1
    p->word = malloc(strlen(s)+1)
    strcpy(p->word, s)
    p->next = bin[h]
    bin[h] = p
```

The *for* loop looks at every node with the same hash value. If the word is found, its count is incremented and the function returns. If the word is not found, the function makes a new node, allocates space and copies the string (experienced C programmers would use *strdup* for the task), and inserts the node at the front of the list.

This C program takes about 2.4 seconds to read its input (the same as the C++ version), but only 0.5 seconds for the insertions (down from 4.9) and only 0.06 seconds to write the output (down from 0.3). The complete run time is 3.0 seconds (down from 7.6), and the processing time is 0.55 seconds (down from 5.2). Our custom-made hash table (in 30 lines of C) is an order of magnitude faster than the maps from the C++ Standard Template Library.

This little exercise illustrates the two main ways to represent sets of words. Balanced search trees operate on strings as indivisible objects; these structures are used in most implementations of the STL's *sets* and *maps*. They always keep the elements in sorted order, so they can efficiently perform operations such as finding a predecessor or reporting the elements in order. Hashing, on the other hand, peeks inside the characters to compute a hash function, and then scatters keys across a big table. It is very fast on the average, but it does not offer the worst-case performance guarantees of balanced trees, or support other operations involving order.

15.2 Phrases

Words are the basic component of documents, and many important problems can be solved by searching for words. Sometimes, however, I search long strings (my documents, or help files, or web pages, or even the entire web) for phrases, such as "substring searching" or "implicit data structures".

How would you search through a large body of text to find "a phrase of several words"? If you had never seen the body of text before, you would have no choice but to start at the beginning and scan through the whole input; most algorithms texts describe many approaches to this "substring searching problem".

Suppose, though, that you had a chance to preprocess the body of text before performing searches. You could make a hash table (or search tree) to index every distinct word of the document, and store a list of every occurrence of each word. Such an "inverted index" allows a program to look up a given word quickly. One can look up phrases by intersecting the lists of the words they contain, but this is subtle to implement and potentially slow. (Some web search engines do, however, take exactly this approach.)

We'll turn now to a powerful data structure and apply it to a small problem: given an input file of text, find the longest duplicated substring of characters in it. For instance, the longest repeated string in "Ask not what your country can do for you, but what you can do for your country" is " can do for you", with " your country" a close second place. How would you write a program to solve this problem?

This problem is reminiscent of the anagram problem that we saw in Section 2.4. If the input string is stored in $c[0..n-1]$, then we could start by comparing every pair of substrings using pseudocode like this

```
maxlen = -1
for i = [0, n)
    for j = (i, n)
        if (thislen = comlen(&c[i], &c[j])) > maxlen
            maxlen = thislen
            maxi = i
            maxj = j
```

The *comlen* function returns the length that its two parameter strings have in common, starting with their first characters:

```
int comlen(char *p, char *q)
    i = 0
    while *p && (*p++ == *q++)
        i++
    return i
```

Because this algorithm looks at all pairs of substrings, it takes time proportional to n^2, at least. We might be able to speed it up by using a hash table to search for words in the phrases, but we'll instead take an entirely new approach.

Our program will process at most *MAXN* characters, which it stores in the array c:

```
#define MAXN 5000000
char c[MAXN], *a[MAXN];
```

We'll use a simple data structure known as a "suffix array"; the structure has been used at least since the 1970's, though the term was introduced in the 1990's. The structure is an array a of pointers to characters. As we read the input, we initialize a so that each element points to the corresponding character in the input string:

```
while (ch = getchar()) != EOF
    a[n] = &c[n]
    c[n++] = ch
c[n] = 0
```

The final element of c contains a null character, which terminates all strings.

The element $a[0]$ points to the entire string; the next element points to the suffix of the array beginning with the second character, and so on. On the input string ''banana'', the array will represent these suffixes:

```
a[0]: banana
a[1]: anana
a[2]: nana
a[3]: ana
a[4]: na
a[5]: a
```

The pointers in the array *a* together point to every suffix in the string, hence the name ''suffix array''.

If a long string occurs twice in the array *c*, it appears in two different suffixes. We will therefore sort the array to bring together equal suffixes (just as sorting brought together anagrams in Section 2.4). The ''banana'' array sorts to

```
a[0]: a
a[1]: ana
a[2]: anana
a[3]: banana
a[4]: na
a[5]: nana
```

We can then scan through this array comparing adjacent elements to find the longest repeated string, which in this case is ''ana''.

We'll sort the suffix array with the *qsort* function:

```
qsort(a, n, sizeof(char *), pstrcmp)
```

The *pstrcmp* comparison function adds one level of indirection to the library *strcmp* function. This scan through the array uses the *comlen* function to count the number of letters that two adjacent words have in common:

```
for i = [0, n)
    if comlen(a[i], a[i+1]) > maxlen
        maxlen = comlen(a[i], a[i+1])
        maxi = i
printf("%.*s\n", maxlen, a[maxi])
```

The *printf* statement uses the ''*'' precision to print *maxlen* characters of the string.

I ran the resulting program to find the longest repeated string in the 807,503 characters in Samuel Butler's translation of Homer's *Iliad*. The program took 4.8 seconds to locate this string:

> whose sake so many of the Achaeans have died at Troy, far from their homes? Go about at once among the host, and speak fairly to them, man by man, that they draw not their ships into the sea.

The text first occurs when Juno suggests it to Minerva as an argument that might keep the Greeks (Achaeans) from departing from Troy; it occurs shortly thereafter when Minerva repeats the argument verbatim to Ulysses. On this and other typical text files of *n* characters, the algorithm runs in $O(n \log n)$ time, due to sorting.

Suffix arrays represent every substring in n characters of input text using the text itself and n additional pointers. Problem 6 investigates how suffix arrays can be used to solve the substring searching problem. We'll turn now to a more subtle application of suffix arrays.

15.3 Generating Text

How can you generate random text? A classic approach is to let loose that poor monkey on his aging typewriter. If the beast is equally likely to hit any lower case letter or the space bar, the output might look like this:

uzlpcbizdmddk njsdzyyvfgxbgjjgbtsak rqvpgnsbyputvqqdtmgltz ynqotqigexjumq-phujcfwn ll jiexpyqzgsdllgcoluphl sefsrvqqytjakmav bfusvirsjl wprwqt

This is pretty unconvincing English text.

If you count the letters in word games (like Scrabble™ or Boggle™), you will notice that there are different numbers of the various letters. There are many more A's, for instance, than there are Z's. A monkey could produce more convincing text by counting the letters in a document — if A occurs 300 times in the text while B occurs just 100 times, then the monkey should be 3 times more likely to type an A than a B. This takes us a small step closer to English:

saade ve mw hc n entt da k eethetocusosselalwo gx fgrsnoh,tvettaf aetnlbilo fc lhd okleutsndyeoshtbogo eet ib nheaoopefni ngent

Most events occur in context. Suppose that we wanted to generate randomly a year's worth of Fahrenheit temperature data. A series of 365 random integers between 0 and 100 wouldn't fool the average observer. We could be more convincing by making today's temperature a (random) function of yesterday's temperature: if it is 85° today, it is unlikely to be 15° tomorrow.

The same is true of English words: if this letter is a Q, then the next letter is quite likely to be a U. A generator can make more interesting text by making each letter a random function of its predecessor. We could, therefore, read a sample text and count how many times every letter follows an A, how many times they follow a B, and so on for each letter of the alphabet. When we write the random text, we produce the next letter as a random function of the current letter. The "order-1" text was made by exactly this scheme:

Order-1: t I amy, vin. id wht omanly heay atuss n macon aresethe hired boutwhe t, tl, ad torurest t plur I wit hengamind tarer-plarody thishand.

Order-2: Ther I the heingoind of-pleat, blur it dwere wing waske hat trooss. Yout lar on wassing, an sit." "Yould," "I that vide was nots ther.

Order-3: I has them the saw the secorrow. And wintails on my my ent, thinks, fore voyager lanated the been elsed helder was of him a very free bottlemarkable,

Order-4: His heard." "Exactly he very glad trouble, and by Hopkins! That it on of the who difficentralia. He rushed likely?" "Blood night that.

We can extend this idea to longer sequences of letters. The order-2 text was made by generating each letter as a function of the two letters preceding it (a letter pair is often called a digram). The digram TH, for instance, is often followed in English by the vowels A, E, I, O, U and Y, less frequently by R and W, and rarely by other letters. The order-3 text is built by choosing the next letter as a function of the three previous letters (a trigram). By the time we get to the order-4 text, most words are English, and you might not be surprised to learn that it was generated from a Sherlock Holmes story ("The Adventure of Abbey Grange"). A classically educated reader of a draft of this column commented that this sequence of fragments reminded him of the evolution from Old English to Victorian English.

Readers with a mathematical background might recognize this process as a Markov chain. One state represents each k-gram, and the odds of going from one to another don't change, so this is a "finite-state Markov chain with stationary transition probabilities".

We can also generate random text at the word level. The dumbest approach is to spew forth the words in a dictionary at random. A slightly better approach reads a document, counts each word, and then selects the next word to be printed with the appropriate probability. (The programs in Section 15.1 use tools appropriate for such tasks.) We can get more interesting text, though, by using Markov chains that take into account a few preceding words as they generate the next word. Here is some random text produced after reading a draft of the first 14 columns of this book:

Order-1: The table shows how many contexts; it uses two or equal to the sparse matrices were not chosen. In Section 13.1, for a more efficient that "the more time was published by calling recursive structure translates to build scaffolding to try to know of selected and testing and more robust and a binary search).

Order-2: The program is guided by verification ideas, and the second errs in the STL implementation (which guarantees good worst-case performance), and is especially rich in speedups due to Gordon Bell. Everything should be to use a macro: for $n = 10,000$, its run time; that point Martin picked up from his desk

Order-3: A Quicksort would be quite efficient for the main-memory sorts, and it requires only a few distinct values in this particular problem, we can write them all down in the program, and they were making progress towards a solution at a snail's pace.

The order 1 text is almost readable aloud, while the order-3 text consists of very long phrases from the original input, with random transitions between them. For purposes of parody, order-2 text is usually juiciest.

I first saw letter-level and word-level order-k approximations to English text in Shannon's 1948 classic *Mathematical Theory of Communication*. Shannon writes,

"To construct [order-1 letter-level text] for example, one opens a book at random and selects a letter at random on the page. This letter is recorded. The book is then opened to another page and one reads until this letter is encountered. The succeeding letter is then recorded. Turning to another page this second letter is searched for and the succeeding letter recorded, etc. A similar process was used for [order-1 and order-2 letter-level text, and order-0 and order-1 word-level text]. It would be interesting if further approximations could be constructed, but the labor involved becomes enormous at the next stage."

A program can automate this laborious task. Our C program to generate order-k Markov chains will store at most five megabytes of text in the array *inputchars*:

```
int k = 2;
char inputchars[5000000];
char *word[1000000];
int nword = 0;
```

We could implement Shannon's algorithm directly by scanning through the complete input text to generate each word (though this might be slow on large texts). We will instead employ the array *word* as a kind of suffix array pointing to the characters, except that it starts only on word boundaries (a common modification). The variable *nword* holds the number of words. We read the file with this code:

```
word[0] = inputchars
while scanf("%s", word[nword]) != EOF
    word[nword+1] = word[nword] + strlen(word[nword]) + 1
    nword++
```

Each word is appended to *inputchars* (no other storage allocation is needed), and is terminated by the null character supplied by *scanf*.

After we read the input, we will sort the *word* array to bring together all pointers that point to the same sequence of k words. This function does the comparisons:

```
int wordncmp(char *p, char* q)
    n = k
    for ( ; *p == *q; p++, q++)
        if (*p == 0 && --n == 0)
            return 0
    return *p - *q
```

It scans through the two strings while the characters are equal. At every null character, it decrements the counter n and returns equal after seeing k identical words. When it finds unequal characters, it returns the difference.

After reading the input, we append k null characters (so the comparison function doesn't run off the end), print the first k words in the document (to start the random output), and call the sort:

```
for i = [0, k)
    word[nword][i] = 0
for i = [0, k)
    print word[i]
qsort(word, nword, sizeof(word[0]), sortcmp)
```

The *sortcmp* function, as usual, adds a level of indirection to its pointers.

Our space-efficient structure now contains a great deal of information about the k-grams in the text. If k is 1 and the input text is "of the people, by the people, for the people", the *word* array might look like this:

```
word[0]: by the
word[1]: for the
word[2]: of the
word[3]: people
word[4]: people, for
word[5]: people, by
word[6]: the people,
word[7]: the people
word[8]: the people,
```

For clarity, this picture shows only the first $k+1$ words pointed to by each element of *word*, even though more words usually follow. If we seek a word to follow the phrase "the", we look it up in the suffix array to discover three choices: "people," twice and "people" once.

We may now generate nonsense text with this pseudocode sketch:

```
phrase = first phrase in input array
loop
    perform a binary search for phrase in word[0..nword-1]
    for all phrases equal in the first k words
        select one at random, pointed to by p
    phrase = word following p
    if k-th word of phrase is length 0
        break
    print k-th word of phrase
```

We initialize the loop by setting *phrase* to the first characters in the input (recall that those words were already printed on the output file). The binary search uses the code in Section 9.3 to locate the first occurrence of *phrase* (it is crucial to find the very first occurrence; the binary search of Section 9.3 does just this). The next loop scans through all equal phrases, and uses Solution 12.10 to select one of them at random. If the k-th word of that phrase is of length zero, the current phrase is the last in the document, so we break the loop.

The complete pseudocode implements those ideas, and also puts an upper bound on the number of words it will generate:

```
phrase = inputchars
for (wordsleft = 10000; wordsleft > 0; wordsleft--)
    l = -1
    u = nword
    while l+1 != u
        m = (l + u) / 2
        if wordncmp(word[m], phrase) < 0
            l = m
        else
            u = m
    for (i = 0; wordncmp(phrase, word[u+i]) == 0; i++)
        if rand() % (i+1) == 0
            p = word[u+i]
    phrase = skip(p, 1)
    if strlen(skip(phrase, k-1)) == 0
        break
    print skip(phrase, k-1)
```

Chapter 3 of Kernighan and Pike's *Practice of Programming* (described in Section 5.9) is devoted to the general topic of "Design and Implementation". They build their chapter around the problem of word-level Markov-text generation because "it is typical of many programs: some data comes in, some data goes out, and the processing depends on a little ingenuity." They give some interesting history of the problem, and implement programs for the task in C, Java, C++, Awk and Perl.

The program in this section compares favorably with their C program for the task. This code is about half the length of theirs; representing a phrase by a pointer to k consecutive words is space-efficient and easy to implement. For inputs of size near a megabyte, the two programs are of roughly comparable speed. Because Kernighan and Pike use a slightly larger structure and make extensive use of the inefficient *malloc*, the program in this column uses an order of magnitude less memory on my system. If we incorporate the speedup of Solution 14 and replace the binary search and sorting by a hash table, the program in this section becomes about a factor of two faster (and increases memory use by about 50%).

15.4 Principles

String Problems. How does your compiler look up a variable name in its symbol table? How does your help system quickly search that whole CD-ROM as you type in each character of your query string? How does a web search engine look up a phrase? These real problems use some of the techniques that we've glimpsed in the toy problems of this column.

Data Structures for Strings. We've seen several of the most important data structures used for representing strings.

Hashing. This structure is fast on the average and simple to implement.

Balanced Trees. These structures guarantee good performance even on perverse inputs, and are nicely packaged in most implementations of the C++ Standard Template Library's *sets* and *maps*.

Suffix Arrays. Initialize an array of pointers to every character (or every word) in your text, sort them, and you have a suffix array. You can then scan through it to find near strings or use binary search to look up words or phrases.

Section 13.8 uses several additional structures to represent the words in a dictionary.

Libraries or Custom-Made Components? The *sets*, *maps* and *strings* of the C++ STL were very convenient to use, but their general and powerful interface meant that they were not as efficient as a special-purpose hash function. Other library components were very efficient: hashing used *strcmp* and suffix arrays used *qsort*. I peeked at the library implementations of *bsearch* and *strcmp* to build the binary search and the *wordncmp* functions in the Markov program.

15.5 Problems

1. Throughout this column we have used the simple definition that words are separated by white space. Many real documents, such as those in HTML or RTF, contain formatting commands. How could you deal with such commands? Are there any other tasks that you might need to perform?

2. On a machine with ample main memory, how could you use the C++ STL *sets* or *maps* to solve the searching problem in Section 13.8? How much memory does it consume compared to McIlroy's structure?

3. How much speedup can you achieve by incorporating the special-purpose *malloc* of Solution 9.2 into the hashing program of Section 15.1?

4. When a hash table is large and the hash function scatters the data well, almost every list in the table has only a few elements. If either of these conditions is violated, though, the time spent searching down the list can be substantial. When a new string is not found in the hash table in Section 15.1, it is placed at the front of the list. To simulate hashing trouble, set *NHASH* to 1 and experiment with this and other list strategies, such as appending to the end of the list, or moving the most recently found element to the front of the list.

5. When we looked at the output of the word frequency programs in Section 15.1, it was most interesting to print the words in decreasing frequency. How would you modify the C and C++ programs to accomplish this task? How would you print only the *M* most common words, where *M* is a constant such as 10 or 1000?

6. Given a new input string, how would you search a suffix array to find the longest match in the stored text? How would you build a GUI interface for this task?

7. Our program for finding duplicated strings was very fast for "typical" inputs, but it can be very slow (greater than quadratic) for some inputs. Time the program on such an input. Do such inputs ever arise in practice?

8. How would you modify the program for finding duplicated strings to find the longest string that occurs more than *M* times?

9. Given two input texts, find the longest string that occurs in both.

10. Show how to reduce the number of pointers in the duplication program by point-ing only to suffixes that start on word boundaries. What effect does this have on the output produced by the program?

11. Implement a program to generate letter-level Markov text.

12. How would you use the tools and techniques of Section 15.1 to generate (order-0 or non-Markov) random text?

13. The program for generating word-level Markov text is at this book's web site. Try it on some of your documents.

14. How could you use hashing to speed up the Markov program?

15. Shannon's quote in Section 15.3 describes the algorithm he used to construct Mar-kov text; implement that algorithm in a program. It gives a good approximation to the Markov frequencies, but not the exact form; explain why not. Implement a program that scans the entire string from scratch to generate each word (and thereby uses the true frequencies).

16. How would you use the techniques of this column to assemble a word list for a dictionary (the problem that Doug McIlroy faced in Section 13.8)? How would you build a spelling checker without using a dictionary? How would you build a grammar checker without using rules of grammar?

17. Investigate how techniques related to k-gram analysis are used in applications such as speech recognition and data compression.

15.6 Further Reading

Many of the texts cited in Section 8.8 contain material on efficient algorithms and data structures for representing and processing strings.

EPILOG TO THE FIRST EDITION

An interview with the author seemed, at the time, to be the best conclusion for the first edition of this book. It still describes the book, so here it is, once again.

Q: Thanks for agreeing to do this interview.
A: No problem — my time is your time.

Q: Seeing how these columns already appeared in *Communications of the ACM*, why did you bother to collect them into a book?
A: There are several little reasons: I've fixed dozens of errors, made hundreds of little improvements, and added several new sections. There are fifty percent more problems, solutions and pictures in the book. Also, it's more convenient to have the columns in one book rather than a dozen magazines. The big reason, though, is that the themes running through the columns are easier to see when they are collected together; the whole is greater than the sum of the parts.

Q: What are those themes?
A: The most important is that thinking hard about programming can be both useful and fun. There's more to the job than systematic program development from formal requirements documents. If this book helps just one disillusioned programmer to fall back in love with his or her work, it will have served its purpose.

Q: That's a pretty fluffy answer. Are there technical threads tying the columns together?
A: Performance is the topic of Part II, and a theme that runs through all columns. Program verification is used extensively in several columns. Appendix 1 catalogs the algorithms in the book.

Q: It seems that most columns emphasize the design process. Can you summarize your advice on that topic?
A: I'm glad you asked. I just happened to prepare a list before this interview. Here are ten suggestions for programmers.

Work on the right problem.
Explore the design space of solutions.
Look at the data.
Use the back of the envelope.
Exploit symmetry.
Design with components.
Build prototypes.
Make tradeoffs when you have to.
Keep it simple.
Strive for elegance.

The points were originally discussed in the context of programming, but they apply to any engineering endeavor.

Q: That raises a point that has bothered me: it's easy to simplify the little programs in this book, but do the techniques scale up to real software?

A: I have three answers: yes, no and maybe. Yes they scale up; Section 3.4 [in the first edition], for instance, describes a huge software project that was simplified down to "just" 80 staff-years. An equally trite answer is no: if you simplify properly, you avoid building jumbo systems and the techniques don't need to scale up. Although there is merit in both views, the truth lies somewhere in between, and that's where the maybe comes in. Some software has to be big, and the themes of this book are sometimes applicable to such systems. The Unix system is a fine example of a powerful whole built out of simple and elegant parts.

Q: There you go talking about another Bell Labs system. Aren't these columns a little too parochial?

A: Maybe a little. I've stuck to material that I've seen used in practice, and that biases the book towards my environment. Phrased more positively, much of the material in these columns was contributed by my colleagues, and they deserve the credit (or blame). I've learned a lot from many researchers and developers within Bell Labs. There's a fine corporate atmosphere that encourages interaction between research and development. So a lot of what you call parochialism is just my enthusiasm for my employer.

Q: Let's come back down to earth. What pieces are missing from this book?

A: I had hoped to include a large system composed of many programs, but I couldn't describe any interesting systems in the ten or so pages of a typical column. At a more general level, I'd like to do future columns on the themes of "computer science for programmers" (like program verification in Column 4 and algorithm design in Column 8) and the "engineering techniques of computing" (like the back-of-the-envelope calculations in Column 7).

Q: If you're so into "science" and "engineering", how come the columns are so light on theorems and tables and so heavy on stories?

A: Watch it — people who interview themselves shouldn't criticize writing styles.

EPILOG TO THE SECOND EDITION

Some traditions are continued for their inherent quality. Others persist anyway.

Q: Welcome back; it's been a long time.

A: Fourteen years.

Q: Let's start where we did before. Why a new edition of the book?

A: I like the book, a lot. It was fun to write, and the readers have been very kind over the years. The principles in the book have stood the test of time, but many examples in the first edition were woefully out of date. Modern readers can't relate to a "huge" computer that has a half-megabyte of main memory.

Q: So what did you change in this edition?

A: Pretty much what I said I changed in the preface. Don't you guys prepare before these interviews?

Q: Oops — sorry. I see that you talk there about how the code for this book is available at the web site.

A: Writing that code was the most fun that I had in working on this edition. I implemented most of the programs in the first edition, but mine were the only eyes to see the real code. For this edition I wrote about 2500 lines of C and C++, to be shown to the whole world.

Q: You call that code ready for public view? I've read some of it; what dreadful style! Microscopic variable names, weird function definitions, global variables that should be parameters, and the list goes on. Aren't you embarrassed to let real software engineers see the code?

A: The style I used can indeed prove fatal in large software projects. This book, however, is not a large software project. It's not even a large book. Solution 5.1 describes the terse coding style and why I chose it. Had I wanted to write a thousand-page book, I would have adopted a lengthier coding style.

Q: Speaking of long code, your *sort.cpp* program measures the C Standard Library *qsort*, the C++ Standard Template Library *sort*, and several hand-made Quicksorts. Can't you make up your mind? Should a programmer use library functions or build code from scratch?

A: Tom Duff gave the best answer to that question: "Whenever possible, steal code." Libraries are great; use them whenever they do the job. Start with your system library, then search other libraries for appropriate functions. In any engineering activity, though, not all artifacts can be all things to all customers. When the library functions don't measure up, you may have to build your own. I hope that the pseudocode fragments in the book (and the real code on the web site) will prove a useful starting point for programmers who have to write their own functions. I think that the scaffolding and the experimental approach of this book will help those programmers to evaluate a variety of algorithms and choose the best one for their application.

Q: Apart from the public code and updating some stories, what is *really* new in this edition?

A: I've tried to confront code tuning in the presence of caches and instruction-level parallelism. At a larger level, the three new columns reflect three major changes that pervade this edition: Column 5 describes real code and scaffolding, Column 13 gives details on data structures, and Column 15 derives advanced algorithms. Most of the ideas in the book have appeared in print before, but the cost model for space in Appendix 3 and the Markov-text algorithm in Section 15.3 are presented here for the first time. The new Markov-text algorithm compares quite favorably to the classic algorithm described by Kernighan and Pike.

Q: There you go with more Bell Labs people. The last time we talked, you were enthusiastic about the place, but you had only been there a few years. Lots has changed at the Labs in the last 14 years; what do you now think about the place and the changes?

A: When I wrote the first columns in the book, Bell Labs was part of the Bell System. When the first edition was published, we were part of AT&T; now we are part of Lucent Technologies. The companies, the telecommunications industry, and the field of computing have all changed dramatically in that period. Bell Labs has kept up with those changes, and has often led the way. I came to the Labs because I enjoy balancing the theoretical and the applied, because I want to build products and write books. The pendulum has swung back and forth during my years at the Labs, but my management has always encouraged a wide range of activities.

A reviewer of the first edition of this book wrote "Bentley's everyday working environment is a programming nirvana. He is a Member of Technical Staff at Bell Labs in Murray Hill, New Jersey, has immediate access to cutting-edge hardware and software technology, and stands in line at the cafeteria with some of the most brilliant software developers in the world." Bell Labs is still that kind of place.

Q: Nirvana every single day of the week?

A: Nirvana many days, and pretty darn nice the others.

APPENDIX 1: **A CATALOG OF ALGORITHMS**

This book covers much of the material in a college algorithms course, but from a different perspective — the emphasis is more on applications and coding than on mathematical analysis. This appendix relates the material to a more typical outline.

Sorting

Problem Definition. The output sequence is an ordered permutation of the input sequence. When the input is a file, the output is usually a distinct file; when the input is an array, the output is usually the same array.

Applications. This list only hints at the diversity of sorting applications.

- Output Requirements. Some users desire sorted output; see Section 1.1 and consider your telephone directory and monthly checking account statement. Functions such as binary search require sorted inputs.

- Collect Equal Items. Programmers use sorting to collect together the equal items in a sequence: the anagram program in Sections 2.4 and 2.8 collects words in the same anagram class. The suffix arrays in Sections 15.2 and 15.3 collect equal text phrases. See also Problems 2.6, 8.10 and 15.8.

- Other Applications. The anagram program in Sections 2.4 and 2.8 uses sorting as a canonical order for the letters in a word, and thereby as a signature of an anagram class. Problem 2.7 sorts to rearrange data on a tape.

General-Purpose Functions. The following algorithms sort an arbitrary n-element sequence.

- Insertion Sort. The program in Section 11.1 has $O(n^2)$ run time in the worst case and for random inputs. The run times of several variants are described in a table in that section. In Section 11.3 Insertion Sort is used to sort an almost-sorted array in $O(n)$ time. It is the only *stable* sort in this book: output elements with equal keys are in the same relative order as in the input.

- Quicksort. The simple Quicksort in Section 11.2 runs in $O(n \log n)$ expected time on an array of n distinct elements. It is recursive and uses logarithmic stack space on the average. In the worst case, it requires $O(n^2)$ time and $O(n)$ stack space. It runs in $O(n^2)$ time on an array of equal elements; the improved version

179

in Section 11.3 has $O(n \log n)$ average run time for *any* array. The table in Section 11.3 presents empirical data on the run time of several implementations of Quicksort. The C Standard Library *qsort* is usually implemented with this algorithm; it is used in Sections 2.8, 15.2 and 15.3 and Solution 1.1. The C++ Standard Library *sort* often uses the algorithm; it is timed in Section 11.3.

- Heapsort. The Heapsort in Section 14.4 runs in $O(n \log n)$ time on any n-element array; it is not recursive and uses only constant extra space. Solutions 14.1 and 14.2 describe faster Heapsorts.

- Other Sorting Algorithms. The Merge Sort algorithm sketched in Section 1.3 is effective for sorting files; a merging algorithm is sketched in Problem 14.4.d. Solution 11.6 gives pseudocode for Selection Sort and Shell Sort.

The run times of several sorting algorithms are described in Solution 1.3.

Special-Purpose Functions. These functions lead to short and efficient programs for certain inputs.

- Radix Sort. McIlroy's bit-string sort in Problem 11.5 can be generalized to sort strings over larger alphabets (bytes, for instance).

- Bitmap Sort. The bitmap sort in Section 1.4 uses the fact that the integers to be sorted are from a small range, contain no duplicates, and have no additional data. Implementation details and extensions are described in Solutions 1.2, 1.3, 1.5 and 1.6.

- Other Sorts. The multiple-pass sort in Section 1.3 reads the input many times to trade time for space. Columns 12 and 13 produce sorted sets of random integers.

Searching

Problem Definition. A search function determines whether its input is a member of a given set, and possibly retrieves associated information.

Applications. Lesk's telephone directory in Problem 2.6 searches to convert an (encoded) name to a telephone number. Thompson's endgame program in Section 10.8 searches a set of chess boards to compute an optimal move. McIlroy's spelling checker in Section 13.8 searches a dictionary to determine whether a word is spelled correctly. Additional applications are described along with the functions.

General-Purpose Functions. The following algorithms search an arbitrary n-element set.

- Sequential Search. Simple and tuned versions of sequential search in an array are given in Section 9.2. Sequential searches in an array and linked list are given in Section 13.2. The algorithm is used in hyphenating words (Problem 3.5), smoothing geographic data (Section 9.2), representing a sparse matrix (Section 10.2), generating random sets (Section 13.2), storing a compressed dictionary (Section 13.8), bin packing (Problem 14.5), and finding all equal text phrases (Section 15.3). The introduction to Column 3 and Problem 3.1 describe two foolish implementations of sequential search.

- Binary Search. The algorithm to search a sorted array in approximately $\log_2 n$ comparisons is described in Section 2.2, and code is developed in Section 4.2. Section 9.3 extends the code to find the first occurrence of many equal items and tunes its performance. Applications include searching for records in a reservation system (Section 2.2), erroneous input lines (Section 2.2), anagrams of an input word (Problem 2.1), telephone numbers (Problem 2.6), the position of a point among line segments (Problem 4.7), the index of an entry in a sparse array (Solution 10.2), a random integer (Problem 13.3), and phrases of words (Sections 15.2 and 15.3). Problems 2.9 and 9.9 discuss the tradeoffs between binary and sequential search.

- Hashing. Problem 1.10 hashes telephone numbers, Problem 9.10 hashes a set of integers, Section 13.4 uses bins to hash a set of integers, and Section 13.8 hashes the words in a dictionary. Section 15.1 hashes to count the words in a document.

- Binary Search Trees. Section 13.3 uses (nonbalanced) binary search trees to represent a set of random integers. Balanced trees typically implement the *set* template in the C++ Standard Template Library, which we used in Sections 13.1 and 15.1 and Solution 1.1.

Special-Purpose Functions. These functions lead to short and efficient programs for certain inputs.

- Key Indexing. Some keys can be used as an index into an array of values. The bins and bit vectors in Section 13.4 both use integer keys as indices. Keys used as indices include telephone numbers (Section 1.4), characters (Solution 9.6), arguments to trigonometric functions (Problem 9.11), indices of sparse arrays (Section 10.2), program counter values (Problem 10.7), chess boards (Section 10.8), random integers (Section 13.4), hash values of a string (Section 13.8), and integer values in priority queues (Problem 14.8). Problem 10.5 reduces space with key indexing and a numerical function.

- Other Methods. Section 8.1 describes how search time was reduced by keeping common elements in a cache. Section 10.1 describes how searching a tax table became simple once the context was understood.

Other Set Algorithms

These problems deal with a collection of n elements that may possibly contain duplicates.

Priority Queues. A priority queue maintains a set of elements under the operations of inserting arbitrary elements and deleting the minimum element. Section 14.3 describes two sequential structes for the task, and gives a C++ class that efficiently implements priority queues using heaps. Applications are described in Problems 14.4, 14.5 and 14.8.

Selection. Problem 2.8 describes a problem in which we must select the kth-smallest element in the set. Solution 11.9 describes an efficient algorithm for the task; alternative algorithms are mentioned in Problems 2.8, 11.1 and 14.4.c.

Algorithms on Strings

Sections 2.4 and 2.8 compute the anagram sets in a dictionary. Solution 9.6 describes several ways to classify characters. Section 15.1 lists the distinct words in a file and also counts the words in a file, first using C++ Standard Template Library components and then with a custom-built hash table. Section 15.2 uses suffix arrays to find the longest repeated substring in a text file, and Section 15.3 uses a variant of suffix arrays to generate random text from a Markov model.

Vector and Matrix Algorithms

Algorithms for swapping subsequences of a vector are discussed in Section 2.3 and Problems 2.3 and 2.4; Solution 2.3 contains code for the algorithms. Problem 2.5 describes an algorithm for swapping nonadjacent subsequences in a vector. Problem 2.7 uses sorting to transpose a matrix represented on tape. Programs for computing the maximum of a vector are described in Problems 4.9, 9.4 and 9.8. Vector and matrix algorithms that share space are described in Sections 10.3 and 14.4. Sparse vectors and matrices are discussed in Sections 3.1, 10.2 and 13.8; Problem 1.9 describes a scheme for initializing sparse vectors that is used in Section 11.3. Column 8 describes five algorithms for computing the maximum-sum subsequence in a vector, and several of the problems in Column 8 deal with vectors and matrices.

Random Objects

Functions for generating pseudorandom integers are used throughout the book; they are implemented in Solution 12.1. Section 12.3 describes an algorithm for "shuffling" the elements of an array. Sections 12.1 through 12.3 describe several algorithms for selecting random subsets of a set (see also Problems 12.7 and 12.9); Problem 1.4 gives an application of the algorithm. Solution 12.10 gives an algorithm for randomly selecting one of an unknown number of objects.

Numerical Algorithms

Solution 2.3 presents the additive Euclidean algorithm for computing the greatest common divisor of two integers. Problem 3.7 sketches an algorithm for evaluating linear recurrences with constant coefficients. Problem 4.9 gives code for an efficient algorithm to raise a number to a positive integer power. Problem 9.11 computes trigonometric functions by table lookup. Solution 9.12 describes Horner's method of evaluating a polynomial. Summing a large set of floating point numbers is described in Problems 11.1 and 14.4.b.

The back-of-the-envelope calculations in Column 7 all start with basic quantities. Those numbers can sometimes be found in a problem specification (such as a requirements document), but other times they must be estimated.

This little quiz is designed to help you evaluate your proficiency as a number guesser. For each question, fill in upper and lower bounds that, *in your opinion*, give you a ninety percent chance of including the true value; try not to make your ranges too narrow or too wide. I estimate that it should take you between five and ten minutes. Please make a good faith effort (and in consideration of the next reader, perhaps a photocopy of this page).

[_____, _____] January 1, 2000, population of the United States in millions.

[_____, _____] The year of Napoleon's birth.

[_____, _____] Length of the Mississippi-Missouri river in miles.

[_____, _____] Maximum takeoff weight in pounds of a Boeing 747 airliner.

[_____, _____] Seconds for a radio signal to travel from the earth to the moon.

[_____, _____] Latitude of London.

[_____, _____] Minutes for a space shuttle to orbit the earth.

[_____, _____] Length in feet between the towers of the Golden Gate Bridge.

[_____, _____] Number of signers of the Declaration of Independence.

[_____, _____] Number of bones in the adult human body.

When you finish this quiz, please turn to the next page for answers and interpretation.

Please answer the questions before you turn the page.

If you have not yet filled in all the guesses yourself, please go back and do so. Here are the answers, from an almanac or similar source.

January 1, 2000, population of the United States is 272.5 million.

Napoleon was born in 1769.

The Mississippi-Missouri river is 3,710 miles long.

Maximum takeoff weight of a B747-400 airliner is 875,000 pounds.

A radio signal travels from the earth to the moon in 1.29 seconds.

Latitude of London is about 51.5 degrees.

A space shuttle orbits the earth in about 91 minutes.

4200 feet between the towers of the Golden Gate Bridge.

56 signers of the Declaration of Independence.

206 bones in the adult human body.

Please count how many of your ranges included the correct answer. Because you used a 90-percent confidence interval, you should have gotten about nine of the ten answers correct.

If you had all ten answers correct, then you may be an excellent estimator. Then again, your ranges may be way too big. You can probably guess which.

If you had six or fewer answers correct, then you are probably as embarrassed as I was when I first took a similar estimation quiz. A little practice couldn't hurt your estimation skills.

If you had seven or eight answers correct, then you are a pretty good guesser. In the future, remember to broaden your 90-percent ranges just a bit.

If you had exactly nine answers correct, then you may be an excellent guesser. Or, you may have given infinite ranges for the first nine questions, and zero for the last question. If so, shame on you.

COST MODELS FOR TIME AND SPACE

Section 7.2 describes two little programs for estimating the time and space consumed by various primitive operations. This appendix shows how those can grow into useful programs for generating one-page time and space estimates. The complete source code for both programs can be found at this book's web site.

The program *spacemod.cpp* produces a model of the space consumed by various constructs in C++. The first part of the program uses a sequence of statements like

```
cout << "sizeof(char)=" << sizeof(char);
cout << " sizeof(short)=" << sizeof(short);
```

to give precise measurements of primitive objects:

```
sizeof(char)=1  sizeof(short)=2  sizeof(int)=4
sizeof(float)=4  sizeof(struct *)=4  sizeof(long)=4
sizeof(double)=8
```

The program also defines a dozen structures, using the simple naming convention illustrated in these examples:

```
struct structc { char c; };
struct structic { int i; char c; };
struct structip { int i; structip *p; };
struct structdc { double d; char c; };
struct structc12 { char c[12]; };
```

The program uses a macro to report the *sizeof* the structure, and then to estimate the number of bytes that *new* allocates in a report like this:

```
structc    1    48 48 48 48 48 48 48 48 48 48
structic   8    48 48 48 48 48 48 48 48 48 48
structip   8    48 48 48 48 48 48 48 48 48 48
structdc   16   64 64 64 64 64 64 64 64 64 64
structcd   16   64 64 64 64 64 64 64 64 64 64
structcdc  24   -3744 4096 64 64 64 64 64 64 64 64
structiii  12   48 48 48 48 48 48 48 48 48 48
```

185

The first number is given by *sizeof*, and the next ten numbers report the differences between successive pointers returned by *new*. This output is typical: most of the numbers are quite consistent, but the allocator skips around every now and then.

This macro makes one line of the report:

```
#define MEASURE(T, text) {                          \
    cout << text << "\t";                           \
    cout << sizeof(T) << "\t";                      \
    int lastp = 0;                                  \
    for (int i = 0; i < 11; i++) {                  \
        T *p = new T;                               \
        int thisp = (int) p;                        \
        if (lastp != 0)                             \
            cout << " " << thisp - lastp; \
        lastp = thisp;                              \
    }                                               \
    cout << "\n";                                   \
}
```

The macro is called with the structure name followed by the same name in quotes, so it can be printed:

```
MEASURE(structc, "structc");
```

(My first draft used a C++ template parameterized by structure type, but measurements were led wildly astray by artifacts of the C++ implementation.)

This table summarizes the output of the program on my machine:

STRUCTURE	*sizeof*	*new* SIZE
int	4	48
structc	1	48
structic	8	48
structip	8	48
structdc	16	64
structcd	16	64
structcdc	24	64
structiii	12	48
structuc	12	48
*structc*12	12	48
*structc*13	13	64
*structc*28	28	64
*structc*29	29	80

The left column of numbers helps us to estimate the *sizeof* structures. We start by summing the *sizeof* the types; that explains the 8 bytes for *structip*. We must also account for the alignment; although its components sum to 10 bytes (two *char*s and a *double*), *structcdc* consumes 24 bytes.

The right column gives us insight into the space overhead of the *new* operator. It appears that any structure with a *sizeof* 12 bytes or less will consume 48 bytes.

Structures with 13 through 28 bytes consume 64 bytes. In general, the allocated block size will be a multiple of 16, with 36 to 47 bytes of overhead. This is surprisingly expensive; other systems that I use consume just 8 bytes of overhead to represent an 8-byte record.

Section 7.2 also describes a little program for estimating the cost of one particular C operation. We can generalize that to the *timemod.c* program that produces a one-page cost model for a set of C operations. (Brian Kernighan, Chris Van Wyk and I built a predecessor of this program in 1991.) The *main* function of that program consists of a sequence of a T (for title) lines followed by M lines to measure the cost of operations:

```
T("Integer Arithmetic");
M({});
M(k++);
M(k = i + j);
M(k = i - j);
    ...
```

Those lines (and a few more like them) produce this output:

```
Integer Arithmetic (n=5000)
    {}              250   261   250   250   251   10
    k++             471   460   471   461   460   19
    k = i + j       491   491   500   491   491   20
    k = i - j       440   441   441   440   441   18
    k = i * j       491   490   491   491   490   20
    k = i / j      2414  2433  2424  2423  2414   97
    k = i % j      2423  2414  2423  2414  2423   97
    k = i & j       491   491   480   491   491   20
    k = i | j       440   441   441   440   441   18
```

The first column gives the operation that is executed inside the loop

```
for i = [1, n]
    for j = [1, n]
        op
```

The next five columns show the raw time in clock clicks (milliseconds on this system) for five executions of that loop (these times are all consistent; inconsistent numbers help to identify suspicious runs). The final column gives the average cost in nanoseconds per operation. The first row of the table says that it takes about ten nanoseconds to execute a loop that contains the null operation. The next row says that incrementing the variable k consumes about 9 additional nanoseconds. All of the arithmetic and logical operations have about the same cost, with the exception of the division and remainder operators, which are an order-of-magnitude more expensive.

This approach gives rough estimates for my machine, and they must not be over-interpreted. I conducted all experiments with optimization disabled. When I enabled that option, the optimizer removed the timing loops and all times were zero.

The work is done by the M macro, which can be sketched in pseudocode as:

```
#define M(op)
    print op as a string
    timesum = 0
    for trial = [0, trials)
        start = clock()
        for i = [1, n]
            fi = i
            for j = [1, n]
                op
        t = clock()-start
        print t
        timesum += t
    print 1e9*timesum / (n*n * trials * CLOCKS_PER_SEC)
```

The complete code for this cost model can be found at this book's web site.

We'll now survey the output of the program on my particular system. Because the clock clicks are all consistent, we will omit them and report only the average time in nanoseconds.

```
Floating Point Arithmetic (n=5000)
  fj=j;                        18
  fj=j; fk = fi + fj           26
  fj=j; fk = fi - fj           27
  fj=j; fk = fi * fj           24
  fj=j; fk = fi / fj           78
Array Operations (n=5000)
  k = i + j                    17
  k = x[i] + j                 18
  k = i + x[j]                 24
  k = x[i] + x[j]              27
```

The floating point operations originally assign the integer j to the floating-point fj (in about 8 nanoseconds); the outer loop assigns i to the floating-point fi. The floating operations themselves cost about as much as their integer counterparts, and the array operations are equally inexpensive.

The next tests give us insight into control flow in general and some sorting operations in particular:

```
Comparisons (n=5000)
  if (i < j) k++              20
  if (x[i] < x[j]) k++        25
Array Comparisons and Swaps (n=5000)
  k = (x[i]<x[k]) ? -1:1      34
  k = intcmp(x+i, x+j)        52
  swapmac(i, j)              41
  swapfunc(i, j)             65
```

The function versions of comparing and swapping each cost about 20 nanoseconds more than their inline counterparts. Section 9.2 compares the cost of computing the maximum of two values with functions, macros and inline code:

```
Max Function, Macro and Inline (n=5000)
  k = (i > j) ? i : j    26
  k = maxmac(i, j)       26
  k = maxfunc(i, j)      54
```

The *rand* function is relatively inexpensive (though recall that the *bigrand* function makes two calls to *rand*), square root is an order of magnitude greater than basic arithmetic operations (though only twice the cost of a division), simple trigonometric operations cost twice that, and advanced trigonometric operations run into microseconds.

```
Math Functions (n=1000)
  k = rand()             40
  fk = j+fi              20
  fk = sqrt(j+fi)       188
  fk = sin(j+fi)        344
  fk = sinh(j+fi)      2229
  fk = asin(j+fi)       973
  fk = cos(j+fi)        353
  fk = tan(j+fi)        465
```

Because those are so pricey, we shrunk the value of n. Memory allocation is more expensive yet, and merits an even smaller n:

```
Memory Allocation (n=500)
  free(malloc(16))      2484
  free(malloc(100))     3044
  free(malloc(2000))    4959
```

My 1982 book *Writing Efficient Programs* was built around 27 rules for code tuning. That book is now out of print, so the rules are repeated here (with only a few small changes), together with examples of how they are used in this book.

Space-For-Time Rules

Data Structure Augmentation. The time required for common operations on data can often be reduced by augmenting the structure with extra information or by changing the information within the structure so that it can be accessed more easily.

In Section 9.2, Wright wanted to find nearest neighbors (by angle) among a set of points on the surface of the globe represented by latitude and longitude, which involved expensive trigonometric operations. Appel augmented her data structure with the x, y and z coordinates, which allowed her to use Euclidean distances with much less compute time.

Store Precomputed Results. The cost of recomputing an expensive function can be reduced by computing the function only once and storing the results. Subsequent requests for the function are then handled by table lookup rather than by computing the function.

The cumulative arrays in Section 8.2 and Solution 8.11 replace a sequence of additions with two table lookups and a subtraction.

Solution 9.7 speeds up a program to count bits by looking up a byte or a word at a time.

Solution 10.6 replaces shifting and logical operations with a table lookup.

Caching. Data that is accessed most often should be the cheapest to access.

Section 9.1 describes how Van Wyk cached the most common size of node to avoid expensive calls to the system storage allocator. Solution 9.2 gives the details on one kind of node cache.

Column 13 caches nodes for lists, bins and binary search trees.

Caching can backfire and increase the run time of a program if locality is not present in the underlying data.

Lazy Evaluation. The strategy of never evaluating an item until it is needed avoids evaluations of unnecessary items.

Time-For-Space Rules

Packing. Dense storage representations can decrease storage costs by increasing the time required to store and retrieve data.

> The sparse array representations in Section 10.2 greatly reduce storage costs by slightly increasing the time to access the structures.
>
> McIlroy's dictionary for a spelling checker in Section 13.8 squeezes 75,000 English words into 52 kilobytes.
>
> Kernighan's arrays in Section 10.3 and the Heapsort in Section 14.4 both use *overlaying* to reduce data space by storing data items that are never simultaneously active in the same memory space.
>
> Although packing sometimes trades time for space, the smaller representations are often also faster to process.

Interpreters. The space required to represent a program can often be decreased by the use of interpreters in which common sequences of operations are represented compactly.

> Section 3.2 uses an interpreter for "form-letter programming" and Section 10.4 uses an interpreter for a simple graphics program.

Loop Rules

Code Motion Out of Loops. Instead of performing a certain computation in each iteration of a loop, it is better to perform it only once, outside the loop.

> Section 11.1 moves an assignment to the variable t out of the main loop of *isort*2.

Combining Tests. An efficient inner loop should contain as few tests as possible, and preferably only one. The programmer should therefore try to simulate some of the exit conditions of the loop by other exit conditions.

> *Sentinels* are a common application of this rule: we place a sentinel at the boundary of a data structure to reduce the cost of testing whether our search has exhausted the structure. Section 9.2 uses a sentinel in sequentially searching an array. Column 13 uses sentinels to yield clean (and incidentally efficient) code for arrays, linked lists, bins and binary search trees. Solution 14.1 places a sentinel at one end of a heap.

Loop Unrolling. Unrolling a loop can remove the cost of modifying loop indices, and also help to avoid pipeline stalls, to reduce branches, and to increase instruction-level parallelism.

> Unrolling a sequential search in Section 9.2 reduces its run time by about 50

percent, and unrolling a binary search in Section 9.3 reduces its run time by between 35 and 65 percent.

Transfer-Driven Loop Unrolling. If a large cost of an inner loop is devoted to trivial assignments, then those assignments can often be removed by repeating the code and changing the use of variables. Specifically, to remove the assignment $i = j$, the subsequent code must treat j as though it were i.

Unconditional Branch Removal. A fast loop should contain no unconditional branches. An unconditional branch at the end of a loop can be removed by "rotating" the loop to have a conditional branch at the bottom.

This operation is usually done by optimizing compilers.

Loop Fusion. If two nearby loops operate on the same set of elements, then combine their operational parts and use only one set of loop control operations.

Logic Rules

Exploit Algebraic Identities. If the evaluation of a logical expression is costly, replace it by an algebraically equivalent expression that is cheaper to evaluate.

Short-Circuiting Monotone Functions. If we wish to test whether some monotone nondecreasing function of several variables is over a certain threshold, then we need not evaluate any of the variables once the threshold has been reached.

A more sophisticated application of this rule exits from a loop as soon as the purpose of the loop has been accomplished. The search loops in Columns 10, 13 and 15 all terminate once they find the desired element.

Reordering Tests. Logical tests should be arranged such that inexpensive and often successful tests precede expensive and rarely successful tests.

Solution 9.6 sketches a series of tests that might be reordered.

Precompute Logical Functions. A logical function over a small finite domain can be replaced by a lookup in a table that represents the domain.

Solution 9.6 describes how the Standard C library character classification functions can be implemented by table lookup.

Boolean Variable Elimination. We can remove boolean variables from a program by replacing the assignment to a boolean variable v by an $if - else$ statement in which one branch represents the case that v is true and the other represents the case that v is false.

Procedure Rules

Collapsing Function Hierarchies. The run times of the elements of a set of functions that (nonrecursively) call themselves can often be reduced by rewriting functions in line and binding the passed variables.

Replacing the max function in Section 9.2 with a macro gives a speedup of almost a factor of two.

Writing the *swap* function inline in Section 11.1 gave a speedup of a factor of almost 3; writing the *swap* inline in Section 11.3 gave less of a speedup.

Exploit Common Cases. Functions should be organized to handle all cases correctly and common cases efficiently.

In Section 9.1, Van Wyk's storage allocator handled all node sizes correctly, but handled the most common node size particularly efficiently.

In Section 6.1, Appel treated the expensive case of near objects with a special-purpose small time step, which allowed the rest of his program to use a more efficient large time step.

Coroutines. A multiple-pass algorithm can often be turned into a single-pass algorithm by use of coroutines.

The anagram program in Section 2.8 uses a pipeline, which can be implemented as a set of coroutines.

Transformations on Recursive Functions. The run time of recursive functions can often be reduced by applying the following transformations:

Rewrite recursion to iteration, as in the lists and binary search trees in Column 13.

Convert the recursion to iteration by using an explicit program stack. (If a function contains only one recursive call to itself, then it is not necessary to store the return address on the stack.)

If the final action of a function is to call itself recursively, replace that call by a branch to its first statement; this is usually known as removing tail recursion. The code in Solution 11.9 is a candidate for this transformation. That branch can often be transformed into a loop. Compilers often perform this optimization.

It is often more efficient to solve small subproblems by use of an auxiliary procedure, rather than by recurring down to problems of size zero or one. The *qsort*4 function in Section 11.3 uses a value of *cutoff* near 50.

Parallelism. A program should be structured to exploit as much of the parallelism as possible in the underlying hardware.

Expression Rules

Compile-Time Initialization. As many variables as possible should be initialized before program execution.

Exploit Algebraic Identities. If the evaluation of an expression is costly, replace it by an algebraically equivalent expression that is cheaper to evaluate.

In Section 9.2, Appel replaced expensive trigonometric operations with multiplications and additions, and also used monotonicity to remove an expensive square root operation.

Section 9.2 replaces an expensive C remainder operator % in an inner loop with a cheaper *if* statement.

We can often multiply or divide by powers of two by shifting left or right. Solution 13.9 replaces an arbitrary division used by bins with a shift. Solution 10.6 replaces a division by 10 with a shift by 4.

In Section 6.1, Appel exploited additional numeric accuracy in a data structure to replace 64-bit floating point numbers with faster 32-bit numbers.

Strength reduction on a loop that iterates through the elements of an array replaces a multiplication by an addition. Many compilers perform this optimization. This technique generalizes to a large class of incremental algorithms.

Common Subexpression Elimination. If the same expression is evaluated twice with none of its variables altered between evaluations, then the second evaluation can be avoided by storing the result of the first and using that in place of the second.

Modern compilers are usually good at eliminating common subexpressions that do not contain function calls.

Pairing Computation. If two similar expressions are frequently evaluated together, then we should make a new procedure that evaluates them as a pair.

In Section 13.1, our first pseudocode always uses *member* and *insert* functions in concert; the C++ code replaces those two functions with an *insert* that does nothing if its argument is already in the set.

Exploit Word Parallelism. Use the full data-path width of the underlying computer architecture to evaluate expensive expressions.

Problem 13.8 shows how bit vectors can operate on many bits at once by operating on *char*s or *int*s.

Solution 9.7 counts bits in parallel.

The following is a complete listing of the C++ integer set representation classes discussed in Column 13. The complete code can be found at this book's web site.

```cpp
class IntSetSTL {
private:
    set<int> S;
public:
    IntSetSTL(int maxelms, int maxval) { }
    int size() { return S.size(); }
    void insert(int t) { S.insert(t);}
    void report(int *v)
    {   int j = 0;
        set<int>::iterator i;
        for (i = S.begin(); i != S.end(); ++i)
            v[j++] = *i;
    }
};


class IntSetArray {
private:
    int n, *x;
public:
    IntSetArray(int maxelms, int maxval)
    {   x = new int[1 + maxelms];
        n = 0;
        x[0] = maxval;
    }
    int size() { return n; }
    void insert(int t)
    {   for (int i = 0; x[i] < t; i++)
            ;
        if (x[i] == t)
            return;
        for (int j = n; j >= i; j--)
            x[j+1] = x[j];
        x[i] = t;
        n++;
    }
```

```
    void report(int *v)
    {   for (int i = 0; i < n; i++)
            v[i] = x[i];
    }
};



class IntSetList {
private:
    int n;
    struct node {
        int val;
        node *next;
        node(int v, node *p) { val = v; next = p; }
    };
    node *head, *sentinel;
    node *rinsert(node *p, int t)
    {   if (p->val < t) {
            p->next = rinsert(p->next, t);
        } else if (p->val > t) {
            p = new node(t, p);
            n++;
        }
        return p;
    }
public:
    IntSetList(int maxelms, int maxval)
    {   sentinel = head = new node(maxval, 0);
        n = 0;
    }
    int size() { return n; }
    void insert(int t) { head = rinsert(head, t); }
    void report(int *v)
    {   int j = 0;
        for (node *p = head; p != sentinel; p = p->next)
            v[j++] = p->val;
    }
};



class IntSetBST {
private:
    int n, *v, vn;
    struct node {
        int val;
        node *left, *right;
        node(int v) { val = v; left = right = 0; }
    };
    node *root;
```

```
    node *rinsert(node *p, int t)
    {   if (p == 0) {
            p = new node(t);
            n++;
        } else if (t < p->val) {
            p->left = rinsert(p->left, t);
        } else if (t > p->val) {
            p->right = rinsert(p->right, t);
        } // do nothing if p->val == t
        return p;
    }
    void traverse(node *p)
    {   if (p == 0)
            return;
        traverse(p->left);
        v[vn++] = p->val;
        traverse(p->right);
    }
public:
    IntSetBST(int maxelms, int maxval) { root = 0; n = 0; }
    int size() { return n; }
    void insert(int t) { root = rinsert(root, t); }
    void report(int *x) { v = x; vn = 0; traverse(root); }
};

class IntSetBitVec {
private:
    enum { BITSPERWORD = 32, SHIFT = 5, MASK = 0x1F };
    int n, hi, *x;
    void set(int i)  {          x[i>>SHIFT] |=  (1<<(i & MASK)); }
    void clr(int i)  {          x[i>>SHIFT] &= ~(1<<(i & MASK)); }
    int  test(int i) { return x[i>>SHIFT] &   (1<<(i & MASK)); }
public:
    IntSetBitVec(int maxelms, int maxval)
    {   hi = maxval;
        x = new int[1 + hi/BITSPERWORD];
        for (int i = 0; i < hi; i++)
            clr(i);
        n = 0;
    }
    int size() { return n; }
    void insert(int t)
    {   if (test(t))
            return;
        set(t);
        n++;
    }
    void report(int *v)
    {   int j = 0;
        for (int i = 0; i < hi; i++)
            if (test(i))
                v[j++] = i;
    }
};
```

```
class IntSetBins {
private:
    int n, bins, maxval;
    struct node {
        int val;
        node *next;
        node(int v, node *p) { val = v; next = p; }
    };
    node **bin, *sentinel;
    node *rinsert(node *p, int t)
    {   if (p->val < t) {
            p->next = rinsert(p->next, t);
        } else if (p->val > t) {
            p = new node(t, p);
            n++;
        }
        return p;
    }
public:
    IntSetBins(int maxelms, int pmaxval)
    {   bins = maxelms;
        maxval = pmaxval;
        bin = new node*[bins];
        sentinel = new node(maxval, 0);
        for (int i = 0; i < bins; i++)
            bin[i] = sentinel;
        n = 0;
    }
    int size() { return n; }
    void insert(int t)
    {   int i = t / (1 + maxval/bins);
        bin[i] = rinsert(bin[i], t);
    }
    void report(int *v)
    {   int j = 0;
        for (int i = 0; i < bins; i++)
            for (node *p = bin[i]; p != sentinel; p = p->next)
                v[j++] = p->val;
    }
};
```

HINTS FOR SELECTED PROBLEMS

Column 1

4. Read Column 12.

5. Consider a two-pass algorithm.

6, 8, 9. Try key indexing.

10. Consider hashing, and don't limit yourself to a computerized system.

11. This problem is for the birds.

12. How do you write without using a pen?

Column 2

1. Think about sorting, binary search and signatures.

2. Strive for an algorithm that runs in linear time.

5. Exploit the identity $cba = (a^r b^r c^r)^r$.

7. Vyssotsky used a system utility and two one-shot programs that he wrote just for this job to rearrange data on tapes.

8. Consider the k smallest elements in the set.

9. The cost of s sequential searches is proportional to sn; the total cost of s binary searches is the cost of the searches plus the time required to sort the table. Before you put too much faith in the constant factors of the various algorithms, see Problem 9.9.

10. How did Archimedes determine that the king's crown wasn't pure gold?

Column 3

2. Use one array to represent the coefficients of the recurrence and another to represent the k previous values. The program consists of a loop within a loop.

4. Only one function need be written from scratch; the other two can call that one.

Column 4

2. Work from a precise invariant. Consider adding two dummy elements to the array to help you initialize your invariant: $x[-1] = -\infty$ and $x[n] = \infty$.

5. If you solve this problem, run to the nearest mathematics department and ask for a Ph.D.

6. Look for an invariant preserved by the process, and relate the initial condition of the can to its terminal condition.

7. Read Section 2.2 again.

9. Try the following loop invariants, which are true immediately before the test in the *while* statement. For vector addition,

$$i \le n \quad \&\& \quad \forall_{1 \le j < i} \ a[j] = b[j] + c[j]$$

and for sequential search,

$$i \le n \quad \&\& \quad \forall_{1 \le j < i} \ x[j] \ne t$$

11. See Solution 11.14 for a recursive function that passes a pointer to an array.

Column 5

3. Search for terms like "mutation testing".

5. What can you accomplish in $O(\log n)$ or $O(1)$ extra comparisons?

6. This book's web site contains a Java program with a GUI for studying sorting algorithms.

9. The tab-separated output format of the scaffolding is designed to be compatible with most spreadsheets. I usually store a series of related experiments on a single page of a spreadsheet, together with graphs of their performance and comments about why I did the experiments and what I learned from each.

Column 6

1. Peek ahead to Section 8.5.

3. Modify the cost model for run times described in Appendix 3 to measure the cost of double-precision operations.

7. Automobile accidents are avoided by measures such as driver training, strict enforcement of speed limits, a minimum drinking age, stiff penalties for drunk driving and a good system of public transportation. If accidents do occur, injuries to passengers can be reduced by the design of the passenger compartment, wearing seat belts (perhaps as mandated by law) and air bags. And if injuries are suffered, their effect can be reduced by paramedics at the scene, rapid evacuation in helicopter ambulances, trauma centers and corrective surgery.

Column 7

5. I first played with the function $(1+x/100)^{72/x}$, then used a spreadsheet to plot $(1+.72/x)^x$. To prove properties about the Rule of 72, recall that $\lim_{n\to\infty} (1+c/n)^n = e^c$, that the natural logarithm of 2 is approximately .693, and that the asymptote is not always the optimal approximation line.

8. Consider especially the designs and programs in Problems 2.7, 8.10, 8.12, 8.13, 9.4, 10.10, 11.6, 12.7, 12.9, 12.11, 13.3, 13.6, 13.11, 15.4, 15.5, 15.7, 15.9 and 15.15 and in Sections 1.3, 2.2, 2.4, 2.8, 10.2, 12.3, 13.2, 13.3, 13.8, 14.3, 14.4, 15.1, 15.2 and 15.3.

Column 8

4. Plot the cumulative sum as a random walk.

7. Floating point addition is not necessarily commutative.

8. In addition to computing the maximum sum in the region, return information about the maximum vectors ending at each side of the array.

10, 11, 12. Use a cumulative array.

13. The obvious algorithm has $O(n^4)$ run time; strive for a cubic algorithm.

Column 9

3. The addition increased k by at most $n-1$, so we know that k is less than $2n$.

9. To make binary search competitive with sequential search even at small values of n, make the comparison operation very expensive (see, for instance, Problem 4.7).

Column 10

1. What code did the compiler generate for accessing packed fields?

5. Mix and match functions and tables.

7. Reduce the data by considering certain ranges of memory to be equivalent. Those ranges might be either fixed-length blocks (say, 64 bytes) or function boundaries.

Column 11

2. Let the loop index i move from high to low, so that it approaches the known value t in $x[l]$.

4. When you have two subproblems to solve, which should you solve right away and which should you leave on the stack to return to later — larger or smaller?

9. Modify Quicksort so that it recurs only on the subrange that contains k.

Column 12

4. Go to a statistician and use the phrases "Coupon Collector's Problem" and "Birthday Paradox".

11. The problem said you *could* use the computer; it didn't say you had to.

Column 13

2. Error checking should test to ensure that an integer to be inserted is in the proper range and that the data structure is not yet full. A destructor should return any allocated storage.

3. Use a binary search to test whether an element is in a sorted array.

Column 14

2. Aim for a Heapsort with this structure.

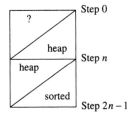

3. See Problem 2, and also consider moving code out of loops.

6. Heaps have implicit pointers from node i to node $2i$; try the same in disk files.

7. Binary search in $x[0..6]$ uses an implicit tree whose root is in $x[3]$. How might the implicit trees of Section 14.1 be used instead?

9. Use the $O(n \log n)$ lower bound on sorting. If both *insert* and *extractmin* run in less than $O(\log n)$ time, then you could sort in less than $O(n \log n)$ time; show how to use the operations to sort that quickly.

Column 15

15. Suppose that we are generating order-1 Markov text from a million-word document that contains the words x, y and z only in the single phrase "$x\ y\ x\ z$". Half the time x should be followed by a y, the other half it should be followed by a z. What odds does Shannon's algorithm give?

16. How could you use counts of k-grams of letters or words?

17. Some commercial speech recognizers are based on trigram statistics.

SOLUTIONS TO SELECTED PROBLEMS

Solutions for Column 1

1. This C program uses the Standard Library *qsort* to sort a file of integers.

```
int intcomp(int *x, int *y)
{    return *x - *y; }

int a[1000000];
int main(void)
{    int i, n=0;
     while (scanf("%d", &a[n]) != EOF)
         n++;
     qsort(a, n, sizeof(int), intcomp);
     for (i = 0; i < n; i++)
         printf("%d\n", a[i]);
     return 0;
}
```

This C++ program uses the *set* container from the Standard Template Library for the same job.

```
int main(void)
{    set<int> S;
     int i;
     set<int>::iterator j;
     while (cin >> i)
         S.insert(i);
     for (j = S.begin(); j != S.end(); ++j)
         cout << *j << "\n";
     return 0;
}
```

Solution 3 sketches the performance of both programs.

2. These functions use the constants to set, clear and test the value of a bit:

```
#define BITSPERWORD 32
#define SHIFT 5
#define MASK 0x1F
#define N 10000000
int a[1 + N/BITSPERWORD];

void set(int i) {        a[i>>SHIFT] |=  (1<<(i & MASK)); }
void clr(int i) {        a[i>>SHIFT] &= ~(1<<(i & MASK)); }
int  test(int i){ return a[i>>SHIFT] &  (1<<(i & MASK)); }
```

a[0] → bits for 1st 32 #s
a[1] → next & so on % 32
i/32

3. This C code implements the sorting algorithm, using the functions defined in Solution 2.

```
int main(void)
{   int i;
    for (i = 0; i < N; i++)
        clr(i);
    while (scanf("%d", &i) != EOF)
        set(i);
    for (i = 0; i < N; i++)
        if (test(i))
            printf("%d\n", i);
    return 0;
}
```

I used the program in Solution 4 to generate a file of one million distinct positive integers, each less than ten million. This table reports the cost of sorting them with the system command-line sort, the C++ and C programs in Solution 1, and the bitmap code:

	SYSTEM SORT	C++/STL	C/qsort	C/bitmaps
Total Secs	89	38	12.6	10.7
Compute Secs	79	28	2.4	.5
Megabytes	.8	70	4	1.25

The first line reports the total time, and the second line subtracts out the 10.2 seconds of input/output required to read and write the files. Even though the general C++ program uses 50 times the memory and CPU time of the specialized C program, it requires just half the code and is much easier to extend to other problems.

4. See Column 12, especially Problem 12.8. This code assumes that *randint(l, u)* returns a random integer in *l..u.*

```
for i = [0, n)
    x[i] = i
for i = [0, k)
    swap(i, randint(i, n-1))
    print x[i]
```

— *Initialize an array*
] *Randomly swap numbers*

k unique #s (oto) from range (n-1)

The *swap* function exchanges the two elements in *x.* The *randint* function is discussed in detail in Section 12.1.

5. Representing all ten million numbers with a bitmap requires that many bits, or 1.25 million bytes. Employing the fact that no phone numbers begin with the digits zero or one reduces the memory to exactly one million bytes. Alternatively, a two-pass algorithm first sorts the integers 0 through 4,999,999 using $5,000,000/8 = 625,000$ words of storage, then sorts 5,000,000 through 9,999,999 in a second pass. A k-pass algorithm sorts at most n nonrepeated positive integers less than n in time kn and space n/k.

6. If each integer appears at most ten times, then we can count its occurrences in a four-bit half-byte (or nybble). Using the solution to Problem 5, we can sort the complete file in a single pass with $10,000,000/2$ bytes, or in k passes with $10,000,000/2k$ bytes.

9. The effect of initializing the vector $data[0..n-1]$ can be accomplished with a signature contained in two additional n-element vectors, $from$ and to, and an integer top. If the element $data[i]$ has been initialized, then $from[i] < top$ and $to[from[i]] = i$. Thus $from$ is a simple signature, and to and top together make sure that $from$ is not accidentally signed by the random contents of memory. Blank entries of $data$ are uninitialized in this picture:

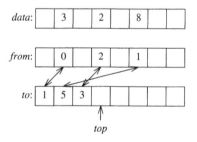

The variable top is initially zero; the array element i is first accessed by the code

```
from[i] = top
to[top] = i
data[i] = 0
top++
```

This problem and solution are from Exercise 2.12 of Aho, Hopcroft and Ullman's *Design and Analysis of Computer Algorithms*, published by Addison-Wesley in 1974. It combines key indexing and a wily signature scheme. It can be used for matrices as well as vectors.

10. The store placed the paper order forms in a 10×10 array of bins, using the last two digits of the customer's phone number as the hash index. When the customer telephoned an order, it was placed in the proper bin. When the customer arrived to retrieve the merchandise, the salesperson sequentially searched through the orders in the appropriate bin — this is classical "open hashing with collision resolution by sequential search". The last two digits of the phone number are quite close to

random and therefore an excellent hash function, while the first two digits would be a horrible hash function — why? Some municipalities use a similar scheme to record deeds in sets of record books.

11. The computers at the two facilities were linked by microwave, but printing the drawings at the test base would have required a printer that was very expensive at the time. The team therefore drew the pictures at the main plant, photographed them, and sent 35mm film to the test station by carrier pigeon, where it was enlarged and printed photographically. The pigeon's 45-minute flight took half the time of the car, and cost only a few dollars per day. During the 16 months of the project the pigeons transmitted several hundred rolls of film, and only two were lost (hawks inhabit the area; no classified data was carried). Because of the low price of modern printers, a current solution to the problem would probably use the microwave link.

12. According to the urban legend, the Soviets solved their problem with a pencil, of course. For background on the true story, see *www.spacepen.com*. The Fisher Space Pen company was founded in 1948, and its writing instruments have been used by the Russian Space Agency, underwater explorers, and Himalayan climbing expeditions.

Solutions for Column 2

A. It is helpful to view this binary search in terms of the 32 bits that represent each integer. In the first pass of the algorithm we read the (at most) four billion input integers and write those with a leading zero bit to one sequential file and those with a leading one bit to another file.

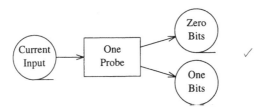

One of those two files contains at most two billion integers, so we next use that file as the current input and repeat the probe process, but this time on the second bit. If the original input file contains n elements, the first pass will read n integers, the second pass at most $n/2$, the third pass at most $n/4$, and so on, so the total running time is proportional to n. The missing integer could be found by sorting the file and then scanning, but that would require time proportional to $n \log n$. This problem was given as an exam by Ed Reingold at the University of Illinois.

B. See Section 2.3.

C. See Section 2.4.

1. To find all anagrams of a given word we first compute its signature. If no preprocessing is allowed then we have to read the entire dictionary sequentially, compute the signature of each word, and compare the two signatures. With preprocessing, we could perform a binary search in a precomputed structure containing (signature, word) pairs sorted by signature. Musser and Saini implement several anagram programs in Chapters 12 through 15 of their *STL Tutorial and Reference Guide*, published by Addison-Wesley in 1996.

2. Binary search finds an element that occurs at least twice by recursively searching the subinterval that contains more than half of the integers. My original solution did not guarantee that the number of integers is halved in each iteration, so the worst-case run time of its $\log_2 n$ passes was proportional to $n \log n$. Jim Saxe reduced that to linear time by observing that the search can avoid carrying too many duplicates. When his search knows that a duplicate must be in a current range of m integers, it will only store $m + 1$ integers on its current work tape; if more integers would have gone on the tape, his program discards them. Although his method frequently ignores input variables, its strategy is conservative enough to ensure that it finds at least one duplicate.

3. This "juggling" code rotates $x[n]$ left by *rotdist*.

```
for i = [0, gcd(rotdist, n))        — open interval
    /* move i-th values of blocks */
    t = x[i]
    j = i
    loop
        k = j + rotdist
        if k >= n
            k -= n          K = (j + rotdist) %. n
        if k == i
            break
        x[j] = x[k]
        j = k
    x[j] = t
```

The greatest common divisor of *rotdist* and n is the number of cycles to be permuted (in terms of modern algebra, it is the number of cosets in the permutation group induced by the rotation).

The next program is from Section 18.1 of Gries's *Science of Programming*; it assumes that the function *swap(a, b, m)* exchanges $x[a..a+m-1]$ with $x[b..b+m-1]$.

```
if rotdist == 0 || rotdist == n
    return
i = p = rotdist
j = n - p
while i != j
    /* invariant:
        x[0  ..p-i  ] in final position
        x[p-i..p-1  ] = a (to be swapped with b)
        x[p  ..p+j-1] = b (to be swapped with a)
        x[p+j..n-1  ] in final position
    */
    if i > j
        swap(p-i, p, j)
        i -= j
    else
        swap(p-i, p+j-i, i)
        j -= i
swap(p-i, p, i)
```

Loop invariants are described in Column 4.

The code is isomorphic to this (slow but correct) additive Euclidean algorithm for computing the greatest common divisor of i and j, which assumes that neither input is zero.

```
int gcd(int i, int j)
    while i != j
        if i > j
            i -= j
        else
            j -= i
    return i
```

Gries and Mills study all three rotation algorithms in "Swapping Sections", Cornell University Computer Science Technical Report 81-452.

4. I ran all three algorithms on a 400MHz Pentium II, with n fixed at 1,000,000 and the rotation distance varying from 1 to 50. This graph plots the average time of 50 runs at each data set:

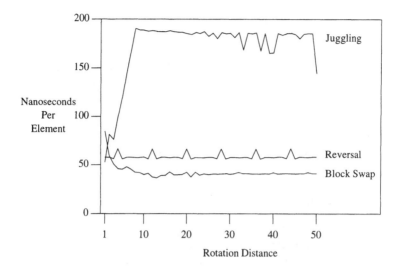

The reversal code has a consistent run time of about 58 nanoseconds per element, except that the time jumps to about 66 for rotation distances of 4, 12, 20 and all later integers congruent to 4 modulo 8. (This is probably an interaction with a cache size of 32 bytes.) The block swap algorithm starts off as the most expensive algorithm (probably due to a function call for swapping single-element blocks), but its good caching behavior makes it the fastest for rotation distances greater than 2. The juggling algorithm starts as the cheapest, but its poor caching behavior (accessing a single element from each 32-byte cache line) drives its time to near 200 nanoseconds at a rotation distance of 8. Its time hovers around 190 nanoseconds, and drops down sporadically (at a rotation distance of 1000, its time drops to 105 nanoseconds, then pops right back up to 190). In the mid 1980's, this same code tickled paging behavior with the rotation distance set to the page size.

6. The signature of a name is its push-button encoding, so the signature of "LESK*M*" is "5375*6*". To find the false matches in a directory, we sign each name with its push-button encoding, sort by signature (and by name within equal signatures), and then sequentially read the sorted file to report any equal signatures with distinct names. To retrieve a name given its push-button encoding we use a structure that contains the signatures and the other data. While we could sort that structure and then look up a push-button encoding by binary search, in a real system we would probably use hashing or a database system.

7. To transpose the row-major matrix, Vyssotsky prepended the column and row to each record, called the system tape sort to sort by column then row, and then removed the column and row numbers with a third program.

8. The *aha!* insight for this problem is that some k-element subset sums to <u>at most t</u> if and only if the subset consisting of the k smallest elements does. That subset can be found in time proportional to $n \log n$ by sorting the original set, or in time proportional to n by using a selection algorithm (see Solution 11.9). When Ullman assigned this as a class exercise, students designed algorithms with both running times mentioned above, as well as $O(n \log k)$, $O(nk)$, $O(n^2)$, and $O(n^k)$. Can you find natural algorithms to go with those running times?

10. Edison filled the shell with water and emptied it into a graduated cylinder. (As the hint may have reminded you, Archimedes also used water to compute volumes; in his day, *aha!* insights were celebrated by shouting *eureka!*)

Solutions for Column 3

1. Each entry in a tax table contains three values: the lower bound for this bracket, the base tax, and the rate at which income over the lower bound is taxed. Including a final sentinel entry in the table with an ''infinite'' lower bound will make the sequential search easier to write and incidentally faster (see Section 9.2); one could also use a binary search. These techniques apply to any piecewise-linear functions.

3. This block letter ''I''

              XXXXXXXXX
              XXXXXXXXX
              XXXXXXXXX
                 XXX
                 XXX
                 XXX
                 XXX
                 XXX
                 XXX
              XXXXXXXXX
              XXXXXXXXX
              XXXXXXXXX

    might be encoded as

              3 lines 9 X
              6 lines 3 blank   3 X   3 blank
              3 lines 9 X

    or more compactly as

              3 9 X
              6 3 b 3 X 3 b
              3 9 X

4. To find the number of days between two dates, compute the number of each day in its respective year, subtract the earlier from the later (perhaps borrowing from the year), and then add 365 times the difference in years plus one for each leap year.

To find the day of the week for a given day, compute the number of days between the given day and a known Sunday, and then use modular arithmetic to convert that to a day of the week. To prepare a calendar for a month in a given year, we need to know how many days there are in the month (take care to handle February correctly) and the day of the week on which the 1st falls. Dershowitz and Reingold wrote an entire book on *Calendrical Calculations* (published by Cambridge University Press in 1997).

5. Because the comparisons take place from the right to the left of the word, it will probably pay to store the words in reverse (right-to-left) order. Possible representations of a sequence of suffixes include a two-dimensional array of characters (which is usually wasteful), a single array of characters with the suffixes separated by a terminator character, and such a character array augmented with an array of pointers, one to each word.

6. Aho, Kernighan and Weinberger give a nine-line program for generating form letters on page 101 of their *Awk Programming Language* (published by Addison-Wesley in 1988).

Solutions for Column 4

1. To show that overflow does not occur we add the conditions $0 \le l \le n$ and $-1 \le u < n$ to the invariant; we can then bound $l + u$. The same conditions can be used to show that elements outside the array bounds are never accessed. We can formally define $mustbe(l, u)$ as $x[l-1] < t$ and $x[u+1] > t$ if we define the fictitious boundary elements $x[-1]$ and $x[n]$ as in Section 9.3.

2. See Section 9.3.

5. For an introduction to this celebrated open problem of mathematics, see B. Hayes's "On the ups and downs of hailstone numbers" in the Computer Recreations column in the January 1984 *Scientific American*. For a more technical discussion, see "The 3x+1 problem and its generalizations" by J. C. Lagarias, in the January 1985 *American Mathematical Monthly*. As this book goes to press, Lagarias has a 30-page bibliography with about a hundred references to the problem at *www.research.att.com/~jcl/3x+1.html*.

6. The process terminates because each step decreases the number of beans in the can by one. It always removes either zero or two white beans from the coffee can, so it leaves invariant the parity (oddness or evenness) of the number of white beans. Thus the last remaining bean is white if and only if the can originally held an odd number of white beans.

7. Because the line segments that form the rungs of the ladder are in increasing y-order, the two that bracket a given point can be found by binary search. The basic comparison in the search tells whether the point is below, on, or above a given line segment; how would you code that function?

8. See Section 9.3.

Solutions for Column 5

1. When I write large programs, I use long names (ten or twenty characters) for my global variables. This column uses short variable names such as x, n and t. In most software projects, the shortest plausible names might be more like *elem*, *nelems* and *target*. I find the short names convenient for building scaffolding and essential for mathematical proofs like that in Section 4.3. Similar rules apply to mathematics: the unfamiliar may want to hear that "the square of the hypotenuse of a right triangle is equal to the sum of the squares of the two adjacent sides", but people working on the problem usually say "$a^2 + b^2 = c^2$".

   I've tried to stick close to Kernighan and Ritchie's C coding style, but I put the first line of code with the opening curly brace of a function and delete other blank lines to save space (a substantial percentage, for the little functions in this book).

   The binary search in Section 5.1 returns an integer that is -1 if the value is not present, and points to the value if it is present. Steve McConnell suggested that the search should properly return two values: a *boolean* telling whether it is present, and an index that is used only if the *boolean* is true:

   ```
   boolean BinarySearch(DataType TargetValue, int *TargetIndex)
   /* precondition: Element[0] <= Element[1] <=
           ... <= Element[NumElements-1]
       postcondition:
           result == false =>
               TargetValue not in Element[0..NumElements-1]
           result == true  =>
               Element[*TargetIndex] == TargetValue
   */
   ```

   Listing 18.3 on page 402 of McConnell's *Code Complete* is a Pascal Insertion Sort that occupies one (large) page; the code and comments are together 41 lines. That style is appropriate for large software projects. Section 11.1 of this book presents the same algorithm in just five lines of code.

   Few of the programs have error checking. Some functions read data from files into arrays of size *MAX*, and *scanf* calls can easily overflow their buffers. Array arguments that should be parameters are instead global variables.

   Throughout this book, I've used shortcuts that are appropriate for textbooks and scaffolding, but not for large software projects. As Kernighan and Pike observe in Section 1.1 of their *Practice of Programming*, "clarity is often achieved through brevity". Even so, most of my code avoids the incredibly dense style illustrated in the C++ code in Section 14.3.

7. For $n = 1000$, searching through the array in sorted order required 351 nanoseconds per search, while searching it in random order raised the average cost to 418 nanoseconds (about a twenty percent slowdown). For $n = 10^6$, the experiment overflows even the L2 cache and the slowdown is a factor of 2.7. For the highly-tuned binary search in Section 8.3, though, the ordered searches zipped right

through an $n = 1000$-element table in 125 nanoseconds each, while the random searches required 266 nanoseconds, a slowdown of over a factor of two.

Solutions for Column 6

4. Want your system to be reliable? Start by building reliability in from the initial design; it is impossible to paste on later. Design your data structures so that information can be recovered if portions of a structure are compromised. Inspect code in reviews and walkthroughs, and test it extensively. Run your software on top of a reliable operating system, and on a redundant hardware system using error-correcting memory. Have in place a plan to recover quickly when your system does fail (and it certainly will fail). Log every failure carefully so that you can learn from each one.

6. "Make it work first before you make it work fast" is usually good advice. However, it took Bill Wulf only a few minutes to convince me that the old truism isn't quite as true as I once thought. He used the case of a document production system that took several hours to prepare a book. Wulf's clincher went like this: "That program, like any other large system, today has ten known, but minor, bugs. Next month, it will have ten different known bugs. If you could choose between removing the ten current bugs or making the program run ten times faster, which would you pick?"

Solutions for Column 7

These solutions include guesses at constants that may be off by a factor of two from their correct values as this book goes to press, but not much further.

1. The Passaic River does not flow at 200 miles per hour, even when falling 80 feet over the beautiful Great Falls in Paterson, New Jersey. I suspect that the engineer really told the reporter that the engorged river was flowing at 200 miles *per day*, five times faster than its typical 40 miles per day, which is just under a leisurely 2 miles per hour.

2. An old removable disk holds 100 megabytes. An ISDN line transmits 112 kilobits per second, or about 50 megabytes per hour. This gives a cyclist with a disk in his pocket about two hours to pedal, or a 15-mile radius of superiority. For a more interesting race, put a hundred DVDs in the cyclist's backpack, and his bandwidth goes up by a factor of 17,000; upgrade the line to ATM at 155 megabits per second, for a factor of 1400 increase. This gives the cyclist another factor of 12, or one day to pedal. (The day after I wrote this paragraph, I walked into a colleague's office to see 200 5-gigabyte write-once media platters in a pile on his desk. In 1999, a terabyte of unwritten media was a stunning sight.)

3. A floppy disk contains 1.44 megabytes. Flat out, my typing is about fifty words (or 300 bytes) per minute. I can therefore fill a floppy in 4800 minutes, or 80 hours. (The input text for this book is only half a megabyte, but it took me substantially longer than three days to type it.)

4. I was hoping for answers along the lines of a ten-nanosecond instruction takes a hundredth of a second, an 11 millisecond disk rotation (at 5400 rpm) takes 3 hours, a 20 msec seek takes 6 hours, and the two seconds to type my name takes about a month. A clever reader wrote, "How long does it take? Exactly the same time as before, if the clock slows down, too."

5. For the rate between 5 and 10 percent, the Rule-of-72 estimate is accurate to within one percent.

6. Since 72/1.33 is approximately 54, we would expect the population to double by 2052 (the UN estimates happily call for the rate to drop substantially).

9. Ignoring slowdown due to queueing, 20 milliseconds (of seek time) per disk operation gives 2 seconds per transaction or 1800 transactions per hour.

10. One could estimate the local death rate by counting death notices in a newspaper and estimating the population of the area they represent. An easier approach uses Little's Law and an estimate of life expectancy; if the life expectancy is 70 years, for instance, then 1/70 or 1.4% of the population dies each year.

11. Peter Denning's proof of Little's Law has two parts. "First, define $\lambda = A/T$, the arrival rate, where A is the number of arrivals during an observation period of length T. Define $X = C/T$, the output rate, where C is the number of completions during T. Let $n(t)$ denote the number in the system at time t in $[0, T]$. Let W be the area under $n(t)$, in units of 'item-seconds', representing the total aggregated waiting time over all items in the system during the observation period. The mean response time per item completed is defined as $R = W/C$, in units of (item-seconds)/(item). The mean number in the system is the average height of $n(t)$ and is $L = W/T$, in units of (item-seconds)/(second). It is now obvious that $L = RX$. This formulation is in terms of the output rate only. There is no requirement for 'flow balance', i.e., that flow in equal flow out (in symbols, $\lambda = X$). If you add that assumption, the formula becomes $L = \lambda \times R$, which is the form encountered in queueing and system theory."

12. When I read that a quarter has "an average life of 30 years", that number seemed high to me; I didn't recall seeing that many old quarters. I therefore dug into my pocket, and found a dozen quarters. Here are their ages in years:

    3 4 5 7 9 9 12 17 17 19 20 34

The average age is 13 years, which is perfectly consistent with a quarter having an average life of about twice that (over this rather uniform distribution of ages). Had I come up with a dozen quarters all less than five years old, I might have dug further into the topic. This time, though, I guessed that the paper had got it right.

The same article reported that "there will be a minimum of 750 million New Jersey quarters made" and also that a new state quarter would be issued every 10 weeks. That multiplies to about four billion quarters per year, or a dozen new quarters for each resident of the United States. A life of 30 years per quarter means that each person has 360 quarters out there. That is too many for pockets alone, but it is plausible if we include piles of change at home and in cars, and a lot in cash registers, vending machines and banks.

Solutions for Column 8

1. David Gries systematically derives and verifies Algorithm 4 in ''A Note on the Standard Strategy for Developing Loop Invariants and Loops'' in *Science of Computer Programming 2*, pp. 207-214.

3. Algorithm 1 uses roughly $n^3/6$ calls to function *max*, Algorithm 2 uses roughly $n^2/2$ calls, and Algorithm 4 uses roughly $2n$ calls. Algorithm 2b uses linear extra space for the cumulative array and Algorithm 3 uses logarithmic extra space for the stack; the other algorithms use only constant extra space. Algorithm 4 is online: it computes its answer in a single pass over the input, which is particularly useful for processing files on disk.

5. If *cumarr* is declared as

```
float *cumarr;
```

then assigning

```
cumarr = realarray+1
```

will mean that *cumarr*$[-1]$ refers to *realarray*$[0]$.

9. Replace the assignment *maxsofar* $=0$ with *maxsofar* $=-\infty$. If the use of $-\infty$ bothers you, *maxsofar* $=x[0]$ does just as well; why?

10. Initialize the cumulative array *cum* so that $cum[i]=x[0]+ \ldots +x[i]$. The subvector $x[l..u]$ sums to zero if $cum[l-1]=cum[u]$. The subvector with the sum closest to zero is therefore found by locating the two closest elements in *cum*, which can be done in $O(n \log n)$ time by sorting the array. That running time is within a constant factor of optimal because any algorithm for solving it can be used to solve the ''Element Uniqueness'' problem of determining whether an array contains duplicated elements (Dobkin and Lipton showed that the problem requires that much time in the worst case on a decision-tree model of computation).

11. The total cost between stations i and j on a linear turnpike is $cum[j]-cum[i-1]$, where *cum* is a cumulative array, as above.

12. This solution uses yet another cumulative array. The loop

```
for i = [1, u]
    x[i] += v
```

is simulated by the assignments

```
cum[u] += v
cum[1-1] -= v
```

which symbolically add v to $x[0..u]$ and then subtract it from $x[0..l-1]$. After all such sums have been taken, we compute the array x by

```
for (i = n-1; i >= 0; i--)
    x[i] = x[i+1] + cum[i]
```

This reduces the worst-case time for n sums from $O(n^2)$ to $O(n)$. This problem arose in gathering statistics on Appel's n-body program described in Section 6.1. Incorporating this solution reduced the run time of the statistics function from four hours to twenty minutes; that speedup would have been inconsequential when the program took a year, but was important when it took just a day.

13. The maximum-sum subarray of an $m \times n$ array can be found in $O(m^2 n)$ time by using the technique of Algorithm 2 in the dimension of length m and the technique of Algorithm 4 in the dimension of length n. The $n \times n$ problem can therefore be solved in $O(n^3)$ time, which was the best result for two decades. Tamaki and Tokuyama published a slightly faster algorithm in the 1998 *Symposium on Discrete Algorithms* (pp. 446-452) that runs in $O(n^3 [(\log \log n)/(\log n)]^{1/2})$ time. They also give an $O(n^2 \log n)$ approximation algorithm for finding a subarray with sum at least half the maximum, and describe applications to database mining. The best lower bound remains proportional to n^2.

Solutions for Column 9

2. These variables help to implement a variant of Van Wyk's scheme. The method uses *nodesleft* to keep track of the number of nodes of size *NODESIZE* pointed to by *freenode*. When that well runs dry, it allocates another group of size *NODE-GROUP*.

```
#define NODESIZE 8
#define NODEGROUP 1000
int nodesleft = 0;
char *freenode;
```

Calls to *malloc* are replaced by calls to this private version:

```
void *pmalloc(int size)
{   void *p;
    if (size != NODESIZE)
        return malloc(size);
    if (nodesleft == 0) {
        freenode = malloc(NODEGROUP*NODESIZE);
        nodesleft = NODEGROUP;
    }
    nodesleft--;
    p = (void *) freenode;
    freenode += NODESIZE;
    return p;
}
```

If the request isn't for the special size, this function immediately calls the system *malloc*. When *nodesleft* drops to zero, it allocates another group. With the same input that was profiled in Section 9.1, the total time dropped from 2.67 to 1.55 seconds, and the time spent in *malloc* dropped from 1.41 to .31 seconds (or 19.7% of the new run time).

If the program also *frees* nodes, then a new variable points to a singly-linked list of free nodes. When a node is freed, it is put on the front of that list. When the list is empty, the algorithm allocates a group of nodes, and links them together on the list.

4. An array of decreasing values forces the algorithm to use roughly 2^n operations.

5. If the binary search algorithms report that they found the search value t, then it is indeed in the table. When applied to unsorted tables, though, the algorithms may sometimes report that t is not present when it is in fact present. In such cases the algorithms locate a pair of adjacent elements that would establish that t is not in the table were it sorted.

6. One might test whether a character is a digit, for instance, with a test such as

```
if c >= '0' && c <= '9'
```

To test whether a character is alphanumeric would require a complex sequence of comparisons; if performance matters, one should put the test most likely to succeed first. It is usually simpler and faster to use a 256-element table:

```
#define isupper(c) (uppertable[c])
```

Most systems store several bits in each element of a table, then extract them with a logical and:

```
#define isupper(c) (bigtable[c] & UPPER)
#define isalnum(c) (bigtable[c] & (DIGIT|LOWER|UPPER))
```

C and C++ programmers might enjoy inspecting the file *ctype.h* to see how their system solves this problem.

7. The first approach is to count the number of one bits in each input unit (perhaps an 8-bit character or perhaps a 32-bit integer), and sum them. To find the number of one bits in a 16-bit integer, one could look at each bit in order, or iterate through the bits that are on (with a statement like $b \mathrel{\&}= (b-1)$), or perform a lookup in a table of, for instance, $2^{16} = 65,536$ elements. What effect will the cache size have on your choice of unit?

The second approach is to count the number of each input unit in the input, and then at the end take the sum of that number multiplied by the number of one bits in that unit.

8. R. G. Dromey wrote this code to compute the maximum element of $x[0..n-1]$, using $x[n]$ as a sentinel:

```
i = 0
while i < n
    max = x[i]
    x[n] = max
    i++
    while x[i] < max
        i++
```

11. Replacing the function evaluations by several 72-element tables decreased the run time of the program on an IBM 7090 from half an hour to a minute. Because the evaluation of helicopter rotor blades required about three hundred runs of the program, those few hundred extra words of memory reduced a week of CPU time to several hours.

12. Horner's method evaluates the polynomial by

```
y = a[n]
for (i = n-1; i >= 0; i--)
    y = x*y + a[i]
```

It uses n multiplications, and is usually twice as fast as the previous code.

Solutions for Column 10

1. Every high-level language instruction that accessed one of the packed fields compiled into many machine instructions; accessing an unpacked field required fewer instructions. By unpacking the records, Feldman slightly increased data space but greatly reduced code space and run time.

2. Several readers suggested storing $(x, y, pointnum)$ triples sorted by y within x; binary search can then be used to look up a given (x, y) pair. The data structure described in the text is easiest to build if the input has been sorted by x values (and within x by y, as above). The structure could be searched more quickly by performing a binary search in the *row* array between values *firstincol*$[i]$ and *firstincol*$[i+1]-1$. Note that those y values appear in increasing order and that the binary search must correctly handle the case of searching an empty subarray.

4. Almanacs store tables of distances between cities as triangular arrays, which reduces their space by a factor of two. Mathematical tables sometimes store only the least significant digits of functions, and give the most significant digits just once, say, for each row of values. Television schedules save space by only stating when shows start (as opposed to listing all shows that are on at any given thirty-minute interval).

5. Brooks combined two representations for the table. The function got to within a few units of the true answer, and the single decimal digit stored in the array gave the difference. After reading this problem and solution, two reviewers of this edition commented that they had recently solved problems by supplementing an approximate function with a difference table.

6. The original file required 300 kilobytes of disk memory. Compressing two digits into one byte reduced that to 150 kilobytes but increased the time to read the file. (This was in the days when a "single-sided, double-density" 5.25-inch floppy disk held 184 kilobytes.) Replacing the expensive / and % operations with a table lookup cost 200 bytes of primary memory but reduced the read time almost to its original cost. Thus 200 bytes of primary memory bought 150 kilobytes of disk. Several readers suggested using the encoding $c = (a << 4)|b$; the values can be decoded by the statements $a = c >> 4$ and $b = c$ & $0xF$. John Linderman observes that "not only are shifting and masking commonly faster than multiplying and dividing, but common utilities like a hex dump could display the encoded data in a readable form".

Solutions for Column 11

1. Sorting to find the minimum or maximum of n floating point numbers is usually overkill. Solution 9 shows how the median can be found more quickly without sorting, but sorting might be easier on some systems. Sorting works well for finding the mode, but hashing can be faster. While the obvious code for finding the mean takes time proportional to n, an approach that first sorts might be able to accomplish the job with greater numerical accuracy; see Problem 14.4.b.

2. Bob Sedgewick observed that Lomuto's partitioning scheme can be modified to work from right to left by using the following invariant:

The partitioning code is then

```
m = u+1
for (i = u; i >= 1; i++)
    if x[i] >= t
        swap(--m, i)
```

Upon termination we know that $x[m]=t$, so we can recur with parameters $(1, m-1)$ and $(m+1, u)$; no additional *swap* is needed. Sedgewick also used $x[l]$ as a sentinel to remove one test from the inner loop:

```
m = i = u+1
do
    while x[--i] < t
        ;
    swap(--m, i)
while i != 1
```

3. To determine the best choice for *cutoff*, I ran the program at all values of *cutoff* from 1 to 100, with n fixed at 1,000,000. This graph plots the results.

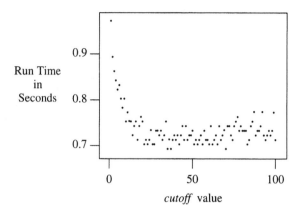

Run Time
in
Seconds

0.9 —

0.8 —

0.7 —

0   50   100

cutoff value

A good value of *cutoff* was 50; values between 30 and 70 give savings to within a few percent of that.

4. See the references cited in Section 11.6.

5. McIlroy's program runs in time proportional to the amount of data to be sorted, which is optimal in the worst case. It assumes that each record in $x[0..n-1]$ has an integer *length* and a pointer to the array $bit[0..length-1]$.

```
void bsort(l, u, depth)
    if l >= u
        return
    for i = [l, u]
        if x[i].length < depth
            swap(i, l++)
    m = l
    for i = [l, u]
        if x[i].bit[depth] == 0
            swap(i, m++)
    bsort(l, m-1, depth+1)
    bsort(m, u, depth+1)
```

The function is originally called by $bsort(0, n-1, 1)$. Beware that this program assigns values to parameters and to variables defining *for* loops. The linear running time depends strongly on the fact that the *swap* operation moves pointers to the bit strings and not the bit strings themselves.

6. This code implements Selection Sort:

```
void selsort()
    for i = [0, n-1)
        for j = [i, n)
            if x[j] < x[i]
                swap(i, j)
```

This code implements Shell Sort:

```
void shellsort()
    for (h = 1; h < n; h = 3*h + 1)
        ;
    loop
        h /= 3
        if (h < 1)
            break
        for i = [h, n)
            for (j = i; j >= h; j -= h)
                if (x[j-h] < x[j])
                    break
                swap(j-h, j)
```

9. This selection algorithm is due to C. A. R. Hoare; the code is a slight modification to *qsort*4.

```
void select1(l, u, k)
        pre l <= k <= u
        post x[l..k-1] <= x[k] <= x[k+1..u]
    if l >= u
        return
    swap(l, randint(l, u))
    t = x[l]; i = l; j = u+1
    loop
        do i++; while i <= u && x[i] < t
        do j--; while x[j] > t
        if i > j
            break
        temp = x[i]; x[i] = x[j]; x[j] = temp
    swap(l, j)
    if j < k
        select1(j+1, u, k)  k-p
    else if j > k
        select1(l, j-1, k)
```

Because the recursion is the last action of the function, it could be transformed into a *while* loop. In Problem 5.2.2-32 of *Sorting and Searching*, Knuth shows that the program uses an average of $3.4n$ comparisons to find the median of n elements; the probabilistic argument is similar in spirit to the worst-case argument in Solution 2.A.

14. This version of Quicksort uses pointers to arrays. Because it uses just the two parameters x and n, I find it even simpler than *qsort*1, so long as the reader understands that the notation $x + j + 1$ denotes the array starting at position $x[j+1]$.

```
void qsort5(int x[], int n)
{    int i, j;
     if (n <= 1)
          return;
     for (i = 1, j = 0; i < n; i++)
          if (x[i] < x[0])
               swap(++j, i, x);
     swap(0, j, x);
     qsort5(x, j);
     qsort5(x+j+1, n-j-1);
}
```

Because it uses pointers into arrays, this function can be implemented in C or C++, but not in Java. We must now also pass the array name (that is, a pointer to the array) to the *swap* function.

Solutions for Column 12

1. These functions return a large (usually 30-bit) random number and a random number in the specified input range, respectively:

   ```
   int bigrand()
   {    return RAND_MAX*rand() + rand(); }

   int randint(int l, int u)
   {    return l + bigrand() % (u-l+1); }
   ```

   RANDMAX convert 2 rand() *digits to base* *RAND-MAX.*

2. To select *m* integers from the range $0..n-1$, choose the number *i* at random in the range, and then report the numbers $i, i+1, ..., i+m-1$, possibly wrapping around to 0. This method chooses each integer with probability m/n, but is strongly biased towards certain subsets.

3. When fewer than $n/2$ integers have been selected so far, the probability that a randomly chosen integer is unselected is greater than $1/2$. That the average number of draws to get an unselected integer is less than 2 follows from the logic that one must toss a coin twice, on the average, to get heads.

4. Let's view the set *S* as a collection of *n* initially empty urns. Each call to *randint* selects an urn into which we throw a ball; if it was previously occupied, the *member* test is true. The number of balls required to ensure that each urn contains at least one ball is known to statisticians as the "Coupon Collector's Problem" (how many baseball cards must I collect to make sure I have all *n*?); the answer is roughly $n \ln n$. The algorithm makes *m* tests when all the balls go into different urns; determining when there are likely to be two balls in one urn is the "Birthday Paradox" (in any group of 23 or more people, two are likely to share a birthday). In general, two balls are likely to share one of *n* urns if there are $O(\sqrt{n})$ balls.

7. To print the values in increasing order one can place the *print* statement after the recursive call, or print $n+1-i$ rather than *i*.

8. To print distinct integers in random order, print each one as it is first generated;

also see Solution 1.4. To print duplicate integers in sorted order, remove the test of whether the integer is already in the set. To print duplicate integers in random order, use the trivial program

```
for i = [0, m)
    print bigrand() % n
```

9. When Bob Floyd studied the set-based algorithm, he was unsettled by the fact that it discards some of the random numbers that it generates. He therefore derived an alternative set-based algorithm, implemented here in C++:

```
void genfloyd(int m, int n)
{   set<int> S;
    set<int>::iterator i;
    for (int j = n-m; j < n; j++) {
        int t = bigrand() % (j+1);
        if (S.find(t) == S.end())
            S.insert(t); // t not in S
        else
            S.insert(j); // t in S
    }
    for (i = S.begin(); i != S.end(); ++i)
        cout << *i << "\n";
}
```

Solution 13.1 implements the same algorithm using a different set interface. Floyd's algorithm originally appeared in *Programming Pearls* in the August 1986 *Communications of the ACM*, and was reprinted as Column 13 of my 1988 *More Programming Pearls*; those references contain a simple proof of its correctness.

10. We always select the first line, we select the second line with probability one half, the third line with probability one third, and so on. At the end of the process, each line has the same probability of being chosen ($1/n$, where n is the total number of lines in the file):

```
i = 0
while more input lines
    with probability 1.0/++i
        choice = this input line
print choice
```

11. I gave this problem, exactly as stated, on a take-home examination in a course on "Applied Algorithm Design". Students who described methods that could compute the answer in just a few minutes of CPU time received zero points. The response "I'd talk to my statistics professor" was worth half credit, and a perfect answer went like this:

The numbers 4..16 have no impact on the game, so they can be ignored. The card wins if 1 and 2 are chosen (in either order) before 3. This happens when 3 is chosen last, which occurs one time out of three. The probability that a random sequence wins is therefore precisely 1/3.

Don't be misled by problem statements; you don't have to use the CPU time just because it's available!

12. Section 5.9 describes Kernighan and Pike's *Practice of Programming*. Section 6.8 of their book describes how they tested a probabilistic program (we'll see a different program for the same task in Section 15.3).

Solutions for Column 13

1. Floyd's algorithm in Solution 12.9 can be implemented using the *IntSet* class in this fashion:

```
void genfloyd(int m, int maxval)
{   int *v = new int[m];
    IntSetSTL S(m, maxval);
    for (int j = maxval-m; j < maxval; j++) {
        int t = bigrand() % (j+1);
        int oldsize = S.size();
        S.insert(t);
        if (S.size() == oldsize) // t already in S
            S.insert(j);
    }
    S.report(v);
    for (int i = 0; i < m; i++)
        cout << v[i] << "\n";
}
```

When *m* and *maxval* are equal, the elements are inserted in increasing order, which is precisely the worst case for binary search trees.

4. This iterative insertion algorithm for linked lists is longer than the corresponding recursive algorithm because it duplicates the case analysis for inserting a node after the *head* and later in the list:

```
void insert(t)
    if head->val == t
        return
    if head->val > t
        head = new node(t, head)
        n++
        return
    for (p = head; p->next->val < t; p = p->next)
        ;
    if p->next->val == t
        return
    p->next = new node(t, p->next)
    n++
```

This simpler code removes that duplication by using a pointer to a pointer:

```
void insert(t)
    for (p = &head; (*p)->val < t; p = &((*p)->next))
        ;
    if (*p)->val == t
        return
    *p = new node(t, *p)
    n++
```

It is just as fast as the previous version. This code works for bins with minor changes, and Solution 7 uses this approach for binary search trees.

5. To replace many allocations with a single one, we need a pointer to the next available node:

```
node *freenode;
```

We allocate all we will ever need when the class is constructed:

```
freenode = new node[maxelms]
```

We peel them off as needed in the insertion function:

```
if (p == 0)
    p = freenode++
    p->val = t
    p->left = p->right = 0
    n++
else if ...
```

The same technique applies to bins; Solution 7 uses it for binary search trees.

6. Inserting nodes in increasing order measures the search costs of arrays and lists, and introduces very little insertion overhead. That sequence will provoke worst-case behavior for bins and binary search trees.

7. The pointers that were *null* in the previous version will now all point to the *sentinel* node. It is initialized in the constructor:

```
root = sentinel = new node
```

The insertion code first puts the target value t into the sentinel node, then uses a pointer to a pointer (as described in Solution 4) to run down the tree until it finds t. At that time it uses the technique of Solution 5 to insert a new node.

```
void insert(t)
    sentinel->val = t
    p = &root
    while (*p)->val != t
        if t < (*p)->val
            p = &((*p)->left)
        else
            p = &((*p)->right)
    if *p == sentinel
        *p = freenode++
        (*p)->val = t
        (*p)->left = (*p)->right = sentinel
        n++
```

The variable *node* is declared and initialized as

```
node **p = &root;
```

9. To replace division with shifting, we initialize the variables with pseudocode like this:

```
goal = n/m
binshift = 1
for (i = 2; i < goal; i *= 2)
    binshift++
nbins = 1 + (n >> binshift)
```

The insertion function starts at this node:

```
p = &(bin[t >> binshift])
```

10. One can mix and match a variety of data structures for representing random sets. Because we have a very good (statistical) idea of how many items each bin will contain, for instance, we might use the insights of Section 13.2 and represent the items in most bins by a small array (we could then spill excess items to a linked list when the bin becomes too full). Don Knuth described an "ordered hash table" for this problem in the May 1986 "Programming Pearls" in *Communications of the ACM* to illustrate his Web system for documenting Pascal programs. That paper is reprinted as Chapter 5 of his 1992 book *Literate Programming*.

Solutions for Column 14

1. The *siftdown* function can be made faster by moving the *swap* assignments to and from the temporary variable out of its loop. The *siftup* function can be made faster by moving code out of loops and by placing a sentinel element in $x[0]$ to remove the test *if $i == 1$*.

2. The modified *siftdown* is a slight modification of the version in the text. The assignment $i = 1$ is replaced with $i = l$, and comparisons to n are replaced with

comparisons to u. The resulting function's run time is $O(\log u - \log l)$. This code builds a heap in $O(n)$ time

```
for (i = n-1; i >= 1; i--)
    /* invariant: maxheap(i+1, n) */
    siftdown(i, n)
    /* maxheap(i, n) */
```

Because $maxheap(l,n)$ is true for all integers $l > n/2$, the bound $n-1$ in the *for* loop can be changed to $n/2$.

3. Using the functions in Solutions 1 and 2, the Heapsort is

```
for (i = n/2; i >= 1; i--)
    siftdown1(i, n)
for (i = n; i >= 2; i--)
    swap(1, i)
    siftdown1(1, i-1)
```

Its running time remains $O(n \log n)$, but with a smaller constant than in the original Heapsort. The sort program at this book's web site implements several versions of Heapsort.

4. Heaps replace an $O(n)$ process by a $O(\log n)$ process in all the problems.

   a. The iterative step in building a Huffman code selects the two smallest nodes in the set and merges them into a new node; this is implemented by two *extract-mins* followed by an *insert*. If the input frequencies are presented in sorted order, then the Huffman code can be computed in linear time; the details are left as an exercise.

   b. A simple algorithm to sum floating point numbers might lose accuracy by adding very small numbers to large numbers. A superior algorithm always adds the two smallest numbers in the set, and is isomorphic to the algorithm for Huffman codes mentioned above.

   c. A million-element heap (minimum at top) represents the million largest numbers seen so far.

   d. A heap can be used to merge sorted files by representing the next element in each file; the iterative step selects the smallest element from the heap and inserts its successor into the heap. The next element to be output from n files can be chosen in $O(\log n)$ time.

5. A heap-like structure is placed over the sequence of bins; each node in the heap tells the amount of space left in the least full bin among its descendants. When deciding where to place a new weight, the search goes left if it can (i.e., the least full bin to the left has enough space to hold it) and right if it must; that requires time proportional to the heap's depth of $O(\log n)$. After the weight is inserted, the path is traversed up to fix the weights in the heap.

6. The common implementation of a sequential file on disk has block i point to block $i+1$. McCreight observed that if node i also points to node $2i$, then an arbitrary

node n can be found in at most $O(\log n)$ accesses. The following recursive function prints the access path.

```
void path(n)
        pre    n >= 0
        post   path to n is printed
    if n == 0
        print "start at 0"
    else if even(n)
        path(n/2)
        print "double to ", n
    else
        path(n-1)
        print "increment to ", n
```

Notice that it is isomorphic to the program for computing x^n in $O(\log n)$ steps given in Problem 4.9.

7. The modified binary search begins with $i = 1$, and at each iteration sets i to either $2i$ or $2i + 1$. The element $x[1]$ contains the median element, $x[2]$ contains the first quartile, $x[3]$ the third quartile, and so on. S. R. Mahaney and J. I. Munro found an algorithm to put an n-element sorted array into "Heapsearch" order in $O(n)$ time and $O(1)$ extra space. As a precursor to their method, consider copying a sorted array a of size $2^k - 1$ into a "Heapsearch" array b: the elements in odd positions of a go, in order, into the last half of the positions of b, positions congruent to 2 modulo 4 go into b's second quarter, and so on.

11. The C++ Standard Template Library supports heaps with operations such as *make_heap, push_heap, pop_heap* and *sort_heap*. One can combine those operations to make a Heapsort as simply as

```
make_heap(a, a+n);
sort_heap(a, a+n);
```

The STL also provides a *priority_queue* adaptor.

Solutions for Column 15

1. Many document systems provide a way to strip out all formatting commands and see a raw text representation of the input. When I played with the string duplication program of Section 15.2 on long texts, I found that it was very sensitive to how the text was formatted. The program took 36 seconds to process the 4,460,056 characters in the King James Bible, and the longest repeated string was 269 characters in length. When I normalized the input text by removing the verse number from each line, so long strings could cross verse boundaries, the longest string increased to 563 characters, which the program found in about the same amount of run time.

3. Because this program performs many searches for each insertion, very little of its time is going to memory allocation. Incorporating the special-purpose memory

allocator reduced the processing time by about 0.06 seconds, for a ten-percent speedup in that phase, but only a two-percent speedup for the entire program.

5. We could add another *map* to the C++ program to associate a sequence of words with each count. In the C program we might sort an array by count, then iterate through it (because some words tend to have large counts, that array will be much smaller than the input file). For typical documents, we might use key indexing and keep an array of linked lists for counts in the range (say) 1..1000.

7. Textbooks on algorithms warn about inputs like "aaaaaaaa", repeated thousands of times. I found it easier to time the program on a file of newlines. The program took 2.09 seconds to process 5000 newlines, 8.90 seconds on 10,000 newlines, and 37.90 seconds on 20,000 newlines. This growth appears to be slightly faster than quadratic, perhaps proportional to roughly $n \log_2 n$ comparisons, each at an average cost proportional to n. A more realistic bad case can be constructed by appending two copies of a large input file.

8. The subarray $a[i..i+M]$ represents $M+1$ strings. Because the array is sorted, we can quickly determine how many characters those $M+1$ strings have in common by calling *comlen* on the first and last strings:

```
comlen(a[i], a[i+M])
```

Code at this book's web site implements this algorithm.

9. Read the first string into the array c, note where it ends, terminate it with a null character, then read in the second string and terminate it. Sort as before. When scanning through the array, use an "exclusive or" to ensure that precisely one of the strings starts before the transition point.

14. This function hashes a sequence of k words terminated by null characters:

```
unsigned int hash(char *)
    unsigned int h = 0
    int n
    for (n = k; n > 0; p++)
        h = MULT * h + *p
        if (*p == 0)
            n--
    return h % NHASH
```

A program at this book's web site uses this hash function to replace binary search in the Markov text generation algorithm, which reduces the $O(n \log n)$ time to $O(n)$, on the average. The program uses a list representation for elements in the hash table to add only *nwords* additional 32-bit integers, where *nwords* is the number of words in the input.

INDEX

To look up algorithms, see also Appendix 1 (A Catalog of Algorithms). To look up code-tuning techniques, see also Appendix 4 (Rules for Code Tuning).

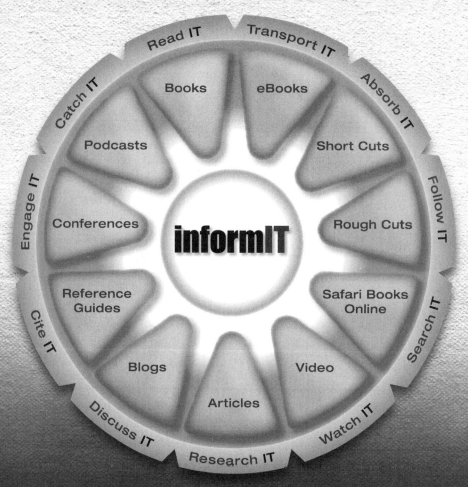

Register
Your Book

at informit.com/register

You may be eligible to receive:
- Advance notice of forthcoming editions of the book
- Related book recommendations
- Chapter excerpts and supplements of forthcoming titles
- Information about special contests and promotions throughout the year
- Notices and reminders about author appearances, tradeshows, and online chats with special guests

Contact us

If you are interested in writing a book or reviewing manuscripts prior to publication, please write to us at:

Editorial Department
Addison-Wesley Professional
75 Arlington Street, Suite 300
Boston, MA 02116 USA
Email: AWPro@aw.com

Visit us on the Web: informit.com/aw